MARGARET COLERICK COLLECTION
THE GOLDEN STAIRCASE

BY LOUEY CHISHOLM

IN FAIRYLAND: Tales Told Again. With 30 coloured pictures by KATHARINE CAMERON. 7s. 6d. net.

THE ENCHANTED LAND: Tales Told Again. With 30 coloured pictures by KATHARINE CAMERON. 7s. 6d. net.

EDITED BY LOUEY CHISHOLM

THE 'TOLD TO THE CHILDREN' SERIES.

THE 'SHOWN TO THE CHILDREN' SERIES.

THE
GOLDEN STAIRCASE

Poems and Verses for Children

CHOSEN BY
LOUEY CHISHOLM

WITH PICTURES BY
M. DIBDIN SPOONER

NEW YORK
G. P. PUTNAM'S SONS
LONDON: T. C. & E. C. JACK

Edinburgh: T. and A. Constable, Printers to His Majesty

TO

BEATRICE BIRNIE SINCLAIR

AND

PHILIP MACKWORTH

PREFACE

My apology for venturing to rush in where even poets have trod with but a measure of success must be that compilers of existing anthologies have had, it seems to me, a more intimate acquaintance with poetry than with the boys and girls for whom their selections have been made. If you talk to a child, you will find that an insight into the working of his little mind, an appreciation of his likes and dislikes, will stand you in better stead than a profound knowledge of your subject. Write, edit or compile a children's book, and again the same holds true. The first qualification for the task is love and knowledge of the little readers.

But time alone can justify the publication of *The Golden Staircase*. When well-worn copies are found on nursery or schoolroom bookshelf, then only shall I feel that I have vindicated my right to compile an anthology for children. My ultimate object is to guide boys and girls to those harvest-fields of poetry in which they may wander at large, but primarily the book has been planned with a view to their enjoyment by the way.

The Golden Staircase has two hundred steps. If a child begins to climb when he is four years old, and climbs twenty steps each year, on his fourteenth birthday he will reach the top. Behind him will descend the staircase from which he has caught glimpses of the merriment and beauty and heroism beyond; before him will stretch those Elysian fields through which his feet have been prepared to roam.

Following the two hundred poems and verses of *The Golden Staircase* are twenty Cradle Songs, which seem to me well within the limits of a little girl's appreciation; and the book ends with a selection of forty Carols, Hymns and Sacred Verses which I hope will appeal to boys and girls alike.

The kindness of authors or their friends, and of publishers, who have allowed me to include copyright poems, I acknowledge below, and to the many who have given this permission with amazing generosity I would tender especial thanks. I hope there may not be, inadvertently, any omission from the list.

Those who have suggested or remonstrated, and those who have copied verses, are too numerous to thank in other than general terms, but I am constrained to mention Miss Mary Steedman and the Rev. W. B. R. Wilson; also Miss Amy Steedman, without whose unfailing help and interest *The Golden Staircase* would still have been in the making.

LOUEY CHISHOLM.

EDINBURGH.

PREFACE

Thanks for the inclusion of copyright poems are due to—
Mrs. Allingham, for *The Fairies* and *Robin Redbreast*, by William Allingham; Miss Alma-Tadema, for *A Blessing for the Blessed, Snowdrops, Frost, The Robin, Little Girls*, and *A Lullaby*; Messrs. D. Appleton and Co., New York, for *Robert of Lincoln*, by William Cullen Bryant; Rev. S. Baring-Gould, for *The Olive Tree*; Canon Beeching, for a verse from *A Boy's Prayer*; Mr. J. J. Bell, for *The Choice, The Lights, On the Quay, The Ships*; Mr. Robert Bridges, for *Gay Robin* and *First Spring Morning*; Miss Abbie Farwell Brown, for *A Lost Playmate*; Miss Kate Bunce, for *The Imps in the Heavenly Meadow*; Messrs. Chatto and Windus, for *Baby*, by George Macdonald; Mrs. Cochran (Sydney Dayre) and the Editor of *St. Nicholas*, for *A Lesson for Mamma*; Messrs. E. P. Dutton and Co., for *The Child of Bethlehem*, by Phillips Brooks; Mrs. Eden and Mrs. Ward, for *Big Smith*, by Juliana H. Ewing; Messrs. C. W. Faulkner and Co., for *The Cats' Tea-Party*, by F. E. Weatherley; Mr. Norman Gale, for *The Fairy Book, Bartholomew*, and *The Bad Boy*; Mr. A. H. P. Graves and the Editor of *St. Nicholas*, for *An Irish Lullaby*; Mr. Anstey Guthrie (F. Anstey) and Messrs. Bradbury, Agnew and Co., for *The Steamship 'Puffin'*; Mrs. Hawkins, for *Kind Shepherd*; Mrs. Henley, for *England, my England*, by W. E. Henley; Miss Elsie Hill and the Editor of *St. Nicholas*, for *When Polly buys a Hat*; Messrs. Houghton, Mifflin and Co., Boston, for *The Enchanted Shirt*, by John Hay; *A Day in June* and *A Christmas Carol*, by J. R. Lowell; *Eventide*, by Caroline Mason; *The Sandpiper*, by Celia Thaxter; *Barbara Frietchie*, by J. G. Whittier; Mrs. Harriet Jay, for *Langley Lane* and *The Green Gnome*, by Robert Buchanan; Mr. Rudyard Kipling (Messrs. Doubleday, Page and Co., and Messrs. Scribner), for *The Camel's Hump* and *Shiv and the Grasshopper*; Mr. John Lane, for *The Rock-a-by Lady*; *Wynken, Blynken, and Nod* and *Little Boy Blue*, by Eugene Field; for *A Child's Evensong*, from *English Poems*, by Richard le Gallienne; for *Harold and Alice*; *Great, Wide, Beautiful World*; *The Wind Whistled Loud*, and *A Pedlar's Caravan*, from *Lilliput Lyrics*, by W. B. Rands; and for *The World's Music* and *Jack Frost*, from *The Child's World*, by Gabriel Setoun; Messrs. Longmans, Green and Co., and Charles Scribner's Sons, New York, for six poems from *A Child's Garden of Verse*, by R. L. Stevenson; Messrs. Macmillan, for *A Christmas Carol*, by Christina Rossetti, and for *The Loss of the Birkenhead*, by Francis Doyle; Mr. Meynell, for *Ex Ore Infantium*, by Francis Thompson; Mr. Henry Newbolt, for *Vitaï Lampada* and *Admirals All*, from *The Island Race*; Moira O'Neill, for *Johneen*, from *Songs of the Glens of Antrim* (Blackwood and Sons); Miss Palgrave, for *A Child's Prayer*, by Francis Palgrave; Judge Parry, for verses from *Katawampus*; Mrs. William Sharp, for *The Bird of Christ, Hushing Song*, and *The Moon-Child*, by Fiona Macleod; Messrs. Charles Scribner's Sons, New York, for *One, Two, Three*, by H. C. Bunner, from *The Poems of H. C. Bunner* (copyright, 1884, 1892, 1896, 1899, by Charles Scribner's Sons); for *Wynken, Blynken and Nod* and *Little Boy Blue*, by Eugene Field, from *A Little Book of Western Verse* (copyright, 1889, by Eugene Field; published by Charles Scribner's Sons); for *Christmas Eve*, and *The Three Kings of Cologne*, by Eugene Field, from *Second Book of Verse* (copyright, 1889, by Julia Sutherland Field, published by Charles Scribner's Sons); for *The Rock-a-by Lady*, by Eugene Field, from *Love-Songs of Childhood* (copyright, 1894, by Eugene Field, published by Charles Scribner's Sons); Messrs. Small, Maynard and Co., for Whitman's *Captain, My Captain*; Rev. C. M. Steedman, for *St. Molios in Arran*; Mrs. Tynan-Hinkson, for *Modereen Rue* and *Chanticleer*; Messrs. Frederick Warne and Co., for *The Jumblies*, by Edward Lear; and it was by the late Mrs. Chesson (Nora Hopper) that leave was given to include *The Blackbird*.

CONTENTS

	PAGE
THE ROBIN	1
BED IN SUMMER	1
MY GARDEN	2
THE LOST PLAYMATE	2
THE LAMPLIGHTER	3
THE STAR	4
THE LAND OF COUNTERPANE	4
THE LITTLE FISH THAT WOULD NOT DO AS IT WAS BID	5
WHO STOLE THE BIRD'S NEST	6
GOOD-NIGHT AND GOOD-MORNING	8
THE LITTLE MAIDEN AND THE LITTLE BIRD	9
THE COW	10
THE COW	10
I'M A MERRY, MERRY SQUIRREL	11
THE CATS' TEA-PARTY	12
THE BIRD'S NEST	13
THE MOUSE AND THE CAKE	13
THE STORY OF LITTLE SUCK-A-THUMB	15
MY SHADOW	15
KINDNESS TO ANIMALS	16
FROST	17
DIRTY JIM	17
THE DEATH OF MASTER TOMMY ROOK	18
HOW DOTH THE LITTLE BUSY BEE	21
MR. NOBODY	21
I WOULD LIKE YOU FOR A COMRADE	22
THE STORY OF AUGUSTUS WHO WOULD NOT HAVE ANY SOUP	23
THE PIN	24

xi

	PAGE
Early Rising	25
Pater's Bathe	26
Hiding	26
Meddlesome Matty	27
Big Smith	29
Wynken, Blynken, and Nod	31
The Pedlar's Caravan	32
The dreadful Story about Harriet and the Matches	33
The Coming of Spring	35
The little Lark	36
Choosing a Name	37
The Fairy Book	38
What became of them	39
Jemima	39
Snowdrops	40
Little Girls	41
A Boy's Aspirations	41
Let Dogs delight to bark and bite	43
A Christmas Visitor	43
The Lost Doll	44
The Jumblies	45
My Kingdom	47
The Spider and the Fly	48
The Cow and the Ass	51
The Pet Lamb	52
Harold and Alice; or, The Reformed Giant	55
The Miller of the Dee	60
The Lark and the Rook	61
The Lamb	62
The Bear's Song	63
A Grace for a Child	64
Lady Moon	64
Seven Times One	65
Try Again	66
A Lesson for Mamma	68

CONTENTS

	PAGE
To J. H.	70
A Night with a Wolf	71
Home for the Holidays	72
Jack Frost	73
Robert of Lincoln	74
The Sparrow's Nest	77
The Grey Squirrels	78
The Village Blacksmith	80
Queen Mab	82
The Camel's Hump	83
The bad Boy	84
The Fairies	86
The Sluggard	87
The Wind in a Frolic	88
Robin Redbreast	90
The Sea-Gull	91
My Heart's in the Highlands	93
When Polly buys a Hat	94
The World's Music	95
One, Two, Three	97
The Babes in the Wood	98
A Boy's Song	103
Hie Away	104
The Sea	104
At Sea	105
The Lights	106
Little Billee	107
Great, wide, beautiful, wonderful World	108
Praise for Mercies	109
First Spring Morning	109
Gay Robin	110
Valentine's Day	111
The Blackbird	111
Going into Breeches	112
A Child's Evensong	114
Hunting Song	115

	PAGE
SING ON, BLYTHE BIRD	116
WEE WILLIE WINKIE	116
CREEP AFORE YE GANG	117
AULD DADDY DARKNESS	118
WEE DAVIE DAYLICHT	119
CHANTICLEER	119
THE GIRL AND HER FAWN	121
THE IMPS IN THE HEAVENLY MEADOW	122
THE WRECK OF THE STEAMSHIP 'PUFFIN'	127
THE CHOICE	131
THE ENCHANTED SHIRT	133
THE FAIRIES OF THE CALDON LOW	135
LLEWELLYN AND HIS DOG	138
THE BATTLE OF BLENHEIM	141
THE INCHCAPE ROCK	143
THE ARAB'S FAREWELL TO HIS STEED	145
BERNARDO DEL CARPIO	148
BERNARD AND ALPHONSO	151
BERNARDO'S REVENGE	153
LOCHINVAR	155
YE MARINERS OF ENGLAND	157
THE PILGRIM FATHERS	158
INCIDENT OF THE FRENCH CAMP	160
HORATIUS	161
THE SLAVE'S DREAM	166
THE GLOVE AND THE LIONS	168
LUCY GRAY; OR SOLITUDE	169
THE WRECK OF THE HESPERUS	171
LORD ULLIN'S DAUGHTER	174
EDINBURGH AFTER FLODDEN	176
SOLDIER, REST!	182
GATHERING-SONG OF DONALD DHU	183
BORDER BALLAD	184
THE CHARGE OF THE LIGHT BRIGADE	185
VITAÏ LAMPADA	186
ADMIRALS ALL	187

CONTENTS

	PAGE
How they brought the Good News from Ghent to Aix	189
The Loss of the Birkenhead	192
The Red Thread of Honour	194
The Battle of the Baltic	197
Nora's Vow	199
From 'As you Like It'	200
From 'The Winter's Tale'	201
From 'King Henry VIII.'	201
From 'The Tempest'	201
Lady Clare	202
The Green Gnome	204
Ballad of Earl Haldan's Daughter	207
Barbara Frietchie	208
King John and the Abbot of Canterbury	210
Hiawatha's Childhood	213
The Pied Piper of Hamelin	216
The Priest and the Mulberry Tree	225
To-day	226
A Boy's Prayer	227
A Farewell	227
Shepherd Boy's Song	228
Pippa's Song	228
The Tiger	228
Nurse's Song	229
The Sandpiper	230
Modereen Rue	231
The Ships	232
On the Quay	234
The Diverting History of John Gilpin	235
The Old Navy	243
O Captain! My Captain!	244
The Burial of Sir John Moore	245
The Eve of Waterloo	246
The Olive Tree	249
Abou Ben Adhem	250
Contentment	251

	PAGE
The Hitchin May-day Song	252
Little Boy Blue	253
The Sands of Dee	254
The Skylark	254
From 'Two Gentlemen of Verona'	255
From 'As You Like It'	256
From 'A Midsummer-Night's Dream'	256
From 'Love's Labour's Lost'	257
Be True	258
The Perfect Life	258
John Grumlie	259
Sir Patrick Spens	260
The Pilgrim	264
To Daffodils	264
The Shepherd to his Love	265
Song	266
Shiv and the Grasshopper	267
St. Molios in Arran	268
Langley Lane	270
Jock o' Hazledean	273
A Day in June	274
An Ode	275
Be Useful	275
Love of Fatherland	275
England, my England	276
The Moon-Child	278
The Forsaken Merman	279
The Gay Goshawk	283
Hynde Etin	288

CRADLE SONGS

Cradle Song	297
Good-night	297
Baby	298
Little Birdie	299

CONTENTS

	PAGE
JOHNEEN	299
BARTHOLOMEW	300
A LULLABY	301
CHRISTMAS EVE	302
AN IRISH LULLABY	303
LULLABY OF AN INFANT CHIEF	303
THE ROCK-A-BY LADY	304
SONG	305
INFANT JOY	305
THE COTTAGER TO HER INFANT	306
LULLABY	306
LULLABY	307
TO A SLEEPING CHILD	308
A CRADLE HYMN	309
HUSHING SONG	310
A BLESSING FOR THE BLESSED	311

CAROLS, HYMNS, AND SACRED VERSE

CRADLE HYMN	315
MARY'S MANGER-SONG	315
AS JOSEPH WAS A-WALKING	316
CAROL	317
A CHRISTMAS CAROL	317
GOD REST YOU MERRY, GENTLEMEN	319
THE FIRST NOWELL	321
THE SON OF GOD IS BORN	322
GOOD KING WENCESLAS	323
A CHRISTMAS CAROL	325
A CHRISTMAS CAROL	326
THE THREE KINGS OF COLOGNE	327
A CHRISTMAS HYMN	328
THE CHILD OF BETHLEHEM	329
CHRISTMAS DAY	330
NEW PRINCE, NEW POMP	331
A HYMN OF THE NATIVITY	332

How Christmas came	334
To his Saviour, a Child; a Present by a Child	334
The Star Song: a Caroll to the King	335
A Carol for Christmas Eve	335
The New-Yeere's Gift	337
A Little Child's Hymn	337
Morning Hymn	338
The Good Shepherd	338
Evening Hymn	339
The Tender Shepherd	340
A Child's Prayer	341
Jesus bids us Shine	341
All Things Bright and Beautiful	342
God, Who hath made the Daisies	343
Psalm XXIII.	344
Early Piety	345
Ex ore Infantium	346
Song	348
Christ and the Little Ones	348
Eventide	350
The God of my Childhood	351
The Bird of Christ	353
A Child's Easter	354
INDEX OF FIRST LINES	357

INDEX OF AUTHORS

	PAGE
ALEXANDER, C. FRANCES	
A Christmas Hymn	328
All Things Bright and Beautiful	342
ALLINGHAM, WILLIAM	
The Fairies	86
Robin Redbreast	90
ALMA-TADEMA, LAURENCE	
The Robin	1
Frost	17
Snowdrops	40
Little Girls	41
A Lullaby	301
A Blessing for the Blessed	311
ANSTEY, F.	
The Wreck of the Steamship Puffin	127
ARNOLD, MATTHEW	
The Forsaken Merman	279
AYTOUN, WILLIAM	
Edinburgh After Flodden	176
BALLANTINE, JAMES	
Creep Afore ye Gang	117
BARING-GOULD, S.	
The Olive Tree	249
Evening Hymn	339
BARNES, WILLIAM	
Lullaby	307
BEECHING, H. C.	
A Boy's Prayer	227

	PAGE
BELL, J. J.	
THE LIGHTS	106
THE CHOICE	131
THE SHIPS	232
ON THE QUAY	234
BLAKE, WILLIAM	
THE LAMB	62
THE TIGER	228
NURSE'S SONG	229
INFANT JOY	305
BONAR, HORATIO	
BE TRUE	258
BONNEY, CALLIE L.	
HOW CHRISTMAS CAME	334
BRIDGES, ROBERT	
FIRST SPRING MORNING	109
GAY ROBIN	110
BROOKS, PHILLIPS	
THE CHILD OF BETHLEHEM	329
BROWN, ABBIE FARWELL	
THE LOST PLAYMATE	2
BROWNING, ROBERT	
INCIDENT OF THE FRENCH CAMP	160
HOW THEY BROUGHT THE GOOD NEWS FROM GHENT TO AIX	189
THE PIED PIPER OF HAMELIN	216
PIPPA'S SONG	228
BRYANT, WILLIAM CULLEN	
ROBERT OF LINCOLN	74
BUCHANAN, ROBERT	
THE GREEN GNOME	204
LANGLEY LANE	270
BUNCE, KATE E.	
THE IMPS IN THE HEAVENLY MEADOW	122
BUNNER, HENRY C.	
ONE, TWO, THREE	97
BUNYAN, JOHN	
SHEPHERD BOY'S SONG	228
THE PILGRIM	264

INDEX OF AUTHORS

	PAGE
BURNS, ROBERT	
My Heart's in the Highlands	93
BYRON, LORD	
The Eve of Waterloo	246
CAMPBELL, THOMAS	
Ye Mariners of England	157
Lord Ullin's Daughter	174
The Battle of the Baltic	197
CARLYLE, THOMAS	
To-day	226
CHILD, L. MARIA	
Who stole the Bird's Nest	6
The Little Maiden and the Little Bird	9
CLOUGH, ARTHUR HUGH	
To a Sleeping Child	308
COLLINS, WILLIAM	
An Ode	275
COOK, ELIZA	
The Mouse and the Cake	13
The Death of Master Tommy Rook	18
Try Again	66
Home for the Holidays	72
COWPER, WILLIAM	
The Diverting History of John Gilpin	235
CRASHAW, RICHARD	
A Hymn of the Nativity	332
CUNNINGHAM, ALLAN	
At Sea	105
DAYRE, SYDNEY	
A Lesson for Mamma	68
DOYLE, SIR FRANCIS H.	
The Loss of the Birkenhead	192
The Red Thread of Honour	194
DUNCAN, MARY L.	
The Tender Shepherd	340

DYER, SIR E.	PAGE
CONTENTMENT	251
EDWARDS, MATILDA B.	
A CHILD'S PRAYER	341
EWING, JULIANA HORATIA	
BIG SMITH	29
FABER, F. W.	
THE GOD OF MY CHILDHOOD	351
FERGUSON, JAMES	
AULD DADDY DARKNESS	118
FIELD, EUGENE	
WYNKEN, BLYNKEN, AND NOD	31
LITTLE BOY BLUE	253
CHRISTMAS EVE	302
THE ROCK-A-BY LADY	304
THE THREE KINGS OF COLOGNE	327
GALE, NORMAN	
THE FAIRY BOOK	38
THE BAD BOY	84
BARTHOLOMEW	300
GALLIENNE, RICHARD LE	
A CHILD'S EVENSONG	114
GANNETT, WILLIAM CHANNING	
MARY'S MANGER-SONG	315
GILL, JULIA	
CHRIST AND THE LITTLE ONES	348
GRAVES, ALFRED PERCEVAL	
AN IRISH LULLABY	303
HASTINGS, LADY FLORA	
EARLY RISING	25
HAWKINS, H. P.	
THE GOOD SHEPHERD	338
HAY, JOHN	
THE ENCHANTED SHIRT	133

INDEX OF AUTHORS

	PAGE
HEBER, BISHOP	
Early Piety	345
HEMANS, FELICIA	
Bernardo Del Carpio	148
The Pilgrim Fathers	158
HENLEY, W. E.	
England, My England	276
HERBERT, GEORGE	
Be Useful	275
Psalm XXIII.	344
HERRICK, ROBERT	
A Grace for a Child	64
To Daffodils	264
To His Savour, a Child; A Present, by a Child	334
The Star Song: A Caroll to the King	335
The New-Yeere's Gift	337
HILL, E.	
When Polly Buys a Hat	94
HOFFMANN, HEINRICH	
The Story of Little Suck-a-Thumb	15
The Story of Augustus who would not have any Soup	23
The Dreadful Story about Harriet and the Matches	33
HOGG, JAMES	
A Boy's Song	103
The Skylark	254
HOOD, E. P.	
God, who hath made the Daisies	343
HOOD, THOMAS	
Queen Mab	82
HOPPER, NORA	
The Blackbird	111
HOUGHTON, LORD	
Good-night and Good-morning	8
Lady Moon	64
HOWITT, MARY	
The Coming of Spring	35
The Spider and the Fly	48
The Sparrow's Nest	77
The Sea-Gull	91
The Fairies of the Caldon Low	135

		PAGE
HOWITT, WILLIAM		
The Grey Squirrels	. . . . . .	78
The Wind in a Frolic	. . . . . .	88
HUNT, LEIGH		
To J. M.	. . . .	70
The Glove and the Lions	. . . . .	168
Abou Ben Adhem	. . . .	250
INGELOW, JEAN		
Seven Times One	. . . .	65
JONSON, BEN		
The Perfect Life	. . . .	258
KINGSLEY, CHARLES		
The Lost Doll	. . . .	44
Valentine's Day	. . . .	111
Ballad of Earl Haldan's Daughter	. . . .	207
A Farewell	. . . .	227
The Sands of Dee	. . . .	254
KIPLING, RUDYARD		
The Camel's Hump	. . . .	83
Shiv and the Grasshopper	. . . . .	267
LAMB, CHARLES		
Choosing a Name	. . . .	37
LAMB, CHARLES and MARY		
Going into Breeches	. . . . . .	112
LEAR, EDWARD		
The Jumblies	. . . .	45
LITTLEDALE, R. F.		
Morning Hymn	. . . .	338
LOCKHART, J. G.		
Bernardo and Alphonso	. . . . .	151
LONGFELLOW, HENRY W.		
The Village Blacksmith	. . . . .	80
The Slave's Dream	. . . .	166
The Wreck of the Hesperus	. . . .	171
Hiawatha's Childhood	. . . . . .	213

INDEX OF AUTHORS

LOWELL, JAMES RUSSELL
    A Day in June 274
    A Christmas Carol 325

LUTHER, MARTIN
    Cradle Hymn 315

MACAULAY, LORD
    Horatius 161

MACDONALD, GEORGE
    Baby 298

MACKAY, CHARLES
    The Miller of the Dee 60

MACLEOD, FIONA
    The Moon-Child 278
    Hushing Song 310
    The Bird of Christ 353

MACLEOD, NORMAN
    I'm a Merry, Merry Squirrel 11

MARLOWE, CHRISTOPHER
    The Shepherd to His Love 265

MARRYAT, CAPTAIN
    The Old Navy 243

MARVELL, ANDREW
    The Girl and her Fawn 121

MASON, CAROLINE
    Eventide 350

MAUGHAN, HENRY NEVILLE
    Song 348

MILLER, EMILY H.
    Jesus bids us shine 341

MILLER, WILLIAM
    Wee Willie Winkie 116

MITCHELL, LANGDON E.
    Carol 317

MOTHERWELL, WILLIAM
    Sing on, Blythe Bird 116

NEWBOLT, HENRY
    Vitaï Lampada 186
    Admirals All 187

NORTON, THE HON. CAROLINE
    The Arab's Farewell to his Steed 145

O'NEILL, MOIRA
    Johneen 299

PALGRAVE, FRANCIS TURNER
    A little Child's Hymn 337

PARKER, ERIC
    My Garden 2

PARRY, JUDGE
    I would like you for a Comrade 22
    Pater's Bathe 26
    The Bear's Song 63

PEACOCK, THOMAS LOVE
    The Priest and the Mulberry Tree 225

PROCTER, BRYAN WALLER
    The Sea 104

RANDS, W. B.
    The Pedlar's Caravan 32
    Harold and Alice; or the Reformed Giant . . 55
    Great, Wide, Beautiful, Wonderful World . . 108
    Lullaby 306

ROSSETTI, CHRISTINA G.
    A Christmas Carol 326
    Christmas Day 330

SCOTT, SIR WALTER
    Hie Away 104
    Hunting Song 115
    Lochinvar 155

INDEX OF AUTHORS xxvii

	PAGE
SCOTT, SIR WALTER—*continued*	
SOLDIER, REST!	182
GATHERING-SONG OF DONALD DHU	183
BORDER BALLAD	184
NORA'S VOW	199
JOCK O' HAZLEDEAN	273
LOVE OF FATHERLAND	275
LULLABY OF AN INFANT CHIEF	303
SETOUN, GABRIEL	
HIDING	26
JACK FROST	73
THE WORLD'S MUSIC	95
SHAKESPEARE, WILLIAM	
FROM 'AS YOU LIKE IT'	200
FROM 'THE WINTER'S TALE'	201
FROM 'KING HENRY VIII.'	201
FROM 'THE TEMPEST'	201
FROM 'TWO GENTLEMEN OF VERONA'	255
FROM 'AS YOU LIKE IT'	256
FROM 'A MIDSUMMER-NIGHT'S DREAM'	256
FROM 'LOVE'S LABOUR'S LOST'	257
SLOSSON, ANNIE	
A CHRISTMAS CAROL	317
A CHILD'S EASTER	354
SMEDLEY, MENELLA BUTE	
A BOY'S ASPIRATIONS	41
SOUTHEY, ROBERT	
THE BATTLE OF BLENHEIM	141
THE INCHCAPE ROCK	143
SOUTHWELL, ROBERT	
NEW PRINCE, NEW POMP	331
SPENCER, THE HON. W. R.	
LLEWELLYN AND HIS DOG	138
STEEDMAN, C. M.	
ST. MOLIOS IN ARRAN	268
STEVENSON, ROBERT LOUIS	
BED IN SUMMER	1
THE LAMPLIGHTER	3
THE LAND OF COUNTERPANE	4
THE COW	10
MY SHADOW	15
MY KINGDOM	47

TAYLOR, ANN
    The Pin 24
    Meddlesome Matty 27

TAYLOR, BAYARD
    A Night with a Wolf 71

TAYLOR, JANE
    The Star 4
    Dirty Jim 17
    The Cow and the Ass 51
    Good-Night 297

TAYLOR, JANE AND ANN
    The little Fish that would not do as it was bid . 5
    The Cow 10
    The little Lark 36

TENNANT, ROBERT
    Wee Davie Daylight 119

TENNYSON, LORD
    The Charge of the Light Brigade 185
    Lady Clare 202
    Song 266
    Little Birdie 299
    Song 305

THACKERAY, W. M.
    Little Billee 107

THAXTER, CELIA
    The Sandpiper 230

THOMPSON, FRANCIS
    Ex Ore Infantium 346

TURNER, ELIZABETH
    The Bird's Nest 13

TYNAN-HINKSON, KATHARINE
    Chanticleer 119
    Modereen Rue 231

UNKNOWN
    Kindness to Animals 16
    Mr. Nobody 21
    What Became of Them? 39

INDEX OF AUTHORS

UNKNOWN—*continued*

Jemima	39
A Christmas Visitor	43
The Lark and the Rook	61
The Babes in the Wood	98
Bernardo's Revenge	153
King John and the Abbot of Canterbury	210
The Hitchin May-Day Song	252
John Grumlie	259
Sir Patrick Spens	260
The Gay Goshawk	283
Hynde Etin	288
Cradle Song	297
As Joseph was A-walking	316
God rest you merry, Gentlemen	319
The First Nowell	321
The Son of God is Born	322
Good King Wenceslas	323
A Carol for Christmas Eve	335

WATTS, ISAAC

How doth the little busy Bee	21
Let Dogs Delight to Bark and Bite	43
The Sluggard	87
Praise for Mercies	109
A Cradle Hymn	309

WEATHERLEY, F. E.

The Cats' Tea-Party	12

WHITMAN, WALT

O Captain! My Captain!	244

WHITTIER, JOHN GREENLEAF

Barbara Frietchie	208

WOLFE, CHARLES

The Burial of Sir John Moore	245

WORDSWORTH, DOROTHY

The Cottager to her Infant	306

WORDSWORTH, WILLIAM

The Pet Lamb	52
Lucy Gray; or Solitude	169

LIST OF PICTURES

THE LAND OF COUNTERPANE. R. L. STEVENSON
Frontispiece, see p. 4

'I was the giant great and still
That sits upon the pillow-hill.'

AT PAGE

GOOD-NIGHT AND GOOD-MORNING. LORD HOUGHTON . . 8

'A fair little girl sat under a tree,
Sewing as long as her eyes could see.'

WYNKEN, BLYNKEN, AND NOD. EUGENE FIELD . . . 32

'All night long their nets they threw
To the stars in the twinkling foam.'

THE LOST DOLL. CHARLES KINGSLEY 44

'I found my poor little doll, dears,
As I played in the heath one day.'

THE LAMB. WILLIAM BLAKE 62

'Little Lamb, who made thee,
Dost thou know who made thee.'

THE CAMEL'S HUMP. RUDYARD KIPLING . . . 84

'Have lifted the hump—
The horrible hump—
The hump that is black and blue!'

THE BABES IN THE WOOD. UNKNOWN 102

'Their pretty lips with blackberries
Were all besmeared and dyed.'

THE IMPS IN THE HEAVENLY MEADOW. KATE BUNCE . 122

'There is a school, where all the angel children
Must work four hours a day.'

xxx

LIST OF PICTURES

AT PAGE

LOCHINVAR. SIR WALTER SCOTT 156

    'He took her soft hand, ere her mother could bar,—
      "Now tread we a measure!" said young Lochinvar.'

LUCY GRAY. WILLIAM WORDSWORTH 170

    'The storm came on before its time;
      She wandered up and down.'

LADY CLARE. LORD TENNYSON 202

    'Yet here's a kiss for my mother dear.'

THE PIED PIPER OF HAMELIN. ROBERT BROWNING . . 222

    'Tripping and skipping, ran merrily after
      The wonderful music with shouting and laughter.'

FROM 'A MIDSUMMER-NIGHT'S DREAM.' WILLIAM SHAKE-
SPEARE 256

    'Newts and blind-worms, do no wrong,
      Come not near our fairy Queen!'

THE FORSAKEN MERMAN. MATTHEW ARNOLD . . . 280

    'Come, dear children, let us away;
      Down and away below!'

BABY. GEORGE MACDONALD 298

    'Where did you come from, baby dear?'

A CAROL FOR CHRISTMAS EVE. UNKNOWN . . . 336

    'In worship low they bent.'

THE GOLDEN STAIRCASE

THE ROBIN

When father takes his spade to dig
   Then Robin comes along;
He sits upon a little twig
   And sings a little song.

Or, if the trees are rather far,
   He does not stay alone,
But comes up close to where we are
   And bobs upon a stone.

             LAURENCE ALMA TADEMA.

BED IN SUMMER

In winter I get up at night
And dress by yellow candle-light.
In summer, quite the other way,
I have to go to bed by day.

I have to go to bed and see
The birds still hopping on the tree,
Or hear the grown-up people's feet
Still going past me in the street.

And does it not seem hard to you,
When all the sky is clear and blue,
And I should like so much to play,
To have to go to bed by day?

             ROBERT LOUIS STEVENSON.

MY GARDEN

Oh, in my garden every day
    It should be always playtime,
And every bird should have a nest,
    And all the world be May-time!

And everywhere would be my own,
    And there would grow together
White winter flowers and buttercups,
    All in the sunny weather.

The rain should never come by day
    To stop the blackbirds' singing;
The wind should only sometimes blow,
    To set the bluebells ringing.

The butterflies would let me come
    And look quite closely at them,
And birds and rabbits sit quite still
    In case I wished to pat them.

And by the walks I'd watch a brook
    Run in and out and under;
And then, could not the flowers do
    Without the rain, I wonder?

Oh, in my garden every day
    It should be always playtime,
And every bird should have a nest,
    And all the world be May-time!

                      ERIC PARKER.

THE LOST PLAYMATE

All in the pleasant afternoon
I saw a pretty baby moon,
And oh! I loved its silver shine;
It was a little friend of mine.

Through rainy days and sunny weather
I thought we two should grow together;
But then, alas! I did not know
How fast a little moon can grow.

And now when I go out to play
I cannot find the moon all day,
But she has grown so big and bright
They let her keep awake all night!

Though I may not sit up to see,
In bed she comes and smiles at me:
But oh! I miss the little moon
Who played there in the afternoon.

ABBIE FARWELL BROWN.

THE LAMPLIGHTER

My tea is nearly ready and the sun has left the sky;
It's time to take the window to see Leerie going by;
For every night at tea-time, and before you take your seat,
With lantern and with ladder he comes posting up the street.

Now Tom would be a driver, and Maria go to sea,
And my papa's a banker and as rich as he can be;
But I, when I am stronger and can choose what I'm to do,
O Leerie, I'll go round at night and light the lamps with you!

For we are very lucky, with a lamp before the door,
And Leerie stops to light it as he lights so many more;
And oh! before you hurry by with ladder and with light
O Leerie, see a little child and nod to him to-night!

ROBERT LOUIS STEVENSON

THE STAR

Twinkle, twinkle, little star,
How I wonder what you are!
Up above the world, so high,
Like a diamond in the sky.

When the blazing sun is gone,
When he nothing shines upon,
Then you show your little light,
Twinkle, twinkle, all the night.

Then the traveller in the dark,
Thanks you for your tiny spark!
He could not see which way to go,
If you did not twinkle so.

In the dark blue sky you keep,
And often through my curtains peep,
For you never shut your eye
Till the sun is in the sky.

As your bright and tiny spark
Lights the traveller in the dark,
Though I know not what you are,
Twinkle, twinkle, little star.

JANE TAYLOR.

THE LAND OF COUNTERPANE

When I was sick and lay a-bed,
I had two pillows at my head,
And all my toys beside me lay
To keep me happy all the day.

And sometimes for an hour or so
I watched my leaden soldiers go,
With different uniforms and drills,
Among the bed-clothes, through the hills;

And sometimes sent my ships in fleets
All up and down among the sheets;
Or brought my trees and houses out,
And planted cities all about.

I was the giant great and still
That sits upon the pillow-hill,
And sees before him, dale and plain,
The pleasant land of counterpane.
ROBERT LOUIS STEVENSON.

THE LITTLE FISH THAT WOULD NOT DO AS IT WAS BID

'DEAR mother,' said a little fish,
  'Pray is not that a fly?
I'm very hungry, and I wish
  You'd let me go and try.'

'Sweet innocent,' the mother cried,
  And started from her nook,
'That horrid fly is put to hide
  The sharpness of the hook.'

Now, as I've heard, this little trout
  Was young and foolish too,
And so he thought he'd venture out,
  To see if it were true.

And round about the hook he played,
  With many a longing look,
And—'Dear me,' to himself he said,
  'I'm sure that's not a hook.

'I can but give one little pluck:
  Let's see, and so I will.'
So on he went, and lo! it stuck
  Quite through his little gill.

And as he faint and fainter grew,
　　With hollow voice he cried,
'Dear mother, had I minded you,
　　I need not now have died.'

　　　　　　　JANE AND ANN TAYLOR.

WHO STOLE THE BIRD'S NEST

'Tu-whit! tu-whit! tu-whee!
Will you listen to me?
Who stole four eggs I laid,
And the nice nest I made?'

'Not I,' said the cow, 'Moo-oo!
Such a thing I'd never do,
I gave you a wisp of hay,
But didn't take your nest away.
Not I,' said the cow, 'Moo-oo!
Such a thing I'd never do.'

'Tu-whit! tu-whit! tu-whee!
Will you listen to me?
Who stole four eggs I laid,
And the nice nest I made?'

'Not I,' said the dog, 'Bow-wow!
I'm not so mean anyhow!
I gave hairs the nest to make,
But the nest I did not take.
Not I,' said the dog, 'Bow-wow!
I'm not so mean anyhow.'

'Tu-whit! tu-whit! tu-whee!
Will you listen to me?
Who stole four eggs I laid,
And the nice nest I made?'

'Coo-coo! Coo-coo! Coo-coo!
Let me speak a few words too!

Who stole that pretty nest
From poor little yellow breast?'

'Not I,' said the sheep, 'Oh no!
I wouldn't treat a poor bird so.
I gave wool the nest to line,
But the nest was none of mine.
Baa! Baa!' said the sheep, 'Oh no!
I wouldn't treat a poor bird so.'

'Tu-whit! tu-whit! tu-whee!
Will you listen to me?
Who stole four eggs I laid,
And the nice nest I made?'

'Coo-coo! Coo-coo! Coo-coo!
Let me speak a few words too!
Who stole that pretty nest
From poor little yellow breast?

'Caw! Caw!' cried the crow;
'I too should like to know
What thief took away
A bird's nest to-day?'

'Cluck! Cluck!' said the hen;
'Don't ask me again,
Why, I haven't a chick
Would do such a trick.
We all gave her a feather,
And she wove them together.
I'd scorn to intrude
On her and her brood.
Cluck! Cluck!' said the hen,
'Don't ask me again.'

'Chirr-a-whirr! Chirr-a-whirr!
All the birds make a stir!
Let us find out his name,
And all cry "For shame!"'

'I would not rob a bird,'
Said little Mary Green;
'I think I never heard
Of anything so mean.'

'It is very cruel too,'
Said little Alice Neal;
'I wonder if he knew
How sad the bird would feel?'

A little boy hung down his head,
And went and hid behind the bed,
For *he* stole that pretty nest
From poor little yellow breast;
And he felt so full of shame,
He didn't like to tell his name.
              L. MARIA CHILD.

GOOD-NIGHT AND GOOD-MORNING

A FAIR little girl sat under a tree,
Sewing as long as her eyes could see:
Then smoothed her work, and folded it right,
And said, 'Dear work, Good-Night! Good-Night!'

Such a number of rooks came over her head,
Crying 'Caw! caw!' on their way to bed:
She said, as she watched their curious flight,
'Little black things, Good-Night! Good-Night!'

The horses neighed, and the oxen lowed;
The sheep's 'Bleat! bleat!' came over the road:
All seeming to say, with a quiet delight,
'Good little girl, Good-Night! Good-Night!'

She did not say to the sun 'Good-Night!'
Though she saw him there, like a ball of light;
For she knew he had God's time to keep
All over the world, and never could sleep.

A fair little girl sat under a tree,
Sewing as long as her eyes could see,

The tall pink foxglove bowed his head—
The violets curtsied and went to bed;
And good little Lucy tied up her hair,
And said, on her knees, her favourite prayer.

And while on her pillow she softly lay,
She knew nothing more till again it was day:
And all things said to the beautiful sun,
'Good-Morning, Good-Morning! our work is begun.'
LORD HOUGHTON.

THE LITTLE MAIDEN AND THE LITTLE BIRD

'LITTLE bird! little bird! come to me!
I have a green cage ready for thee—
Beauty-bright flowers I'll bring thee anew,
And fresh, ripe cherries, all wet with dew.'

'Thanks, little maiden, for all thy care,—
But I love dearly the clear, cool air,
And my snug little nest in the old oak tree.'
'Little bird! little bird! stay with me.'

'Nay, little damsel! away I'll fly
To greener fields and warmer sky;
When spring returns with pattering rain,
You'll hear my merry song again.'

'Little bird! little bird! who'll guide thee
Over the hills and over the sea?
Foolish one! come in the house to stay,
For I'm very sure you'll lose your way.'

'Ah, no, little maiden! God guides me
Over the hills and over the sea;
I will be free as the rushing air,
And sing of sunshine everywhere.'
L. MARIA CHILD.

THE COW

Thank you, pretty cow, that made
Pleasant milk to soak my bread,
Every day, and every night,
Warm, and fresh, and sweet, and white.

Do not chew the hemlock rank,
Growing on the weedy bank;
But the yellow cowslips eat,
They will make it very sweet.

Where the purple violet grows,
Where the bubbling water flows,
Where the grass is fresh and fine
Pretty cow, go there and dine.

JANE AND ANN TAYLOR.

THE COW

The friendly cow all red and white,
   I love with all my heart:
She gives me cream with all her might,
   To eat with apple tart.

She wanders lowing here and there,
   And yet she cannot stray,
All in the pleasant open air,
   The pleasant light of day;

And blown by all the winds that pass,
   And wet with all the showers,
She walks among the meadow grass
   And eats the meadow flowers.

ROBERT LOUIS STEVENSON.

I'M A MERRY, MERRY SQUIRREL

(From *The Gold Thread*)

' I'M a merry, merry squirrel,
All day I leap and whirl
   Through my home in the old beech-tree;
If you chase me, I will run
In the shade and in the sun,
   But you never, never can catch me!
For round a bough I'll creep,
   Playing hide-and-seek so sly,
Or through the leaves bo-peep,
   With my little shining eye.
Ha, ha, ha! ha, ha, ha! ha, ha, ha!

Up and down I run and frisk,
With my bushy tail to whisk
   All who mope in the old beech-trees;
How droll to see the owl,
As I make him wink and scowl,
   When his sleepy, sleepy head I tease!
And I waken up the bat,
   Who flies off with a scream,
For he thinks that I'm the cat
   Pouncing on him in his dream.
Ha, ha, ha! ha, ha, ha! ha, ha, ha!

Through all the summer long
I never want a song,
   From my birds in the old beech-trees;
I have singers all the night,
And, with the morning bright,
   Come my busy, humming, fat brown bees.
When I've nothing else to do,
   With the nursing birds I sit,
And we laugh at the cuckoo
   A-cuckooing to her tit!
Ha, ha, ha! ha, ha, ha! ha, ha, ha!

When winter comes with snow,
And its cruel tempests blow
    All the leaves from my old beech-trees;
Then beside the wren and mouse
I furnish up a house,
    Where like a prince I live at my ease!
What care I for hail or sleet,
    With my hairy cap and coat;
And my tail across my feet,
    Or wrapp'd about my throat!
Ha, ha, ha! ha, ha, ha! ha, ha, ha!

NORMAN MACLEOD.

THE CATS' TEA-PARTY

FIVE little pussy-cats, invited out to tea,
Cried: 'Mother, let us go—Oh, do! for good we'll surely be.
We'll wear our bibs and hold our things as you have shown us how—
Spoons in right paws, cups in left—and make a pretty bow;
We'll always say, "Yes, if you please," and "Only half of that."'
'Then go, my darling children,' said the happy Mother Cat.
The five little pussy-cats went out that night to tea,
Their heads were smooth and glossy, their tails were swinging free;
They held their things as they had learned, and tried to be polite,—
With snowy bibs beneath their chins they were a pretty sight.
But, alas, for manners beautiful, and coats as soft as silk!
The moment that the little kits were asked to take some milk,

They dropped their spoons, forgot to bow, and—oh,
    what do you think?
They put their noses in the cups and all began to
    drink!
Yes, every naughty little kit set up a miou for more,
Then knocked the tea-cups over, and scampered through
    the door.
F. E. WEATHERLEY.

THE BIRD'S NEST

ELIZA and Anne were extremely distress'd
To see an old bird fly away from her nest,
    And leave her poor young ones alone;
The pitiful chirping they heard from the tree
Made them think it as cruel as cruel could be,
    Not knowing for what she had flown.

But, when with a worm in her bill she return'd,
They smil'd on each other, soon having discern'd
    She had not forsaken her brood;
But like their dear mother was careful and kind,
Still thinking of them, though she left them behind
    To seek for them suitable food.
ELIZABETH TURNER.

THE MOUSE AND THE CAKE

A MOUSE found a beautiful piece of plum-cake,
The richest and sweetest that mortal could make;
'Twas heavy with citron and fragrant with spice,
And covered with sugar all sparkling as ice.

' My stars!' cried the mouse, while his eye beamed with
    glee,
' Here's a treasure I've found; what a feast it will be:

But, hark! there's a noise, 'tis my brothers at play;
So I'll hide with the cake, lest they wander this way.

'Not a bit shall they have, for I know I can eat
Every morsel myself, and I'll have such a treat';
So off went the mouse, as he held the cake fast,
While his hungry young brothers went scampering past.

He nibbled, and nibbled, and panted, but still
He kept gulping it down till he made himself ill;
Yet he swallowed it all, and 'tis easy to guess,
He was soon so unwell that he groaned with distress.

His family heard him, and as he grew worse,
They sent for the doctor, who made him rehearse
How he'd eaten the cake to the very last crumb,
Without giving his playmates and relatives some.

'Ah me!' cried the doctor, 'advice is too late,
You must die before long, so prepare for your fate;
If you had but divided the cake with your brothers,
'Twould have done you no harm, and been good for the others.

'Had you shared it, the treat had been wholesome enough;
But eaten by one, it was dangerous stuff;
So prepare for the worst'; and the word had scarce fled,
When the doctor turned round, and the patient was dead.

Now all little people the lesson may take,
And some large ones may learn from the mouse and the cake,
Not to be over-selfish with what we may gain;
Or the best of our pleasures may turn into pain.

ELIZA COOK.

THE STORY OF LITTLE SUCK-A-THUMB

    ONE day Mamma said: 'Conrad, dear,
I must go out and leave you here.
But mind now, Conrad, what I say,
Don't suck your thumb while I'm away.
The great tall tailor always comes
To little boys that suck their thumbs;
And ere they dream what he's about,
He takes his great sharp scissors out
And cuts their thumbs clean off—and then,
You know, they never grow again.'

Mamma had scarcely turn'd her back,
The thumb was in, alack! alack!

The door flew open, in he ran,
The great long red-legg'd scissor-man.
Oh! children, see! the tailor's come
And caught out little Suck-a-Thumb.
Snip! Snap! Snip! the scissors go;
And Conrad cries out—Oh! Oh! Oh!
Snip! Snap! Snip! They go so fast,
That both his thumbs are off at last.

Mamma comes home; there Conrad stands,
And looks quite sad, and shows his hands:—
'Ah!' said Mamma, 'I knew he'd come
To naughty little Suck-a-Thumb.'
HEINRICH HOFFMANN.

MY SHADOW

I HAVE a little shadow that goes in and out with me,
And what can be the use of him is more than I can
    see

He is very, very like me from the heels up to the head;
And I see him jump before me, when I jump into my
    bed.

The funniest thing about him is the way he likes to
    grow—
Not at all like proper children, which is always very
    slow;
For he sometimes shoots up taller, like an indiarubber
    ball,
And he sometimes gets so little that there's none of
    him at all.

He hasn't got a notion of how children ought to play,
And can only make a fool of me in every sort of way.
He stays so close beside me, he's a coward you can see;
I'd think shame to stick to nursie as that shadow
    sticks to me!

One morning, very early, before the sun was up,
I rose and found the shining dew on every buttercup;
But my lazy little shadow, like an arrant sleepy-head,
Had stayed at home behind me and was fast asleep in
    bed!

ROBERT LOUIS STEVENSON.

KINDNESS TO ANIMALS

Little children, never give
Pain to things that feel and live:
Let the gentle robin come
For the crumbs you save at home,—
As his meat you throw along
He'll repay you with a song;
Never hurt the timid hare
Peeping from her green grass lair,
Let her come and sport and play
On the lawn at close of day;

THE GOLDEN STAIRCASE

The little lark goes soaring high
To the bright windows of the sky,
Singing as if 'twere always spring,
And fluttering on an untired wing,—
Oh! let him sing his happy song,
Nor do these gentle creatures wrong.

UNKNOWN.

FROST

The flowers in the garden
  Are very cold at night;
When I look out of window
  Their beds are hard and white.

The primrose and the scilla,
  The merry crocus too—
O! Jane, if we were flowers,
  What should we children do?

We'd have to sleep all naked
  Beneath the windy trees;
Yet we should die, I know it,
  With even a chemise. . . .

LAURENCE ALMA TADEMA.

DIRTY JIM

There was one little Jim,
'Tis reported of him,
  And must be to his lasting disgrace,
That he never was seen
With hands at all clean,
  Nor yet ever clean was his face.

His friends were much hurt
To see so much dirt,
    And often they made him quite clean;
But all was in vain,
He got dirty again,
    And not at all fit to be seen.

It gave him no pain
To hear them complain,
    Nor his own dirty clothes to survey:
His indolent mind
No pleasure could find
    In tidy and wholesome array.

The idle and bad
Like this little lad,
    May love dirty ways, to be sure;
But good boys are seen
To be decent and clean,
    Although they are ever so poor.

                  JANE TAYLOR.

THE DEATH OF MASTER TOMMY ROOK

A PAIR of steady Rooks
Chose the safest of all nooks,
In the hollow of a tree to build their home;
And while they kept within,
They did not care a pin
For any roving sportsman who might come.

Their family of five
Were all happy and alive;
And Mrs. Rook was careful as could be,
To never let them out,
Till she looked all round about,
And saw that they might wander far and free.

She had talked to every one
    Of the dangers of a gun,
And fondly begged that none of them would stir
    To take a distant flight,
    At morning, noon, or night,
Before they prudently asked leave of her.

But one fine sunny day,
    Toward the end of May,
Young Tommy Rook began to scorn her power,
    And said that he would fly
    Into the field close by,
And walk among the daisies for an hour.

'Stop, stop!' she cried, alarmed,
    'I see a man that's armed,
And he will shoot you, sure as you are seen;
    Wait till he goes, and then,
    Secure from guns and men,
We all will have a ramble on the green.'

But Master Tommy Rook,
    With a very saucy look,
Perched on a twig, and plumed his jetty breast;
    Still talking all the while,
    In a very pompous style,
Of doing just what he might like the best.

'I don't care one bit,' said he,
    'For any gun you see;
I am tired of the cautions you bestow:
    I mean to have my way,
    Whatever you may say,
And shall not ask when I may stay or go.'

'But my son,' the mother cried,
    'I only wish to guide
Till you are wise, and fit to go alone;

I have seen much more of life,
Of danger, woe, and strife,
Than you, my child, can possibly have known.

'Just wait ten minutes here,
Let that man disappear;
I am sure he means to do some evil thing;
I fear you may be shot,
If you leave this sheltered spot,
So, pray, come back, and keep beside my wing.'

But Master Tommy Rook
Gave another saucy look,
And chattered out, 'Don't care! don't care! don't care!'
And off he flew with glee,
From his brothers in the tree,
And lighted on the field so green and fair.

He hopped about and found
All pleasant things around;
He strutted through the daisies,—but, alas!
A loud shot—Bang! was heard,
And the wounded, silly bird
Rolled over, faint and dying, on the grass.

'There, there, I told you so,'
Cried his mother in her woe,
'I warned you, with a parent's thoughtful truth;
And you see that I was right,
When I tried to stop your flight,
And said you needed me to guide your youth.'

Poor Master Tommy Rook
Gave a melancholy look,
And cried, just as he drew his latest breath:
'Forgive me, mother dear,
And let my brothers hear,
That disobedience caused my cruel death.'

Now when his lot was told,
　The Rooks, both young and old,
All said he should have done as he was bid;
　That he well deserved his fate;
　And I, who now relate
His hapless story, really think he did.

ELIZA COOK.

HOW DOTH THE LITTLE BUSY BEE

How doth the little busy bee
　Improve each shining hour,
And gather honey all the day
　From every opening flow'r!

How skilfully she builds her cell!
　How neat she spreads the wax!
And labours hard to store it well
　With the sweet food she makes.

In works of labour or of skill,
　I would be busy too;
For Satan finds some mischief still
　For idle hands to do.

In books, or work, or healthful play,
　Let my first years be past,
That I may give for ev'ry day
　Some good account at last.

ISAAC WATTS.

MR. NOBODY

I KNOW a funny little man,
　As quiet as a mouse,
Who does the mischief that is done
　In everybody's house!

There's no one ever sees his face,
   And yet we all agree
That every plate we break was cracked
   By Mr. Nobody.

'Tis he who always tears our books,
   Who leaves the door ajar,
He pulls the buttons from our shirts,
   And scatters pins afar;
That squeaking door will always squeak,
   For, prithee, don't you see,
We leave the oiling to be done
   By Mr. Nobody.

He puts damp wood upon the fire,
   That kettles cannot boil;
His are the feet that bring in mud,
   And all the carpets soil.
The papers always are mislaid,
   Who had them last but he?
There's no one tosses them about
   But Mr. Nobody.

The finger-marks upon the door
   By none of us are made;
We never leave the blinds unclosed,
   To let the curtains fade.
The ink we never spill; the boots
   That lying round you see
Are not our boots;—they all belong
   To Mr. Nobody.

UNKNOWN.

I WOULD LIKE YOU FOR A COMRADE

(From Katawampus)

I WOULD like you for a comrade, for I love you, that I do,
I never met a little girl as amiable as you;

I would teach you how to dance and sing, and how to
    talk and laugh,
If I were not a little girl and you were not a calf.

I would like you for a comrade, you should share my
    barley meal,
And butt me with your little horns just hard enough to
    feel;
We would lie beneath the chestnut-trees and watch the
    leaves uncurl,
If I were not a clumsy calf and you a little girl.

JUDGE PARRY.

THE STORY OF AUGUSTUS WHO WOULD NOT HAVE ANY SOUP

Augustus was a chubby lad;
Fat, ruddy cheeks Augustus had;
And everybody saw with joy
The plump and hearty, healthy boy.
He ate and drank as he was told,
And never let his soup get cold.
But one day, one cold winter's day,
He scream'd out—'Take the soup away!
O take the nasty soup away!
I won't have any soup to-day.'

Next day begins his tale of woes,
Quite lank and lean Augustus grows.
Yet though he feels so weak and ill,
The naughty fellow cries out still—
'Not any soup for me, I say:
O take the nasty soup away!
I won't have any soup to-day.'

The third day comes; O what a sin!
To make himself so pale and thin.
Yet, when the soup is put on table,
He screams, as loud as he is able,—

'Not any soup for me, I say:
O take the nasty soup away!
I won't have any soup to-day.'

Look at him, now the fourth day's come!
He scarcely weighs a sugar-plum;
He's like a little bit of thread,
And on the fifth day, he was—dead!

HEINRICH HOFFMANN.

THE PIN

'DEAR me! what signifies a pin!
　　I'll leave it on the floor;
My pincushion has others in,
　　Mamma has plenty more:
A miser will I never be,'
Said little heedless Emily.

So tripping on to giddy play
　　She left the pin behind,
For Betty's broom to whisk away,
　　Or some one else to find;
She never gave a thought, indeed,
To what she might to-morrow need.

Next day a party was to ride,
　　To see an air-balloon!
And all the company beside
　　Were dressed and ready soon:
But she, poor girl, she could not stir,
For just a pin to finish her.

'Twas vainly now, with eye and hand,
　　She did to search begin;
There was not one—not one, the band
　　Of her pelisse to pin!
She cut her pincushion in two,
But not a pin had slidden through!

At last, as, hunting on the floor,
    Over a crack she lay,
The carriage rattled to the door,
    Then rattled fast away.
Poor Emily! she was not in,
For want of just—a single pin!

There's hardly anything so small,
    So trifling, or so mean,
That we may never want at all,
    For service unforeseen:
And those who venture wilful waste,
May woful want expect to taste.

ANN TAYLOR.

EARLY RISING

Get up, little sister, the morning is bright,
And the birds are all singing to welcome the light;
The buds are all op'ning—the dew's on the flower;
If you shake but a branch, see, there falls quite a shower.

By the side of their mothers, look, under the trees,
How the young fawns are skipping about as they please;
And by all those rings on the water, I know,
The fishes are merrily swimming below.

The bee, I dare say, has been long on the wing,
To get honey from every flower of the spring;
For the bee never idles, but labours all day,
And thinks, wise little insect, work better than play.

The lark's singing gaily; it loves the bright sun,
And rejoices that now the gay spring is begun;
For the spring is so cheerful, I think 'twould be wrong
If we do not feel happy to hear the lark's song.

Get up, for when all things are merry and glad,
Good children should never be lazy and sad;
For God gives us daylight, dear sister, that we
May rejoice like the lark, and may work like the bee.
LADY FLORA HASTINGS.

PATER'S BATHE

(From Katawampus)

You can take a tub with a rub and a scrub in a two-foot tank of tin,
You can stand and look at the whirling brook and think about jumping in;
You can chatter and shake in the cold black lake, but the kind of bath for me,
Is to take a dip from the side of a ship, in the trough of the rolling sea.

You may lie and dream in the bed of a stream when an August day is dawning,
Or believe 'tis nice to break the ice on your tub of a winter morning;
You may sit and shiver beside the river, but the kind of bath for me,
Is to take a dip from the side of a ship, in the trough of the rolling sea.
JUDGE PARRY.

HIDING

When the table-cloth is laid
  And the cups are on the table;
When the tea and toast are made,
  That's a happy time for Mabel.

Stealing to her mother's side,
   In her ear she whispers low,
'When papa comes in I'll hide;
   Do not tell him where I go.'

On her knees upon the floor;
   In below the sofa creeping;
When she hears him at the door
   She pretends that she is sleeping.
'Where is Mabel?' father cries,
   Looking round and round about.
Then he murmurs in surprise,
   'Surely Mabel can't be out.'

First he looks behind his chair,
   Then he peers below the table,
Seeking, searching everywhere,
   All in vain for little Mabel.
But at last he thinks he knows,
   And he laughs and shakes his head;
Says to mother, 'I suppose
   Mabel has been put to bed.'

But when he sits down to tea,
   From beneath the sofa creeping,
Mabel climbs upon his knee,
   Claps her hands: 'I was not sleeping.'
Father whispers, 'Where's my girl's
   Very secret hiding-place?'
But she only shakes her curls,
   Laughing, smiling in his face.

                      GABRIEL SETOUN.

MEDDLESOME MATTY

ONE ugly trick has often spoiled
   The sweetest and the best;
Matilda, though a pleasant child,
   One ugly trick possessed,

Which, like a cloud before the skies,
Hid all her better qualities.

Sometimes she'd lift the tea-pot lid,
  To peep at what was in it;
Or tilt the kettle, if you did
  But turn your back a minute.
In vain you told her not to touch,
Her trick of meddling grew so much.

Her grandmamma went out one day,
  And by mistake she laid
Her spectacles and snuff-box gay
  Too near the little maid;
'Ah! well,' thought she, 'I'll try them on,
As soon as grandmamma is gone.'

Forthwith she placed upon her nose
  The glasses large and wide;
And looking round, as I suppose,
  The snuff-box, too, she spied:
'Oh! what a pretty box is that;
I'll open it,' said little Matt.

'I know that grandmamma would say,
  "Don't meddle with it, dear";
But then, she's far enough away,
  And no one else is near:
Besides, what can there be amiss
In opening such a box as this?'

So thumb and finger went to work
  To move the stubborn lid,
And presently a mighty jerk
  The mighty mischief did;
For all at once, ah! woful case,
The snuff came puffing in her face.

Poor eyes and nose, and mouth beside,
  A dismal sight presented;

In vain, as bitterly she cried,
    Her folly she repented.
In vain she ran about for ease;
    She could do nothing now but sneeze.

She dashed the spectacles away,
    To wipe her tingling eyes,
And as in twenty bits they lay,
    Her grandmamma she spies.
'Hey-day! and what's the matter now?'
Says grandmamma, with lifted brow.

Matilda, smarting with the pain,
    And tingling still, and sore,
Made many a promise to refrain
    From meddling evermore.
And 'tis a fact, as I have heard,
She ever since has kept her word.

ANN TAYLOR.

BIG SMITH

Are you a Giant, great big man, or is your real name Smith?
Nurse says you've got a hammer that you hit bad children with.
I'm good to-day, and so I've come to see if it is true
That you can turn a red-hot rod into a horse's shoe.

Why do you make the horses' shoes of iron instead of leather?
Is it because they are allowed to go out in bad weather?
If horses should be shod with iron, Big Smith, will you shoe mine?
For now I may not take him out, excepting when it's fine.

Although he's not a real live horse, I'm very fond of him;
His harness won't take off and on, but still it's new and trim.
His tail is hair, he has four legs, but neither hoofs nor heels;
I think he'd seem more like a horse without these yellow wheels.

They say that Dapple-grey's not yours, but don't you wish he were?
My horse's coat is only paint, but his is soft grey hair;
His face is big and kind, like yours, his forelock white as snow—
Shan't you be sorry when you've done his shoes and he must go?

I do so wish, Big Smith, that I might come and live with you;
To rake the fire, to heat the rods, to hammer two and two.
To be so black, and not to have to wash unless I choose;
To pat the dear old horses, and to mend their poor old shoes!

When all the world is dark at night, you work among the stars,
A shining shower of fireworks beat out of red-hot bars.
I've seen you beat, I've heard you sing, when I was going to bed;
And now your face and arms looked black, and now were glowing red.

The more you work, the more you sing, the more the bellows roar;
The falling stars, the flying sparks, stream shining more and more.
You hit so hard, you look so hot, and yet you never tire;
It must be very nice to be allowed to play with fire.

I long to beat and sing and shine, as you do, but instead
I put away my horse, and Nurse puts me away to bed.
I wonder if you go to bed; I often think I'll keep
Awake and see, but, though I try, I always fall asleep.

I know it's very silly, but I sometimes am afraid
Of being in the dark alone, especially in bed.
But when I see your forge-light come and go upon
    the wall,
And hear you through the window, I am not afraid
    at all.

I often hear a trotting horse, I sometimes hear it stop;
I hold my breath — you stay your song — it's at the
    blacksmith's shop.
Before it goes, I'm apt to fall asleep, Big Smith, it's
    true;
But then I dream of hammering that horse's shoes
    with you!

                    JULIANA HORATIA EWING.

WYNKEN, BLYNKEN, AND NOD

Wynken, Blynken, and Nod one night
    Sailed off in a wooden shoe—
Sailed on river of crystal light,
    Into a sea of dew.
'Where are you going, and what do you wish?'
    The old moon asked the three.
'We have come to fish for the herring-fish
    That live in this beautiful sea;
      Nets of silver and gold have we!'
        Said Wynken, Blynken, and Nod.

The old moon laughed and sang a song,
    As they rocked in the wooden shoe,
And the wind that sped them all night long
    Ruffled the waves of dew.

The little stars were the herring-fish
   That lived in that beautiful sea—
'Now cast your nets wherever you wish—
   But never afeared are we';
   So cried the stars to the fishermen three:
      Wynken, Blynken, and Nod.

All night long their nets they threw
   To the stars in the twinkling foam—
Then down from the skies came the wooden shoe,
   Bringing the fishermen home;
'Twas all so pretty a sail, it seemed
   As if it could not be,
And some folks thought 'twas a dream they'd dreamed
   Of sailing that beautiful sea—
   But I shall name you the fishermen three:
      Wynken, Blynken, and Nod.

Wynken and Blynken are two little eyes,
   And Nod is a little head,
And the wooden shoe that sailed the skies
   Is a wee one's trundle-bed.
So shut your eyes while mother sings
   Of wonderful sights that be,
And you shall see the beautiful things
   As you rock on the misty sea,
   Where the old shoe rocked the fishermen three:
      Wynken, Blynken, and Nod.
                           EUGENE FIELD.

THE PEDLAR'S CARAVAN

I wish I lived in a caravan,
With a horse to drive, like a pedlar-man!
Where he comes from nobody knows,
Or where he goes to, but on he goes!

ALL NIGHT LONG THEIR NETS THEY THREW
FOR THE FISH IN THE TWINKLING FOAM—

THE GOLDEN STAIRCASE

His caravan has windows two,
And a chimney of tin, that the smoke comes
    through;
He has a wife, with a baby brown,
And they go riding from town to town.

Chairs to mend, and delf to sell!
He clashes the basins like a bell;
Tea-trays, baskets ranged in order,
Plates, with alphabets round the border!

The roads are brown, and the sea is green,
But his house is like a bathing-machine;
The world is round, and he can ride,
Rumble and slash, to the other side!

With the pedlar-man I should like to roam,
And write a book when I came home;
All the people would read my book,
Just like the Travels of Captain Cook!

W. B. RANDS.

THE DREADFUL STORY ABOUT HARRIET AND THE MATCHES

It almost makes me cry to tell
What foolish Harriet befell.
Mamma and Nurse went out one day
And left her all alone at play;
Now, on the table close at hand,
A box of matches chanc'd to stand;
And kind Mamma and Nurse had told her
That, if she touch'd them, they should scold her.
But Harriet said: 'Oh, what a pity!
For, when they burn, it is so pretty;
They crackle so, and spit, and flame;
Mamma, too, often does the same.'

    The pussy-cats heard this,
    And they began to hiss,
    And stretch their claws
    And raise their paws;
    'Me-ow,' they said, ' me-ow, me-o,
    You'll burn to death, if you do so.'

But Harriet would not take advice,
She lit a match, it was so nice!
It crackled so, it burn'd so bright,
It filled her with immense delight.
She jump'd for joy and ran about
And was too pleas'd to put it out.

    The pussy-cats saw this
    And said : ' Oh, naughty, naughty Miss!'
    And stretch'd their claws
    And rais'd their paws:
    ''Tis very, very wrong, you know,
    Me-ow, me-o, me-ow, me-o,
    You will be burnt, if you do so.'

And see! oh! what a dreadful thing!
The fire has caught her apron-string;
Her apron burns, her arms, her hair;
She burns all over, everywhere.

    Then how the pussy-cats did mew,
    What else, poor pussies, could they do?
    They scream'd for help, 'twas all in vain!
    So then, they said: 'We'll scream again;
    Make haste, make haste, me-ow, me-o,
    She'll burn to death, we told her so.'

So she was burnt, with all her clothes,
And arms, and hands, and eyes, and nose:
Till she had nothing more to lose
Except her little scarlet shoes;
And nothing else but these were found
Among her ashes on the ground.

And when the good cats sat beside
The smoking ashes, how they cried!
'Me-ow, me-oo, me-ow, me-oo,
What will Mamma and Nursy do?'
Their tears ran down their cheeks so fast,
They made a little pond at last.

HEINRICH HOFFMANN.

THE COMING OF SPRING

I AM coming, little maiden,
With the pleasant sunshine laden,
With the honey for the bee,
With the blossom for the tree,
With the flower and with the leaf—
Till I come the time is brief.

I am coming, I am coming.
Hark! the little bee is humming;
See the lark is soaring high
In the bright and sunny sky;
And the gnats are on the wing—
Little maiden, now is Spring.

See the yellow catkins cover
All the slender willows over,
And on mossy banks so green
Starlike primroses are seen,
And their clustering leaves below
White and purple violets grow.

Hark! the little lambs are bleating,
And the cawing rooks are meeting
In the elms, a noisy crowd,
And all birds are singing loud,
And the first white butterfly
In the sun goes flitting by.

Little maiden, look around thee.
Green and flowery fields surround thee,
Every little stream is bright,
All the orchard trees are white,
And each small and waving shoot
Has for thee sweet flower or fruit.

Turn thy eyes to earth and heaven.
God, for thee, the spring hath given,
Taught the birds their melodies,
Clothed the earth and cleared the skies.
For thy pleasure or thy food
Pour thy soul in gratitude,
So mayst thou 'mid blessings dwell.
Little maiden, fare thee well.
MARY HOWITT.

THE LITTLE LARK

I HEAR a pretty bird, but hark!
　I cannot see it anywhere.
Oh! it is a little lark,
　Singing in the morning air.
Little lark, do tell me why
You are singing in the sky?

Other little birds at rest,
　Have not yet begun to sing;
Every one is in its nest,
　With its head behind its wing:
Little lark, then, tell me why
You're so early in the sky?

You look no bigger than a bee,
　In the middle of the blue;
Up above the poplar-tree,
　I can hardly look at you:
Little lark, do tell me why
You are mounted up so high?

THE GOLDEN STAIRCASE

'Tis to watch the silver star,
   Sinking slowly in the skies;
And beyond the mountain far,
   See the glorious sun arise:
Little lady, this is why
I am mounted up so high.

'Tis to sing a merry song
   To the pleasant morning light;
Why stay in my nest so long,
   When the sun is shining bright?
Little lady, this is why
I sing so early in the sky.

To the little birds below,
   I do sing a merry tune;
And I let the ploughman know
   He must come to labour soon.
Little lady, this is why
I am singing in the sky.

              JANE AND ANN TAYLOR.

CHOOSING A NAME

I HAVE got a new-born sister;
I was nigh the first that kissed her.
When the nursing woman brought her
To papa, his infant daughter,
How papa's dear eyes did glisten!—
She will shortly be to christen:
And papa has made the offer,
I shall have the naming of her.

Now I wonder what would please her,
Charlotte, Julia, or Louisa?
Ann and Mary, they're too common;
Joan's too formal for a woman;
Jane's a prettier name beside;
But we had a Jane that died.

They would say, if 'twas Rebecca,
That she was a little Quaker.
Edith's pretty, but that looks
Better in old English books;
Ellen's left off long ago;
Blanche is out of fashion now.

None that I have named as yet
Are so good as Margaret.
Emily is neat and fine.
What do you think of Caroline?
How I'm puzzled and perplext
What to choose or think of next!
I am in a little fever
Lest the name that I shall give her
Should disgrace her or defame her;
I will leave papa to name her.

CHARLES LAMB.

THE FAIRY BOOK

In summer, when the grass is thick, if mother has the time,
She shows me with her pencil how a poet makes a rhyme,
And often she is sweet enough to choose a leafy nook,
Where I cuddle up so closely when she reads the Fairy-book.

In winter, when the corn's asleep, and birds are not in song,
And crocuses and violets have been away too long,
Dear mother puts her thimble by in answer to my look,
And I cuddle up so closely when she reads the Fairy-book.

And mother tells the servants that of course they must
    contrive
To manage all the household things from four till
    half-past five,
For we really cannot suffer interruption from the cook,
When we cuddle close together with the happy Fairy-
    book.

NORMAN GALE.

WHAT BECAME OF THEM?

He was a rat, and she was a rat,
    And down in one hole they did dwell,
And both were as black as a witch's cat,
    And they loved one another well.

He had a tail, and she had a tail,
    Both long and curling and fine;
And each said, 'Yours is the finest tail
    In the world, excepting mine.'

He smelt the cheese, and she smelt the cheese,
    And they both pronounced it good;
And both remarked it would greatly add
    To the charms of their daily food.

So he ventured out, and she ventured out,
    And I saw them go with pain;
But what befell them I never can tell,
    For they never came back again.

UNKNOWN.

JEMIMA

There was a little girl, and she wore a little curl
    Right down the middle of her forehead,
When she was good, she was very, very good,
    But when she was bad, she was horrid!

One day she went upstairs, while her parents, unawares,
  In the kitchen down below were occupied with meals,
And she stood upon her head, on her little truckle bed,
  And she then began hurraying with her heels.

Her mother heard the noise, and thought it was the boys
  A-playing at a combat in the attic,
But when she climbed the stair and saw Jemima there,
  She took and she did whip her most emphatic.

UNKNOWN.

SNOWDROPS

LITTLE ladies, white and green,
  With your spears about you,
Will you tell us where you've been
  Since we lived without you?

You are sweet, and fresh, and clean,
  With your pearly faces;
In the dark earth where you've been
  There are wondrous places:

Yet you come again, serene,
  When the leaves are hidden;
Bringing joy from where you've been,
  You return unbidden—

Little ladies, white and green,
  Are you glad to cheer us?
Hunger not for where you've been,
  Stay till Spring be near us!

LAURENCE ALMA TADEMA.

LITTLE GIRLS

If no one ever marries me,—
   And I don't see why they should,
For nurse says I'm not pretty,
   And I'm seldom very good—

If no one ever marries me
   I shan't mind very much,
I shall buy a squirrel in a cage,
   And a little rabbit-hutch;

I shall have a cottage near a wood,
   And a pony all my own,
And a little lamb, quite clean and tame,
   That I can take to town;

And when I'm getting really old,—
   At twenty eight or nine—
I shall buy a little orphan girl
   And bring her up as mine.

LAURENCE ALMA TADEMA.

A BOY'S ASPIRATIONS

I was four yesterday: when I'm quite old,
I'll have a cricket-ball made of pure gold;
I'll carve the roast meat, and help soup and fish;
I'll get my feet wet whenever I wish;

I'll never go to bed till twelve o'clock;
I'll make a mud pie in a clean frock;
I'll whip naughty boys with a new birch;
I'll take my guinea-pig always to church;

I'll spend a hundred pounds every day;
I'll have the alphabet quite done away;
I'll have a parrot without a sharp beak;
I'll see a pantomime six times a week;

I'll have a rose-tree, always in bloom;
I'll keep a dancing bear in Mamma's room;
I'll spoil my best clothes, and not care a pin;
I'll have no visitors ever let in;

I'll go at liberty upstairs or down;
I'll pin a dishcloth to the cook's gown;
I'll light the candles, and ring the big bell;
I'll smoke Papa's pipe, feeling quite well;

I'll have a ball of string, fifty miles long;
I'll have a whistle as loud as the gong;
I'll scold the housemaid for making a dirt;
I'll cut my fingers without being hurt;

I'll have my pinafores quite loose and nice;
I'll wear great fishing-boots like Captain Rice;
I'll have a pot of beer at the girls' tea;
I'll have John taught to say 'Thank you,' to me;

I'll never stand up to show that I'm grown;
No one shall say to me, 'Don't throw a stone!'
I'll drop my butter'd toast on the new chintz;
I'll have no governess giving her hints!

I'll have a nursery up in the stars;
I'll lean through windows without any bars;
I'll sail without my nurse in a big boat;
I'll have no comforters tied round my throat;

I'll have a language with not a word spell'd;
I'll ride on horseback without being held;
I'll hear Mamma say, 'My boy, good as gold!'
When I'm a grown-up man sixty years old.

MENELLA BUTE SMEDLEY.

LET DOGS DELIGHT TO BARK AND BITE

    Let dogs delight to bark and bite,
        For God hath made them so;
    Let bears and lions growl and fight,
        For 'tis their nature, too.

    But, children, you should never let
        Such angry passions rise;
    Your little hands were never made
        To tear each other's eyes.

    Let love through all your actions run,
        And all your words be mild;
    Live like the Blessed Virgin's Son,
        That sweet and lovely Child.

    His soul was gentle as a lamb;
        And, as His stature grew,
    He grew in favour both with man,
        And God His Father, too.

    Now Lord of all, He reigns above,
        And from His heavenly throne
    He sees what children dwell in love,
        And marks them for His own.
                      ISAAC WATTS.

A CHRISTMAS VISITOR

He comes in the night! he comes in the night!
    He softly, silently comes;
While the little brown heads on the pillows so white
    Are dreaming of bugles and drums.

He cuts through the snow like a ship through the foam,
    While the white flakes around him whirl;
Who tells him I know not, but he findeth the home
    Of each good little boy and girl.

His sleigh it is long, and deep, and wide;
  It will carry a host of things,
While dozens of drums hang over the side,
  With the sticks sticking under the strings.

And yet not the sound of a drum is heard,
  Not a bugle blast is blown,
As he mounts to the chimney-top like a bird,
  And drops to the hearth like a stone.

The little red stockings he silently fills,
  Till the stockings will hold no more;
The bright little sleds for the great snow hills
  Are quickly set down on the floor.

Then Santa Claus mounts to the roof like a bird,
  And glides to his seat in the sleigh;
Not the sound of a bugle or drum is heard
  As he noiselessly gallops away.

He rides to the East, and he rides to the West,
  Of his goodies he touches not one;
He eateth the crumbs of the Christmas feast
  When the dear little folks are done.

Old Santa Claus doeth all that he can;
  This beautiful mission is his;
Then, children, be good to the little old man
  When you find who the little man is.

UNKNOWN.

THE LOST DOLL

(From The Water Babies)

I ONCE had a sweet little doll, dears,
  The prettiest doll in the world;
Her cheeks were so red and so white, dears,
  And her hair was so charmingly curled.

I found my poor little doll, dears,
As I played on the heath one day

But I lost my poor little doll, dears,
    As I played in the heath one day;
And I cried for her more than a week, dears,
    But I never could find where she lay.

I found my poor little doll, dears,
    As I played in the heath one day;
Folks say she is horribly changed, dears,
    For her paint is all washed away,
And her arm trodden off by the cows, dears,
    And her hair not the least bit curled:
Yet for old sake's sake she is still, dears,
    The prettiest doll in the world.

                      CHARLES KINGSLEY.

THE JUMBLIES

They went to sea in a Sieve, they did,
    In a Sieve they went to sea:
In spite of all their friends could say,
On a winter's morn, on a stormy day,
    In a Sieve they went to sea!
And when the Sieve turned round and round,
And every one cried, 'You'll all be drowned!'
They called aloud, 'Our Sieve ain't big,
But we don't care a button! we don't care a fig!
    In a Sieve we'll go to sea!'
      Far and few, far and few,
Are the lands where the Jumblies live;
Their heads are green, and their hands are blue,
And they went to sea in a Sieve.

They sailed away in a Sieve, they did,
    In a sieve they sailed so fast,
With only a beautiful pea-green veil
Tied with a riband by way of a sail,
    To a small tobacco-pipe mast;

And every one said, who saw them go,
'Oh, won't they be soon upset, you know!
For the sky is dark, and the voyage is long,
And happen what may, it's extremely wrong
    In a sieve to sail so fast!'
       Far and few, far and few,
Are the lands where the Jumblies live;
Their heads are green, and their hands are blue,
And they went to sea in a Sieve.

The water it soon came in, it did,
    The water it soon came in;
So to keep them dry, they wrapped their feet
In a pinky paper all folded neat,
    And they fastened it down with a pin.
And they passed the night in a crockery-jar,
And each of them said, 'How wise we are!
Though the sky be dark, and the voyage be long,
Yet we never can think we were rash or wrong,
    While round in our Sieve we spin!'
       Far and few, far and few,
Are the lands where the Jumblies live;
Their heads are green, and their hands are blue,
And they went to sea in a Sieve.

And all night long they sailed away;
    And when the sun went down,
They whistled and warbled a moony song
To the echoing sound of a coppery gong,
    In the shade of the mountains brown.
'O Timballo! How happy we are,
When we live in a Sieve and a crockery-jar,
And all night long in the moonlight pale,
We sail away with a pea-green sail,
    In the shade of the mountains brown!'
       Far and few, far and few,
Are the lands where the Jumblies live;
Their heads are green, and their hands are blue,
And they went to sea in a Sieve.

THE GOLDEN STAIRCASE 47

They sailed to the Western Sea, they did,
   To a land all covered with trees,
And they bought an Owl, and a useful Cart,
And a pound of Rice, and a Cranberry Tart,
   And a hive of silvery Bees.
And they bought a Pig, and some green Jackdaws,
And a lovely Monkey with lollipop paws,
And forty bottles of Ring-Bo-Ree,
   And no end of Stilton Cheese.
      Far and few, far and few,
Are the lands where the Jumblies live;
Their heads are green, and their hands are blue,
And they went to sea in a Sieve.

And in twenty years they all came back,
   In twenty years or more,
And every one said, 'How tall they've grown!
For they've been to the Lakes, and the Terrible
     Zone,
   And the hills of the Chankly Bore';
And they drank their health, and gave them a
     feast
Of dumplings made of beautiful yeast;
And every one said, 'If we only live,
We too will go to sea in a Sieve,—
   To the hills of the Chankly Bore!'
      Far and few, far and few,
Are the lands where the Jumblies live;
Their heads are green, and their hands are blue,
And they went to sea in a Sieve.
                  EDWARD LEAR.

MY KINGDOM

   Down by a shining water well
   I found a very little dell,
      No higher than my head.

The heather and the gorse about
In summer bloom were coming out,
  Some yellow and some red.

I called the little pool a sea;
The little hills were big to me;
  For I am very small.
I made a boat, I made a town,
I searched the caverns up and down,
  And named them one and all.

And all about was mine, I said,
The little sparrows overhead,
  The little minnows too.
This was the world, and I was king;
For me the bees came by to sing,
  For me the swallows flew.

I played there were no deeper seas,
Nor any wider plains than these,
  Nor other kings than me.
At last I heard my mother call
Out from the house at evenfall,
  To call me home to tea.

And I must rise and leave my dell,
And leave my dimpled water well,
  And leave my heather blooms.
Alas! and as my home I neared,
How very big my nurse appeared,
  How great and cool the rooms!

              ROBERT LOUIS STEVENSON.

THE SPIDER AND THE FLY

'WILL you walk into my parlour?' said the Spider to the Fly,—
''Tis the prettiest little parlour that ever you did spy;

THE GOLDEN STAIRCASE

The way into my parlour is up a winding stair,
And I have many curious things to show when you are there.'
'Oh no, no,' said the little Fly, 'to ask me is in vain,
For who goes up your winding stair can ne'er come down again.'

'I'm sure you must be weary, dear, with soaring up so high;
Will you rest upon my little bed?' said the Spider to the Fly.
'There are pretty curtains drawn around, the sheets are fine and thin,
And if you like to rest a while, I'll snugly tuck you in!'
'Oh no, no,' said the little Fly, 'for I've often heard it said,
They never, never wake again, who sleep upon your bed!'

Said the cunning Spider to the Fly: 'Dear friend, what can I do
To prove the warm affection I've always felt for you?
I have, within my pantry, good store of all that's nice;
I'm sure you're very welcome—will you please to take a slice?'
'Oh no, no,' said the little Fly, 'kind sir, that cannot be,
I've heard what's in your pantry, and I do not wish to see!'

'Sweet creature,' said the Spider, 'you're witty and you're wise;
How handsome are your gauzy wings, how brilliant are your eyes!
I have a little looking-glass upon my parlour shelf,
If you'll step in one moment, dear, you shall behold yourself.'
'I thank you, gentle sir,' she said, 'for what you're pleased to say,
And bidding you good-morning now, I'll call another day.'

The Spider turned him round about, and went into his den,
For well he knew the silly Fly would soon come back again;
So he wove a subtle web, in a little corner sly,
And set his table ready, to dine upon the Fly.
Then he came out to his door again, and merrily did sing,—
'Come hither, hither, pretty Fly, with the pearl and silver wing;
Your robes are green and purple, there's a crest upon your head;
Your eyes are like the diamond bright, but mine are dull as lead!'

Alas, alas! how very soon this silly little Fly,
Hearing his wily, flattering words, came slowly flitting by:
With buzzing wings she hung aloft, then near and nearer drew,—
Thinking only of her brilliant eyes, and green and purple hue,
Thinking only of her crested head—poor foolish thing! At last,
Up jumped the cunning Spider, and fiercely held her fast;
He dragged her up his winding stair, into his dismal den,
Within his little parlour—but she ne'er came out again!
And now, dear little children, who may this story read,
To idle, silly, flattering words, I pray you, ne'er give heed:
Unto an evil counsellor close heart, and ear, and eye,
And take a lesson from this tale, of the Spider and the Fly.

MARY HOWITT.

THE COW AND THE ASS

Beside a green meadow a stream used to flow,
So clear, you might see the white pebbles below;
To this cooling brook the warm cattle would stray,
To stand in the shade on a hot summer's day.

A cow, quite oppressed by the heat of the sun,
Came here to refresh, as she often had done,
And, standing quite still, stooping over the stream,
Was musing, perhaps; or perhaps she might dream.

But soon a brown ass, of respectable look,
Came trotting up also, to taste of the brook,
And to nibble a few of the daisies and grass:
'How d'ye do?' said the Cow;—
  'How d'ye do?' said the Ass.

'Take a seat,' said the Cow, gently waving her hand;
'By no means, dear Madam,' said he, 'while you stand.'
Then, stooping to drink, with a complaisant bow,
'Ma'am, your health,' said the Ass:
  'Thank you, Sir,' said the Cow.

When a few of these compliments more had been
    passed,
They laid themselves down on the herbage at last;
And waiting politely, (as gentlemen must),
The ass held his tongue, that the cow might speak first.

Then with a deep sigh, she directly began,
'Don't you think, Mr. Ass, we are injured by man?
'Tis a subject which lies with a weight on my mind:
We really are greatly oppressed by mankind.

'Pray, what is the reason—I see none at all—
That I always must go when Jane chooses to call?
Whatever I'm doing—'tis certainly hard—
I'm forced to leave off, to be milked in the yard.

'I've no will of my own, but must do as they please,
And give them my milk to make butter and cheese;

Sometimes I endeavour to kick down the pail,
Or give her a box on the ear with my tail!'

'But, Ma'am,' said the Ass, 'not presuming to teach—
Oh dear! I beg pardon—pray finish your speech;
Excuse my mistake,' said the complaisant swain;
'Go on, and I'll not interrupt you again.'

'Why, Sir, I was just then about to observe,
Those hard-hearted tyrants no longer I'll serve;
But leave them for ever to do as they please,
And look somewhere else for their butter and cheese.'

Ass waited a moment, his answer to scan,
And then, 'Not presuming to teach,' he began,
'Permit me to say, since my thoughts you invite,
I always saw things in a different light.

'That you afford man an important supply,
No ass in his senses would ever deny:
But then, in return, 'tis but fair to allow,
They are of some service to you, Mistress Cow.

''Tis their pleasant meadow in which you repose,
And they find you a shelter from winterly snows.
For comforts like these, we're indebted to man;
And for him, in return, should do all that we can.'

The cow, upon this, cast her eyes on the grass,
Not pleased to be schooled in this way by an ass:
'Yet,' said she to herself, 'though he's not very bright,
I really believe that the fellow is right!'

JANE TAYLOR.

THE PET LAMB

The dew was falling fast, the stars began to blink;
I heard a voice; it said, 'Drink, pretty creature, drink!'
And, looking o'er the hedge, before me I espied
A snow-white mountain-lamb with a Maiden at its side.

No other sheep were near; the lamb was all alone,
And by a slender cord was tethered to a stone;
With one knee on the grass did the little Maiden kneel,
While to that mountain-lamb she gave its evening meal.

The lamb, while from her hand he thus his supper took,
Seemed to feast with head and ears; and his tail with pleasure shook.
'Drink, pretty creature, drink,' she said in such a tone
That I almost received her heart into my own.

'Twas little Barbara Lewthwaite, a child of beauty rare!
I watched them with delight, they were a lovely pair.
Now with her empty can the Maiden turned away:
But ere ten yards were gone her footsteps did she stay.

Towards the lamb she looked, and from that shady place
I unobserved could see the working of her face:
If Nature to her tongue could measured numbers bring,
Thus, thought I, to her lamb that little Maid might sing:

'What ails thee, Young One? what? Why pull so at thy cord?
Is it not well with thee? well both for bed and board?
Thy plot of grass is soft, and green as grass can be;
Rest, little Young One, rest; what is 't that aileth thee?

'What is it thou wouldst seek? What is wanting to thy heart?
Thy limbs are they not strong? And beautiful thou art:
This grass is tender grass; these flowers they have no peers;
And that green corn all day is rustling in thy ears!

'If the sun be shining hot, do but stretch thy woollen
    chain,
This beech is standing by, its covert thou canst gain;
For rain and mountain-storms! the like thou need'st
    not fear,
The rain and storm are things that scarcely can come
    here.

'Rest, little Young One, rest; thou hast forgot the day
When my father found thee first in places far away;
Many flocks were on the hills, but thou wert owned by
    none,
And thy mother from thy side for evermore was gone.

'He took thee in his arms, and in pity brought thee
    home:
A blessed day for thee! then whither wouldst thou
    roam?
A faithful nurse thou hast; the dam that did thee yean
Upon the mountain-tops no kinder could have been.

'Thou know'st that twice a day I have brought thee in
    this can
Fresh water from the brook, as clear as ever ran;
And twice in the day, when the ground is wet with dew,
I bring thee draughts of milk, warm milk it is, and new.

'Thy limbs will shortly be twice as stout as they are
    now,
Then I'll yoke thee to my cart like a pony in the
    plough;
My playmate thou shalt be; and when the wind is cold,
Our hearth shall be thy bed, our house shall be thy fold.

It will not, will not rest!—Poor creature, can it be
That 'tis thy mother's heart which is working so in thee?
Things that I know not of belike to thee are dear,
And dreams of things which thou canst neither see nor
    hear.

Alas, the mountain-tops that look so green and fair!
I've heard of fearful winds and darkness that come
 there;
The little brooks that seem all pastime and all play,
When they are angry, roar like lions for their prey.

'Here thou need'st not dread the raven in the sky;
Night and day thou art safe,—our cottage is hard by.
Why bleat so after me? Why pull so at thy chain?
Sleep—and at break of day I will come to thee again!'

—As homeward through the lane I went with lazy feet,
This song to myself did I oftentimes repeat;
And it seemed, as I retraced the ballad line by line,
That but half of it was hers, and one half of it was
 mine.

Again, and once again, did I repeat the song;
'Nay,' said I, 'more than half to the damsel must
 belong,
For she looked with such a look, and she spake with
 such a tone,
That I almost received her heart into my own.'
WILLIAM WORDSWORTH.

HAROLD AND ALICE; OR, THE REFORMED GIANT

I

The Giant sat on a rock up high,
 With the wind in his shaggy hair;
And he said, 'I have drained the dairies dry,
 And stripped the orchards bare;

'I have eaten the sheep, with the wool on their
 backs,'
 (A nasty Giant was he,)
'The eggs and the shells, the honey, the wax,
 The fowls, and the cock-turkey;

'And now I think I could eat a score
  Of babies so plump and small;
And if, after that, I should want any more,
  Their brothers and sisters and all.

'To-morrow I'll do it. Ha! what was that?'
  Said he, for a sound he heard;
'Was it fluttering owl or pattering rat,
  Or bough to the breeze that stirred?'

Oh, it was neither rat nor owl,
  Giant! nor shaking leaf;
Young Harold has heard your scheme so foul,
  And it may come to grief!

One thing which you ate has escaped your
      mind,—
  Young Harold's guinea-pig dear;
And he has crept up to try and find
  His pet, and he shakes with fear;

He has hid himself in a corner, you know,
  To listen and look about;
And if to the village to-morrow you go,
  You may find the babes gone out!

II

Now, when to the village came Harold back
  And told his tale so wild,
Then every mother she cried, 'Good lack!
  My child! preserve my child!'

And every father took his sword
  And sharpened it on a stone;
But little Harold said never a word,
  Having a plan of his own.

He laid six harrows outside the stile
  That led to the village green,
Then on them a little hay did pile,
  For the prongs not to be seen.

THE GOLDEN STAIRCASE

A toothsome sucking-pig he slew,
    And thereby did it lay;
For why? Because young Harold knew
    The Giant would pass that way.

Then he went in and said his prayers,—
    Not to lie down to sleep;
But at his window up the stairs
    A watch all night did keep,

Till the little stars all went pale to bed,
    Because the sun was out,
And the sky in the east grew dapple-red,
    And the little birds chirped about.

III

Now all the village was early awake,
    And, with short space to pray,
Their preparations they did make,
    To bear the babes away.

The horses were being buckled in,—
    The little ones looked for a ride,—
When on came the Giant, as ugly as Sin,
    With a terrible six-yard stride.

Then every woman and every child
    To scream aloud began;
Young Harold up at his watch-tower smiled,
    And his sword drew every man;

For now the Giant, fierce and big,
    Came near to the stile by the green,
But when he saw that luscious pig,
    His lips grew wet between!

Now, left foot, right foot, step it again,
    He trod on—the harrow spikes!
And how he raged and roared with pain
    He may describe who likes.

At last he fell, and as he lay
    Loud bellowing on the ground,
The stalwart men of the village, they
    With drawn swords danced around.

'O spare my life, I you entreat!
    I will be a Giant good!
O take out these thorns that prick my feet,
    Which now are bathed in blood!'

Then the little village maids did feel
    For this Giant so shaggy-haired,
And to their parents they did kneel,
    Saying, 'Let his life be spared!'

His bleeding wounds the maids did bind;
    They framed a litter strong
With all the hurdles they could find;
    Six horses drew him along;

And all the way to his castle rude
    Up high in the piny rocks,
He promised to be a Giant good—
    The cruel, crafty fox!

IV

'O mother, lend me your largest tub!'—
    'Why, daughter? tell me quick!'—
'O mother, to make a syllabub
    For the Giant who is so sick.'

Now in fever-fit the Giant lay,
    From the pain in his wounded feet,
And hoping soon would come the day
    When he might the babies eat.

'O mother, dress me in white, I beg,
    With flowers and pretty gear;
For Mary and Madge, and Jess and Peg,
    And all my playmates dear,

THE GOLDEN STAIRCASE

'We go to the Giant's this afternoon,
   To carry him something nice,—
A custard three times as big as the moon,
   With sugar and wine and spice.'

'O daughter, your father shall go with you;
   Suppose the Giant is well,
And eats you up, what shall we do?'
   Then her thought did Alice tell:—

'No, mother dear; we go alone,
   And Heaven for us will care;
If the Giant bad has a heart of stone,
   We will soften it with prayer!'

Now, when the Giant saw these maids,
   Drest all in white, draw near,
He twitched his monstrous shoulder-blades,
   And dropped an honest tear!

'Dear Giant, a syllabub nice we bring,
   Pray let us tuck you in!'
The Giant said, 'Sweet innocent thing!
   'Oh, I am a lump of sin!

'Go home, and say to the man of prayer
   To make the church-door wide,
For I next Sunday will be there,
   And kneel, dears, at your side.

'Tell brave young Harold I forgive
   Him for the harrow-spikes;
And I will do, please Heaven I live,
   What penance the prayer-man likes.

'Set down, my dears, the syllabub,
   And as I better feel,
I'll try and eat a fox's cub
   At my next mid-day meal;

'And all my life the village I'll keep
  From harmful vermin free;
But never more will eat up the sheep,
  The honey, or cock-turkey!'

V

Now Sunday came, and in the aisle
  Did kneel the Giant tall;
The priest could not forbear a smile,
  The church it looked so small!

And as the Giant walked away,
  He knocked off the roof with his head;
But he quarried stones on the following day,
  To build another instead.

And it was high and broad and long,
  And a hundred years it stood,
To tell of the Giant so cruel and strong
  That kindness had made good.

And when Harold and Alice were married there,
  A handsome sight was seen;
For the bridegroom was brave, and the bride
  was fair—
  LONG LIVE OUR GRACIOUS QUEEN!

W. B. RANDS.

THE MILLER OF THE DEE

THERE dwelt a miller hale and bold,
  Beside the river Dee;
He wrought and sang from morn to night,
  No lark more blithe than he;
And this the burden of his song
  For ever used to be,—
'I envy nobody, no, not I,
  And nobody envies me!'

THE GOLDEN STAIRCASE

'Thou'rt wrong, my friend!' said old King Hal,
  'Thou'rt wrong as wrong can be;
For could my heart be light as thine,
  I'd gladly change with thee.
And tell me now what makes thee sing
  With voice so loud and free,
While I am sad, though I'm the king,
  Beside the river Dee?'

The miller smiled and doff'd his cap:
  'I earn my bread,' quoth he;
'I love my wife, I love my friends,
  I love my children three;
I owe no penny I cannot pay;
  I thank the river Dee,
That turns the mill that grinds the corn,
  To feed my babes and me.'

'Good friend,' said Hal, and sigh'd the while,
  'Farewell! and happy be;
But say no more, if thou'dst be true,
  That no one envies thee.
Thy mealy cap is worth my crown,—
  Thy mill my kingdom's fee!—
Such men as thou are England's boast,
  O miller of the Dee!'

CHARLES MACKAY.

THE LARK AND THE ROOK

'GOOD-NIGHT, Sir Rook!' said a little Lark.
'The daylight fades, it will soon be dark.
I've bathed my wings in the sun's last ray,
I've sung my hymn to the parting day;
So now I haste to my quiet nook
In yon dewy meadow—good-night, Sir Rook!'

'Good-night, poor Lark,' said his titled friend,
With a haughty toss and a distant bend;
'I also go to my rest profound,
But not to sleep on the cold, damp ground.
The fittest place for a bird like me
Is the topmost bough of yon tall pine-tree.

'I opened my eyes at peep of day
And saw you taking your upward way,
Dreaming your fond, romantic dreams,
An ugly speck in the sun's bright beams;
Soaring too high to be seen or heard,
And I said to myself: "What a foolish bird!"

'I trod the park with a princely air,
I filled my crop with the richest fare;
I cawed all day 'mid a lordly crew,
And I made more noise in the world than you!
The sun shone forth on my ebon wing;
I looked and wondered—good-night, poor thing!'

'Good-night, once more,' said the Lark's sweet voice,
'I see no cause to repent my choice;
You build your nest in the lofty pine,
But is your slumber more sweet than mine?
You make more noise in the world than I,
But whose is the sweeter minstrelsy?'

UNKNOWN.

THE LAMB

Little Lamb, who made thee,
Dost thou know who made thee,
Gave thee life and bade thee feed
By the stream and o'er the mead;
Gave thee clothing of delight,
Softest clothing, woolly, bright;

Little lamb, who made thee? — Doest thou know who made thee?

Gave thee such a tender voice,
Making all the vales rejoice?
   Little Lamb, who made thee?
   Dost thou know who made thee?

   Little Lamb, I'll tell thee;
   Little Lamb, I'll tell thee:
He is callèd by thy name,
For He calls Himself a Lamb.
He is meek, and He is mild,
He became a little child.
I a child and thou a lamb,
We are callèd by His name.
   Little Lamb, God bless thee!
   Little Lamb, God bless thee!
WILLIAM BLAKE.

THE BEAR'S SONG

(From Katawampus)

OH, the mother she loves her only son,
While he makes eyes at the curranty bun,
And the slippery, slimy, sea-side snake
Loves soothing syrup and seedy cake.
   'Tis nothing to the love I feel
   For thee, thou little savoury seal.

The tide may follow the master moon,
And the dish run away with the silver spoon,
The ice may weep for the noonday sun,
And three times seven be twenty-one.
   'Tis nothing to the love I feel
   For thee, thou little savoury seal.

Oh, savoury seal with the silent eye,
We will feast ourselves on cod-liver pie,

Oh, savoury seal with the loving heart,
We will feast on turnips and treacle tart.
Life shall be one unending meal,
For you and me, my savoury seal.

JUDGE PARRY.

A GRACE FOR A CHILD

Here a little child I stand,
Heaving up my either hand;
Cold as paddocks though they be,
Here I lift them up to Thee,
For a Benison to fall
On our meat, and on us all.   Amen.

ROBERT HERRICK.

LADY MOON

'I see the moon, and the moon sees me,
God bless the moon, and God bless me.'

Old Rhyme.

Lady Moon, Lady Moon, where are you roving?
　　Over the sea.
Lady Moon, Lady Moon, whom are you loving?
　　All that love me.

Are you not tired with rolling, and never
　　Resting to sleep?
Why look so pale and so sad, as forever
　　Wishing to weep.

Ask me not this, little child, if you love me;
　　You are too bold;
I must obey my dear Father above me,
　　And do as I'm told.

Lady Moon, Lady Moon, where are you roving?
  Over the sea.
Lady Moon, Lady Moon, whom are you loving?
  All that love me.
LORD HOUGHTON.

SEVEN TIMES ONE

There's no dew left on the daisies and clover,
 There's no rain left in heaven;
I've said my 'seven times' over and over,
 Seven times one are seven.

I am old, so old, I can write a letter;
 My birthday lessons are done;
The lambs play always, they know no better;
 They are only one times one.

O moon! in the night I have seen you sailing
 And shining so round and low;
You were bright! ah, bright! but your light is
  failing—
 You are nothing now but a bow.

You moon, have you done something wrong in
  heaven
 That God has hidden your face?
I hope if you have you will soon be forgiven
 And shine again in your place.

O velvet bee, you're a dusty fellow,
 You've powdered your legs with gold!
O brave marsh mary-buds, rich and yellow,
 Give me your money to hold!

O columbine, open your golden wrapper,
 Where two twin turtle-doves dwell!
O cuckoopint, toll me the purple clapper
 That hangs in your clear green bell!

And show me your nest with the young ones
    in it;
  I will not steal them away;
I am old! you may trust me, linnet, linnet,
  I am seven times one to-day.

JEAN INGELOW.

TRY AGAIN

King Bruce of Scotland flung himself down
  In a lonely mood to think;
'Tis true he was monarch, and wore a crown,
  But his heart was beginning to sink.

For he had been trying to do a great deed,
  To make his people glad;
He had tried and tried, but couldn't succeed;
  And so he became quite sad.

He flung himself down in low despair,
  As grieved as man could be;
And after a while as he pondered there,
  'I'll give it all up,' said he.

Now just at the moment, a spider dropped,
  With its silken, filmy clue;
And the King, in the midst of his thinking, stopped
  To see what the spider would do.

'Twas a long way up to the ceiling dome,
  And it hung by a rope so fine;
That how it would get to its cobweb home,
  King Bruce could not divine.

It soon began to cling and crawl
  Straight up with strong endeavour;
But down it came with a slippery sprawl,
  As near to the ground as ever.

THE GOLDEN STAIRCASE

Up, up it ran, not a second to stay,
    To utter the least complaint;
Till it fell still lower, and there it lay,
    A little dizzy and faint.

Its head grew steady—again it went,
    And travelled a half yard higher;
'Twas a delicate thread it had to tread,
    And a road where its feet would tire.

Again it fell and swung below,
    But again it quickly mounted;
Till up and down, now fast, now slow,
    Nine brave attempts were counted.

'Sure,' cried the King, 'that foolish thing
    Will strive no more to climb;
When it toils so hard to reach and cling,
    And tumbles every time.'

But up the insect went once more,
    Ah me! 'tis an anxious minute;
He's only a foot from his cobweb door,
    Oh say, will he lose or win it?

Steadily, steadily, inch by inch,
    Higher and higher he got;
And a bold, little run at the very last pinch
    Put him into his native cot.

'Bravo, bravo!' the King cried out,
    'All honour to those who try;
The spider up there, defied despair;
    He conquered, and why shouldn't I?'

And Bruce of Scotland braced his mind,
    And gossips tell the tale,
That he tried once more as he tried before,
    And that time did not fail.

Pay goodly heed, all ye who read,
    And beware of saying 'I can't';
'Tis a cowardly word, and apt to lead
    To Idleness, Folly, and Want.

Whenever you find your heart despair
    Of doing some goodly thing;
Con over this strain, try bravely again,
    And remember the Spider and King!

ELIZA COOK.

A LESSON FOR MAMMA

DEAR mother, if you just could be
A tiny little girl like me,
And I your mother, you would see
    How nice I'd be to you.
I'd always let you have your way;
I'd never frown at you and say,
    'You are behaving ill to-day;
    Such conduct will not do.'

I'd always give you jelly-cake
For breakfast, and I'd never shake
My head and say, 'You must not take
    So very large a slice.'
I'd never say, 'My dear, I trust
You will not make me say you *must*
Eat up your oatmeal'; or 'The crust,
    You'll find, is very nice.'

I'd buy you candy every day;
I'd go down town with you, and say,
'What would my darling like? You may
    Have anything you see.'

THE GOLDEN STAIRCASE

I'd never say, 'My pet, you know
'Tis bad for health and teeth, and so
I cannot let you have it. No;
    It would be wrong in me.'

And every day I'd let you wear
Your nicest dress, and never care
If it should get a great big tear;
    I'd only say to you,
    'My precious treasure, never mind,
For little clothes *will* tear, I find.'
Now, mother, wouldn't that be kind?
    That's just what *I* should do.

I'd never say, 'Well, just a *few*!'
I'd let you stop your lessons too;
I'd say, 'They are too hard for you,
    Poor child, to understand.'
I'd put the books and slates away;
You shouldn't do a thing but play,
And have a party every day;
    Ah-h-h! wouldn't that be grand!

But, mother dear, you cannot grow
Into a little girl, you know,
And I can't be your mother; so
    The only thing to do,
Is just for you to try and see
How very, very nice 'twould be
For *you* to do all this for *me*,
    Now, mother, *couldn't* you?

SYDNEY DAYRE.

TO J. H.

FOUR YEARS OLD:—A NURSERY SONG

One cannot turn a minute,
But mischief—there you're in it,
A-getting at my books, John,
With mighty bustling looks, John;
Or poking at the roses
In midst of which your nose is;
Or climbing on a table,
No matter how unstable,
And turning up your quaint eye
And half-shut teeth with 'Mayn't I?'
Or else you're off at play, John,
Just as you'd be all day, John,
With hat or not, as happens,
And there you dance, and clap hands,
Or on the grass go rolling,
Or plucking flowers, or bowling,
And getting me expenses
With losing balls o'er fences;
And see what flow'rs the weather
Has render'd fit to gather;
And, when we home must jog, you
Shall ride my back, you rogue you.
Your hat adorn'd with fir-leaves,
Horse-chestnut, oak, and vine-leaves;
And so, with green o'erhead, John,
Shall whistle home to bed, John.
—But see, the sun shines brightly;
Come, put your hat on rightly,
And we'll among the bushes,
And hear your friends the thrushes.

LEIGH HUNT.

A NIGHT WITH A WOLF

Little one, come to my knee!
   Hark, how the rain is pouring
Over the roof, in the pitch-black night,
   And the wind in the woods a-roaring!

Hush, my darling, and listen,
   Then pay for the story with kisses;
Father was lost in the pitch-black night,
   In just such a storm as this is!

High up on the lonely mountains,
   Where the wild men watched and waited;
Wolves in the forest, and bears in the bush,
   And I on my path belated.

The rain and the night together
   Came down, and the wind came after,
Bending the props of the pine-tree roof,
   And snapping many a rafter.

I crept along in the darkness,
   Stunned, and bruised, and blinded,
Crept to a fir with thick-set boughs,
   And a sheltering rock behind it.

There, from the blowing and raining,
   Crouching, I sought to hide me:
Something rustled, two green eyes shone,
   And a wolf lay down beside me.

Little one, be not frightened;
   I and the wolf together,
Side by side, through the long, long night
   Hid from the awful weather.

His wet fur pressed against me;
   Each of us warmed the other;
Each of us felt, in the stormy dark,
   That beast and man was brother.

    And when the falling forest
      No longer crashed in warning,
    Each of us went from our hiding-place,
      Forth in the wild, wet morning.

    Darling, kiss me in payment!
      Hark, how the wind is roaring;
    Father's house is a better place
      When the stormy rain is pouring!
                      BAYARD TAYLOR.

HOME FOR THE HOLIDAYS

Home for the Holidays, here we go;
Bless me, the train is exceedingly slow!
Pray, Mr. Engineer, get up your steam,
And let us be off, with a puff and a scream!
We have two long hours to travel, you say;
Come, Mr. Engineer, gallop away!
Two hours more! why, the sun will be down,
Before we reach dear old London town!
And then, what a number of fathers and mothers,
And uncles and aunts, and sisters and brothers,
Will be there to meet us—oh! do make haste,
For I'm sure, Mr. Guard, we have no time to waste:
Thank goodness we shan't have to study and stammer
Over Latin and sums, and that nasty French Grammar;
Lectures, and classes, and lessons are done,
And now we'll have nothing but frolic and fun.
Home for the Holidays, here we go;
But this Fast train is really exceedingly slow!

We shall have sport when Christmas comes,
When 'snap-dragon' burns our fingers and thumbs.
We'll hang mistletoe over our dear little cousins,
And pull them beneath it and kiss them by dozens:

THE GOLDEN STAIRCASE 73

We shall have games at 'Blind-man's Buff,'
And noise and laughter, and romping enough:
We'll crown the plum-pudding with bunches of bay,
And roast all the chestnuts that come in our way;
And when Twelfth-night falls, we'll have such a cake
That as we stand round it the table shall quake.
We'll draw 'King and Queen,' and be happy together,
And dance old 'Sir Roger' with hearts like a feather.
Home for the Holidays, here we go;
But this Fast train is really exceedingly slow!

Home for the Holidays! here we go!
But really this train is exceedingly slow;
Yet stay! I declare here is London at last;
The Park is right over the tunnel just past.
Huzza! huzza! I can see my papa!
I can see George's uncle, and Edward's mamma!
And Fred, there's your brother! look! look! there he
    stands;
They see us, they see us, they're waving their hands!
Why don't the train stop, what are they about?
Now, now it is steady,—oh! pray let us out;
A cheer for old London, a kiss for mamma,
We're home for the Holidays. Now, Huzza!

ELIZA COOK.

JACK FROST

  THE door was shut, as doors should be,
    Before you went to bed last night;
  Yet Jack Frost has got in, you see,
    And left your window silver white.

  He must have waited till you slept;
    And not a single word he spoke,
  But pencilled o'er the panes and crept
    Away again before you woke.

And now you cannot see the trees
  Nor fields that stretch beyond the lane;
But there are fairer things than these
  His fingers traced on every pane.

Rocks and castles towering high;
  Hills and dales and streams and fields;
And knights in armour riding by,
  With nodding plumes and shining shields.

And here are little boats, and there
  Big ships with sails spread to the breeze;
And yonder, palm-trees waving fair
  On islands set in silver seas.

And butterflies with gauzy wings;
  And herds of cows and flocks of sheep;
And fruit and flowers and all the things
  You see when you are sound asleep.

For, creeping softly underneath
  The door when all the lights are out,
Jack Frost takes every breath you breathe
  And knows the things you think about.

He paints them on the window-pane
  In fairy lines with frozen steam;
And when you wake, you see again
  The lovely things you saw in dream.
                    GABRIEL SETOUN.

ROBERT OF LINCOLN

Merrily swinging on briar and weed,
  Near to the nest of his little dame,
Over the mountain-side or the mead,
  Robert of Lincoln is telling his name:

Bob-o'-link, bob-o'-link,
　　　Spink, spank, spink;
Snug and safe is that nest of ours,
Hidden among the summer flowers,
　　　Chee, chee, chee.

Robert of Lincoln is gayly drest,
　　Wearing a bright wedding-coat;
White are his shoulders and white his crest,
　　Hear him call in his merry note:
　　　Bob-o'-link, bob-o'-link,
　　　Spink, spank, spink;
Look, what a nice new coat of mine,
Sure there never was bird so fine.
　　　Chee, chee, chee.

Robert of Lincoln's Quaker wife,
　　Pretty and quiet with plain brown wings,
Passing at home a patient life,
　　Broods in the grass while her husband sings:
　　　Bob-o'-link, bob-o'-link,
　　　Spink, spank, spink;
Brood, kind creature; you need not fear
Thieves and robbers, while I am here.
　　　Chee, chee, chee.

Modest and shy as a nun is she;
　　One weak chirp is her only note.
Braggart and prince of braggarts is he,
　　Pouring boasts from his little throat;
　　　Bob-o'-link, bob-o'-link,
　　　Spink, spank, spink;
Never was I afraid of man;
Catch me, cowardly knaves, if you can!
　　　Chee, chee, chee.

Robert of Lincoln at length is made
　　Sober with work, and silent with care;
Off is his holiday garment laid,
　　Half forgotten that merry air:

Bob-o'-link, bob-o'-link,
　　Spink, spank, spink;
Nobody knows but my mate and I
Where our nest and our nestlings lie.
　　Chee, chee, chee.

Six white eggs on a bed of hay,
　　Flecked with purple, a pretty sight!
There as the mother sits all day,
　　Robert is singing with all his might:
　　　Bob-o'-link, bob-o'-link,
　　　Spink, spank, spink;
Nice good wife, that never goes out,
Keeping house while I frolic about.
　　Chee, chee, chee.

Soon as the little ones chip the shell
　　Six wide mouths are open for food;
Robert of Lincoln bestirs him well,
　　Gathering seeds for the hungry brood.
　　　Bob-o'-link, bob-o'-link,
　　　Spink, spank, spink;
This new life is likely to be
Hard for a gay young fellow like me.
　　Chee, chee, chee!

Summer wanes; the children are grown;
　　Fun and frolic no more he knows;
Robert of Lincoln's a humdrum crone;
　　Off he flies, and we sing as he goes:
　　　Bob-o'-link, bob-o'-link,
　　　Spink, spank, spink;
When you can pipe that merry old strain,
Robert of Lincoln, come back again.
　　Chee, chee, chee.

　　　　　　　　WILLIAM CULLEN BRYANT.

THE SPARROW'S NEST

Nay, only look what I have found!
A Sparrow's Nest upon the ground;
A Sparrow's Nest, as you may see,
Blown out of yonder old elm-tree.

And what a medley thing it is!
I never saw a nest like this,—
Not neatly wove with decent care,
Of silvery moss and shining hair;

But put together, odds and ends,
Picked up from enemies and friends;
See, bits of thread, and bits of rag,
Just like a little rubbish bag!

Here is a scrap of red and brown,
Like the old washer-woman's gown;
And here is muslin, pink and green,
And bits of calico between.

Oh, never thinks the lady fair,
As she goes by with dainty air,
How the pert Sparrow overhead,
Has robbed her gown to make its bed!

See, hair of dog and fur of cat,
And rovings of a worsted mat,
And shreds of silk, and many a feather,
Compacted cunningly together!

Well, here has hoarding been, and hiving,
And not a little good contriving,
Before a home of peace and ease
Was fashioned out of things like these!

Think, had these odds and ends been brought
To some wise man renowned for thought,
Some man, of men a very gem,
Pray, what could he have done with them?

If we had said, 'Here, sir, we bring
You many a worthless little thing,
Just bits and scraps, so very small,
That they have scarcely size at all;

'And out of these, you must contrive
A dwelling large enough for five;
Neat, warm, and snug; with comfort stored;
Where five small things may lodge and board.'

How would the man of learning vast
Have been astonished and aghast;
And vowed that such a thing had been
Ne'er heard of, thought of, much less seen!

Ah! man of learning, you are wrong!
Instinct is, more than wisdom, strong;
And He who made the Sparrow, taught
This skill beyond your reach of thought.

And here, in this uncostly nest,
Five little creatures have been blest;
Nor have kings known, in palaces,
Half their contentedness in this—
Poor, simple dwelling as it is!

MARY HOWITT.

THE GREY SQUIRRELS

When in my youth I travellèd
  Throughout each north countrie,
Many a strange thing did I hear,
  And many a strange thing see.

. . . . . .

But nothing was there that pleased me more
  Than when, in autumn brown,
I came, in the depths of the pathless woods,
  To the Grey Squirrels' town.

There were hundreds that in the hollow boles
    Of the old, old trees did dwell,
And laid up store, hard by their door,
    Of the sweet mast as it fell.

But soon the hungry wild swine came,
    And with thievish snouts dug up
Their buried treasure, and left them not
    So much as an acorn cup!

Then did they chatter in angry mood,
    And one and all decree,
Into the forests of rich stone-pine
    Over hill and dale to flee.

Over hill and dale, over hill and dale,
    For many a league they went,
Like a troop of undaunted travellers
    Governed by one consent.

But the hawk and eagle, and peering owl,
    Did dreadfully pursue;
And the further the Grey Squirrels went,
    The more their perils grew;
When lo! to cut off their pilgrimage,
    A broad stream lay in view.

But then did each wondrous creature show
    His cunning and bravery;
With a piece of the pine-bark in his mouth,
    Unto the stream came he,

And boldly his little bark he launched,
    Without the least delay;
His bushy tail was his upright sail,
    And he merrily steered away.

Never was there a lovelier sight
    Than that Grey Squirrels' fleet;
And with anxious eyes I watched to see
    What fortune it would meet.

Soon had they reached the rough mid-stream,
   And ever and anon
I grieved to behold some small bark wrecked,
   And its little steersman gone.

But the main fleet stoutly held across;
   I saw them leap to shore;
They entered the woods with a cry of joy,
   For their perilous march was o'er.
WILLIAM HOWITT.

THE VILLAGE BLACKSMITH

UNDER a spreading chestnut tree
   The village smithy stands;
The smith, a mighty man is he,
   With large and sinewy hands;
And the muscles of his brawny arms
   Are strong as iron bands.

His hair is crisp, and black, and long,
   His face is like the tan;
His brow is wet with honest sweat,
   He earns whate'er he can,
And looks the whole world in the face,
   For he owes not any man.

Week in, week out, from morn till night,
   You can hear his bellows blow;
You can hear him swing his heavy sledge,
   With measured beat and slow,
Like a sexton ringing the village bell,
   When the evening sun is low.

And children coming home from school
   Look in at the open door;
They love to see the flaming forge,
   And hear the bellows roar,
And catch the burning sparks that fly
   Like chaff from a threshing-floor.

He goes on Sunday to the church,
   And sits among his boys;
He hears the parson pray and preach,
   He hears his daughter's voice,
Singing in the village choir,
   And it makes his heart rejoice.

It sounds to him like her mother's voice,
   Singing in Paradise!
He needs must think of her once more,
   How in the grave she lies;
And with his hard, rough hand he wipes
   A tear out of his eyes.

Toiling,—rejoicing,—sorrowing,
   Onward through life he goes;
Each morning sees some task begun,
   Each evening sees its close;
Something attempted, something done,
   Has earned a night's repose.

Thanks, thanks to thee, my worthy friend,
   For the lesson thou hast taught!
Thus at the flaming forge of life
   Our fortunes must be wrought;
Thus on its sounding anvil shaped
   Each burning deed and thought!

                HENRY W. LONGFELLOW.

QUEEN MAB

A LITTLE fairy comes at night,
  Her eyes are blue, her hair is brown,
With silver spots upon her wings,
  And from the moon she flutters down.

She has a little silver wand,
  And when a good child goes to bed
She waves her wand from right to left,
  And makes a circle round its head.

And then it dreams of pleasant things,
  Of fountains filled with fairy fish,
And trees that bear delicious fruit
  And bow their branches at a wish:

Of arbours filled with dainty scents
  From lovely flowers that never fade;
Bright flies that glitter in the sun,
  And glow-worms shining in the shade:

And talking birds with gifted tongues,
  For singing songs and telling tales,
And pretty dwarfs to show the way
  Through fairy hills and fairy dales.

But when a bad child goes to bed,
  From left to right she weaves her rings,
And then it dreams all through the night
  Of only ugly, horrid things!

Then lions come with glaring eyes,
  And tigers growl, a dreadful noise,
And ogres draw their cruel knives,
  To shed the blood of girls and boys.

Then stormy waves rush on to drown,
  Or raging flames come scorching round,
Fierce dragons hover in the air,
  And serpents crawl along the ground.

Then wicked children wake and weep,
  And wish the long black gloom away;
But good ones love the dark, and find
  The night as pleasant as the day.

                    THOMAS HOOD.

THE CAMEL'S HUMP

(From Just-So Stories)

The camel's hump is an ugly lump
  Which well you may see at the Zoo;
But uglier yet is the hump we get
  From having too little to do.

Kiddies and grown-ups too-oo-oo,
If we haven't enough to do-oo-oo,
    We get the hump—
    Cameelious hump—
The hump that is black and blue!

We climb out of bed with a frousy head
  And a snarly-yarly voice;
We shiver and scowl, and we grunt and we growl
  At our bath and our boots and our toys;

And there ought to be a corner for me
(And I know there is one for you)
    When we get the hump—
    Cameelious hump—
The hump that is black and blue!

The cure for this ill is not to sit still,
  Or frowst with a book by the fire;
But to take a large hoe and a shovel also,
  And dig till you gently perspire;

And then you will find that the sun and the wind,
And the Djinn of the Garden too,
    Have lifted the hump—
    The horrible hump—
The hump that is black and blue!

I get it as well as you-oo-oo
If I haven't enough to do-oo-oo,
    We all get hump—
    Cameelious hump—
Kiddies and grown-ups too!
RUDYARD KIPLING.

THE BAD BOY

ONCE a little round-eyed lad
Determined to be very bad.

He called his porridge nasty pap,
And threw it all in nurse's lap.

His gentle sister's cheek he hurt,
He smudged his pinny in the dirt.

He found the bellows, and he blew
The pet canary right in two!

And when he went to bed at night
He would not say his prayers aright.

This pained a lovely twinkling star
That watched the trouble from afar.

She told her bright-faced friends, and soon
The dreadful rumour reached the moon.

The moon, a gossiping old dame,
Told Father Sun the bad boy's shame.

And then the giant sun began
A very satisfactory plan.

LIFTED THE HUMP—THE HORRIBLE HUMP—
THE HUMP THAT IS BLACK AND BLUE!

THE GOLDEN STAIRCASE

Upon the naughty rebel's face
He would not pour his beamy grace.

He would not stroke the dark-brown strands
With entertaining shiny hands.

The little garden of the boy
Seemed desert, missing heaven's joy.

But all his sister's tulips grew
Magnificent with shine and dew.

Where'er he went he found a shade,
But light was poured upon the maid.

He also lost, by his disgrace,
That indoors sun, his mother's face.

His father sent him up to bed
With neither kiss nor pat for head.

And in his sleep he had such foes,
Bad fairies pinched his curling toes—

They bit his ears, they pulled his hairs,
They threw him three times down the stairs.

Oh little boys who would not miss
A father's and a mother's kiss,

Who would not cause a sister pain,
Who want the sun to shine again,

Who want sweet beams to tend the plot,
Where grows the pet forget-me-not,

Who hate a life of streaming eyes,
Be good, be merry, and be wise.

NORMAN GALE.

THE FAIRIES

Up the airy mountain,
Down the rushy glen,
We daren't go a-hunting,
For fear of little men;
Wee folk, good folk,
Trooping all together;
Green jacket, red cap,
And white owl's feather!

Down along the rocky shore
Some make their home,
They live on crispy pancakes
Of yellow tide-foam;
Some in the reeds
Of the black mountain-lake,
With frogs for their watch-dogs,
All night awake.

High on the hilltop
The old King sits;
He is now so old and grey,
He's nigh lost his wits.
With a bridge of white mist
Columbkill he crosses,
On his stately journeys
From Slieveleague to Rosses;
Or going up with music
On cold, starry nights,
To sup with the Queen
Of the gay Northern Lights.

They stole little Bridget
For seven years long;
When she came down again
Her friends were all gone.
They took her lightly back,

Between the night and morrow,
They thought that she was fast asleep,
But she was dead with sorrow.
They have kept her ever since
Deep within the lake,
On a bed of flag-leaves,
Watching till she wake.

By the craggy hillside,
Through the mosses bare,
They have planted thorn-trees
For pleasure, here and there.
Is any man so daring
As dig them up in spite,
He shall find their sharpest thorns
In his bed at night.

Up the airy mountain,
Down the rushy glen,
We daren't go a-hunting,
For fear of little men;
Wee folk, good folk,
Trooping all together,
Green jacket, red cap,
And white owl's feather!

WILLIAM ALLINGHAM.

THE SLUGGARD

'Tis the voice of the Sluggard; I heard him complain,
'You have waked me too soon; I must slumber again';
As the door on its hinges, so he on his bed
Turns his sides, and his shoulders, and his heavy head.

'A little more sleep and a little more slumber';
Thus he wastes half his days, and his hours without
    number;

And when he gets up he sits folding his hands,
Or walks about saunt'ring, or trifling he stands.

I pass'd by his garden, and saw the wild brier,
The thorn and the thistle, grow broader and higher;
The clothes that hang on him are turning to rags;
And his money still wastes till he starves or he begs.

I made him a visit, still hoping to find
That he took better care for improving his mind.
He told me his dreams, talk'd of eating and drinking:
But he scarce reads his Bible, and never loves thinking.

Said I then to my heart, 'Here's a lesson for me,
This man's but a picture of what I might be;
But thanks to my friends for their care in my breeding,
Who taught me betimes to love working and reading.'

ISAAC WATTS.

THE WIND IN A FROLIC

THE Wind one morning sprang up from sleep,
Saying, 'Now for a frolic! now for a leap!
Now for a mad-cap galloping chase!
I'll make a commotion in every place!

So it swept with a bustle right through a great town,
Cracking the signs and scattering down
Shutters; and whisking, with merciless squalls,
Old women's bonnets and gingerbread stalls.

There never was heard a much lustier shout,
As the apples and oranges trundled about;
And the urchins that stand with their thievish eyes
For ever on watch, ran off each with a prize.

Then away to the fields it went, blustering and
    humming,
And the cattle all wondered what monster was coming.
It plucked by the tails the grave, matronly cows,
And tossed the colts' manes all over their brows;
Till, offended at such an unusual salute,
They all turned their backs, and stood sulky and mute.

So on it went, capering and playing its pranks,—
Whistling with reeds on the broad river's banks,
Puffing the birds as they sat on the spray,
Or the traveller grave on the king's highway.
It was not too nice to hustle the bags
Of the beggar, and flutter his dirty rags;
'Twas so bold, that it feared not to play its joke
With the doctor's wig or the gentleman's cloak.
Through the forest it roared, and cried gaily, 'Now,
You sturdy old oaks, I'll make you bow!'
And it made them bow without more ado,
Or it cracked their great branches through and through.

Then it rushed like a monster on cottage and farm;
Striking their dwellers with sudden alarm;
And they ran out like bees in a midsummer swarm:
There were dames with their kerchiefs tied over their
    caps,
To see if their poultry were free from mishaps;
The turkeys they gobbled, the geese screamed aloud,
And the hens crept to roost in a terrified crowd;
There was rearing of ladders, and logs were laid on,
Where the thatch from the roof threatened soon to be
    gone.

But the Wind had swept on, and met in a lane
With a school boy, who panted and struggled in vain;
For it tossed him and twirled him, then passed—and he
    stood
With his hat in a pool and his shoes in the mud!

Then away went the Wind in its holiday glee,
And now it was far on the billowy sea;
And the lordly ships felt its staggering blow,
And the little boats darted to and fro.

But, lo! it was night, and it sank to rest
On the sea-birds' rock in the gleaming west,
Laughing to think, in its frolicsome fun,
How little of mischief it really had done.

WILLIAM HOWITT.

ROBIN REDBREAST

Good-bye, good-bye to Summer!
  For Summer's nearly done;
The garden smiling faintly,
  Cool breezes in the sun;
Our Thrushes now are silent,
  Our Swallows flown away,—
But Robin's here, in coat of brown,
  And ruddy breast-knot gay.
    Robin, Robin Redbreast,
      O Robin dear!
    Robin singing sweetly
      In the falling of the year.

Bright yellow, red, and orange,
  The leaves come down in hosts;
The trees are Indian Princes,
  But soon they'll turn to Ghosts
The scanty pears and apples
  Hang russet on the bough,
It's Autumn, Autumn, Autumn late,
  'Twill soon be Winter now.
    Robin, Robin Redbreast,
      O Robin dear!
    And welaway! my Robin,
      For pinching times are near.

The fireside for the Cricket,
  The wheatstack for the Mouse,
When trembling night-winds whistle
  And moan all round the house;
The frosty ways like iron,
  The branches plumed with snow,—
Alas! in Winter dead and dark,
  Where can poor Robin go?
    Robin, Robin Redbreast,
      O Robin dear!
    And a crumb of bread for Robin,
      His little heart to cheer.
            WILLIAM ALLINGHAM.

THE SEA-GULL

Oh, the white Sea-gull, the wild Sea-gull,
  A joyful bird is he,
As he lies like a cradled thing at rest
  In the arms of a sunny sea!
The little waves rock to and fro,
  And the white Gull lies asleep,
As the fisher's bark, with breeze and tide,
  Goes merrily over the deep.
The ship, with her fair sails set, goes by,
  And her people stand to note
How the Sea-gull sits on the rocking waves,
  As if in an anchored boat.

The sea is fresh, the sea is fair,
  And the sky calm overhead,
And the Sea-gull lies on the deep, deep sea,
  Like a king in his royal bed!
Oh, the white Sea-gull, the bold Sea-gull,
  A joyful bird is he,
Throned like a king, in calm repose
  On the breast of the heaving sea!

The waves leap up, the wild wind blows,
    And the Gulls together crowd,
And wheel about, and madly scream
    To the deep sea roaring loud.
And let the sea roar ever so loud,
    And the winds pipe ever so high,
With a wilder joy the bold Sea-gull
    Sends forth a wilder cry.—

For the Sea-gull, he is a daring bird,
    And he loves with the storm to sail;
To ride in the strength of the billowy sea,
    And to breast the driving gale!
The little boat, she is tossed about,
    Like a sea-weed, to and fro;
The tall ship reels like a drunken man,
    As the gusty tempests blow.

But the Sea-gull laughs at the fear of man,
    And sails in a wild delight
On the torn-up breast of the night-black sea,
    Like a foam-cloud, calm and white.
The waves may rage and the winds may roar,
    But he fears not wreck nor need;
For he rides the sea, in its stormy strength,
    As a strong man rides his steed!

Oh, the white Sea-gull, the bold Sea-gull!
    He makes on the shore his nest,
And he tries what the inland fields may be;
    But he loveth the sea the best!
And away from land a thousand leagues,
    He goes 'mid surging foam;
What matter to him is land or shore,
    For the sea is his truest home!

And away to the north, 'mid ice-rocks stern,
    And amid the frozen snow,
To a sea that is lone and desolate,
    Will the wanton Sea-gull go.

For he careth not for the winter wild,
　　Nor those desert regions chill;
In the midst of the cold, as on calm blue seas,
　　The Sea-gull hath his will!

And the dead whale lies on the northern shores,
　　And the seal, and the sea-horse grim,
And the death of the great sea-creatures makes
　　A full, merry feast for him!
Oh, the wild Sea-gull, the bold Sea-gull!
　　As he screams in his wheeling flight;
As he sits on the waves in storm or calm,
　　All cometh to him aright!
All cometh to him as he liketh best;
　　Nor any his will gainsay;
And he rides on the waves like a bold young king,
　　That was crowned but yesterday!
　　　　　　　　　　　　MARY HOWITT.

MY HEART'S IN THE HIGHLANDS

My heart's in the Highlands, my heart is not here;
My heart's in the Highlands a-chasing the deer;
Chasing the wild deer, and following the roe,
My heart's in the Highlands wherever I go.
Farewell to the Highlands, farewell to the North,
The birthplace of valour, the country of worth;
Wherever I wander, wherever I rove,
The hills of the Highlands for ever I love.

Farewell to the mountains high covered with snow;
Farewell to the straths and green valleys below;
Farewell to the forests and wild hanging woods;
Farewell to the torrents and loud-pouring floods.
My heart's in the Highlands, my heart is not here,
My heart's in the Highlands a-chasing the deer;
Chasing the wild deer, and following the roe,
My heart's in the Highlands wherever I go.
　　　　　　　　　　　　ROBERT BURNS.

WHEN POLLY BUYS A HAT

When Father goes to town with me to buy my Sunday hat,
We can't afford to waste much time in doing things like that;
We walk into the nearest shop, and Father tells them then,
'Just bring a hat you think will fit a little girl of ten!'

It may be plain, it may be fine with lace and flowers too;
If it just 'feels right' on my head we think that it will do;
It may be red or brown or blue, with ribbons light or dark;
We put it on—and take the car that goes to Central Park.

When Mother buys my hat for me, we choose the shape with care;
We ask if it's the best they have, and if they're sure 't will wear;
And when the trimming's rather fine, why, Mother shakes her head
And says, 'Please take the feathers off—we'd like a bow instead!'

But oh, when Sister buys my hats, you really do not know
The hurry and the worry that we have to undergo!
How many times I've heard her say,—and shivered where I sat,—
'I think I'll go to town to-day, and buy that child a hat!'

They bring great hats with curving brims, but I'm too tall for those;
And hats that have no brims at all, which do not suit my nose;

I walk about, and turn around, and struggle not to
    frown;
And wish I had long curly hair like Angelina Brown.

Till when at last the daylight goes, and I'm so tired
    then,
I hope I'll never, never need another hat again,
And when I've quite made up my mind that shopping
    is the worst
Of all my tasks—then Sister buys the hat that we saw
    first!

And so we take it home with us as quickly as we may,
And Sister lifts it from the box and wonders what
    they'll say;
And I—I peep into the glass, and (promise not to tell!)
I smile, because I really think it suits me very well;

Then slip into the library as quiet as can be,
And this is what my Brother says when first he looks
    at me:
'Upon—my—word! I never saw a queerer sight than
    that!
Don't tell me this outrageous thing is Polly's Sunday
    hat!'
E. HILL.

THE WORLD'S MUSIC

The world's a very happy place,
   Where every child should dance and sing,
And always have a smiling face,
   And never sulk for anything.

I waken when the morning's come,
   And feel the air and light alive
With strange sweet music like the hum
   Of bees about their busy hive.

The linnets play among the leaves
   At hide-and-seek, and chirp and sing;
While, flashing to and from the eaves,
   The swallows twitter on the wing.

And twigs that shake, and boughs that sway;
   And tall old trees you could not climb;
And winds that come, but cannot stay,
   Are singing gaily all the time.

From dawn to dark the old mill-wheel
   Makes music, going round and round;
And dusty-white with flour and meal,
   The miller whistles to its sound.

The brook that flows beside the mill,
   As happy as a brook can be,
Goes singing its own song until
   It learns the singing of the sea.

For every wave upon the sands
   Sings songs you never tire to hear,
Of laden ships from sunny lands
   Where it is summer all the year.

And if you listen to the rain
   When leaves and birds and bees are dumb,
You hear it pattering on the pane
   Like Andrew beating on his drum.

The coals beneath the kettle croon,
   And clap their hands and dance in glee;
And even the kettle hums a tune
   To tell you when it's time for tea.

The world is such a happy place
   That children, whether big or small,
Should always have a smiling face
   And never, never sulk at all.

                       GABRIEL SETOUN.

ONE, TWO, THREE

It was an old, old, old, old lady,
   And a boy that was half-past three,
And the way that they played together
   Was beautiful to see.

She couldn't go romping and jumping,
   And the boy no more could he;
For he was a thin little fellow,
   With a thin little twisted knee.

They sat in the yellow sunlight,
   Out under the maple tree,
And the game that they played I'll tell you,
   Just as it was told to me.

It was Hide-and-Go-Seek they were playing,
   Though you'd never have known it to be—
With an old, old, old, old lady,
   And a boy with a twisted knee.

The boy would bend his face down
   On his little sound right knee,
And he guessed where she was hiding
   In guesses One, Two, Three.

'You are in the china closet!'
   He would cry and laugh with glee—
It wasn't the china closet,
   But he still had Two and Three.

'You are up in papa's big bedroom,
   In the chest with the queer old key,'
And she said: 'You are warm and warmer;
   But you are not quite right,' said she.

'It can't be the little cupboard
　　Where mamma's things used to be—
So it must be in the clothes-press, gran'ma,'
　　And he found her with his Three.

Then she covered her face with her fingers,
　　That were wrinkled and white and wee,
And she guessed where the boy was hiding,
　　With a One and a Two and a Three.

And they never had stirred from their places
　　Right under the maple tree—
This old, old, old, old lady,
　　And the boy with the lame little knee—
This dear, dear, dear old lady,
　　And the boy who was half-past three.

　　　　　　　　　　HENRY C. BUNNER.

THE BABES IN THE WOOD

Now ponder well, you parents dear,
　　These words which I shall write;
A doleful story you shall hear,
　　In time brought forth to light.
A gentleman of good account
　　In Norfolk dwelt of late,
Who did in honour far surmount
　　Most men of his estate.

Sore sick he was, and like to die,
　　No help his life could save;
His wife by him as sick did lie,
　　And both possessed one grave.
No love between these two was lost,
　　Each was to other kind;
In love they lived, in love they died,
　　And left two babes behind.

The one a fine and pretty boy,
   Not passing three years old;
The other a girl more young than he,
   And framed in beauty's mould.
The father left his little son,
   As plainly doth appear,
When he to perfect age should come,
   Three hundred pounds a year.

And to his little daughter, Jane,
   Five hundred pounds in gold,
To be paid down on marriage-day,
   Which might not be controlled.
But if the children chance to die
   Ere they to age should come,
Their uncle should possess their wealth;
   For so the will did run.

'Now, brother,' said the dying man,
   'Look to my children dear;
Be good unto my boy and girl,
   No friends else have they here:
To God and you I recommend
   My children dear this day;
But little while be sure we have
   Within this world to stay.

'You must be father and mother both,
   And uncle all in one;
God knows what will become of them
   When I am dead and gone.'
With that bespake their mother dear,
   'Oh brother kind,' quoth she,
'You are the man must bring our babes
   To wealth or misery:

'And if you keep them carefully,
   Then God will you reward;
But if you otherwise should deal,
   God will your deeds regard.'

With lips as cold as any stone,
   They kissed their children small:
'God bless you both, my children dear!'
   With that the tears did fall.

These speeches then their brother spoke,
   To this sick couple there:
'The keeping of your little ones,
   Sweet sister, do not fear:
God never prosper me nor mine,
   Nor ought else that I have,
If I do wrong your children dear,
   When you are laid in grave.'

The parents being dead and gone,
   The children home he takes,
And brings them straight unto his house,
   Where much of them he makes.
He had not kept these pretty babes
   A twelvemonth and a day,
But, for their wealth, he did devise
   To make them both away.

He bargained with two ruffians strong,
   Which were of furious mood,
That they should take these children young,
   And slay them in a wood.
He told his wife an artful tale,
   He would the children send,
To be brought up in fair London,
   With one that was his friend.

Away then went those pretty babes
   Rejoicing at their tide,
Rejoicing in a merry mind,
   They should on cock-horse ride.
They prate and prattle pleasantly
   As they rode on the way,
To those that should their butchers be,
   And work their lives' decay.

THE GOLDEN STAIRCASE

So that the pretty speech they had
   Made Murder's heart relent;
And they that undertook the deed
   Full sore did now repent.
Yet one of them more hard of heart
   Did vow to do his charge,
Because the wretch that hired him
   Had paid him very large.

The other won't agree thereto,
   So here they fall to strife;
With one another they did fight,
   About the children's life;
And he that was of mildest mood
   Did slay the other there,
Within an unfrequented wood;
   The babes did quake for fear!

He took the children by the hand,
   Tears standing in their eye,
And bade them straightway follow him
   And look they did not cry.
And two long miles he led them on,
   While they for food complain;
'Stay here,' quoth he; 'I'll bring you bread
   When I come back again.'

These pretty babes, with hand in hand,
   Went wandering up and down;
But never more could see the man
   Approaching from the town:
Their pretty lips with blackberries
   Were all besmeared and dyed;
And when they saw the darksome night
   They sat them down and cried.

Thus wandered these poor innocents,
   Till death did end their grief;
In one another's arms they died,
   As wanting due relief:

No burial this pretty pair
    Of any man receives,
Till Robin Redbreast piously
    Did cover them with leaves.

And now the heavy wrath of God
    Upon their uncle fell;
Yea, fearful fiends did haunt his house,
    His conscience felt an hell:
His barns were fired, his goods consumed,
    His lands were barren made,
His cattle died within the field,
    And nothing with him stayed.

And in a voyage to Portugal
    Two of his sons did die;
And to conclude, himself was brought
    To want and misery:
He pawned and mortgaged all his land
    Ere seven years came about;
And now at length this wicked act
    Did by this means come out:

The fellow that did take in hand
    These children for to kill,
Was for a robbery judged to die,
    Such was God's blessed will;
So did confess the very truth,
    As here hath been displayed;
Their uncle having died in gaol,
    Where he for debt was laid.

You that executors be made
    And overseers eke
Of children that be fatherless
    And infants mild and meek;
Take you example by this thing,
    And yield to each his right,
Lest God with such like misery
    Your wicked minds requite.

UNKNOWN.

THEIR PRETTYE LIPPES WITH BLACKBERRIES
WERE ALL BESMEAR'D AND DYED

A BOY'S SONG

Where the pools are bright and deep,
Where the grey trout lies asleep,
Up the river and o'er the lea—
That's the way for Billy and me.

Where the blackbird sings the latest,
Where the hawthorn blooms the sweetest,
Where the nestlings chirp and flee—
That's the way for Billy and me.

Where the mowers mow the cleanest,
Where the hay lies thick and greenest;
There to trace the homeward bee—
That's the way for Billy and me.

Where the hazel bank is steepest,
Where the shadow falls the deepest,
Where the clustering nuts fall free—
That's the way for Billy and me.

Why the boys should drive away
Little sweet maidens from the play,
Or love to banter and fight so well,
That's the thing I never could tell.

But this I know, I love to play,
Through the meadow, among the hay;
Up the water and o'er the lea,
That's the way for Billy and me.

There let us walk, there let us play,
Through the meadow among the hay,
Up the water and over the lea—
That's the way for Billy and me.

JAMES HOGG.

HIE AWAY

(From Waverley)

Hie away, hie away
Over bank and over brae,
Where the copsewood is the greenest,
Where the fountains glisten sheenest,
Where the lady-fern grows strongest,
Where the morning dew lies longest,
Where the black-cock sweetest sips it,
Where the fairy latest trips it:
Hie to haunts right seldom seen,
Lovely, lonesome, cool, and green,
Over bank and over brae,
Hie away, hie away.

SIR WALTER SCOTT.

THE SEA

The Sea! the Sea! the open Sea!
The blue, the fresh, the ever free!
Without a mark, without a bound,
It runneth the earth's wide regions round.
It plays with the clouds; it mocks the skies;
Or like a cradled creature lies.

I'm on the Sea! I'm on the Sea!
I am where I would ever be;
With the blue above, and the blue below,
And silence wheresoe'er I go;
If a storm should come and awake the deep,
What matter? I shall ride and sleep.

I love (oh, how I love!) to ride
On the fierce, foaming, bursting tide,
When every mad wave drowns the moon,
Or whistles aloft his tempest tune,
And tells how goeth the world below,
And why the south-west blasts do blow.

I never was on the dull, tame shore,
But I loved the great Sea more and more,
And backwards flew to her billowy breast,
Like a bird that seeketh its mother's nest;
And a mother she was and is to me;
For I was born on the open Sea!

The waves were white, and red the morn,
In the noisy hour when I was born;
And the whale it whistled, the porpoise rolled,
And the dolphins bared their backs of gold;
And never was heard such an outcry wild
As welcomed to life the Ocean-child!

I've lived since then, in calm and strife,
Full fifty summers a sailor's life,
With wealth to spend, and power to range,
But never have sought, nor sighed for change;
And Death, whenever he comes to me,
Shall come on the wide unbounded Sea!

BRYAN WALLER PROCTER.

AT SEA

A WET sheet and a flowing sea,
   A wind that follows fast,
And fills the white and rustling sail,
   And bends the gallant mast;
And bends the gallant mast, my boys,
   While, like the eagle free,
Away the good ship flies, and leaves
   Old England on the lee.

O for a soft and gentle wind!
   I heard a fair one cry;
But give to me the snoring breeze,
   And white waves heaving high;

And white waves heaving high, my boys,
   The good ship tight and free—
The world of waters is our home,
   And merry men are we.

There's tempest in yon hornèd moon,
   And lightning in yon cloud;
But hark the music, mariners!
   The wind is piping loud;
The wind is piping loud, my boys,
   The lightning flashing free—
While the hollow oak our palace is,
   Our heritage the sea.

ALLAN CUNNINGHAM.

THE LIGHTS

I KNOW the ships that pass by day:
I guess their business, grave or gay,
   And spy their flags, and learn their names,
     And whence they come and where they go—
   But in the night I only know
Some little starry flames.

And yet I think these jewelled lights
Have meanings full as noonday sights:
   For every emerald signs to me
     That ship and souls are harbour near,
   And every ruby rich and clear
Proclaims them bound for sea.

And all the yellow diamonds set
On mast and deck and hull in jet
   Have meanings real as day can show:
     They tell of care, of watchful eyes,
      Of labour, slumber, hopes, and sighs—
   Of human joy and woe.

O ships that come and go by night,
God's blessing be on every light!   J. J. BELL.

LITTLE BILLEE

There were three sailors of Bristol city
   Who took a boat and went to sea.
But first with beef and captain's biscuits
   And pickled pork they loaded she.

There was gorging Jack and guzzling Jimmy,
   And the youngest he was little Billee.
Now when they got as far as the Equator,
   They'd nothing left but one split pea.

Says gorging Jack to guzzling Jimmy,
   'I am extremely hungaree.'
To gorging Jack says guzzling Jimmy,
   'We've nothing left, us must eat we.'

Says gorging Jack to guzzling Jimmy,
   'With one another we shouldn't agree!
There's little Bill, he's young and tender,
   We're old and tough, so let's eat he.'

'O! Billy, we're going to kill and eat you,
   So undo the button of your chemie.'
When Bill received this information,
   He used his pocket-handkerchie.

'First let me say my catechism,
   Which my poor mammy taught to me.'
'Make haste, make haste,' says guzzling Jimmy,
   While Jack pulled out his snickersnee.

So Billy went up to the main-top gallant mast,
   And down he fell on his bended knee.
He scarce had come to the twelfth commandment,
   When up he jumps. 'There's land I see:

'Jerusalem and Madagascar,
   And North and South Amerikee:
There's a British flag a-riding at anchor,
   With Admiral Napier, K.C.B.'

So when they got aboard of the Admiral's,
   He hanged fat Jack and flogged Jimmee;
But as for little Bill, he made him
   The Captain of a Seventy-three!

W. M. THACKERAY.

GREAT, WIDE, BEAUTIFUL, WONDERFUL WORLD

GREAT, wide, beautiful, wonderful World,
With the wonderful water round you curled,
And the wonderful grass upon your breast—
World, you are beautifully drest.

The wonderful air is over me,
And the wonderful wind is shaking the tree,
It walks on the water, and whirls the mills,
And talks to itself on the tops of the hills.

You friendly Earth! how far do you go,
With the wheat-fields that nod and the rivers that flow,
With cities and gardens, and cliffs and isles,
And people upon you for thousands of miles?

Ah, you are so great, and I am so small,
I tremble to think of you, World, at all;
And yet, when I said my prayers to-day,
A whisper inside me seemed to say,
'You are more than the Earth, though you are such a dot:
You can love and think, and the Earth can not!'

W. B. RANDS.

PRAISE FOR MERCIES

Whene'er I take my walks abroad,
   How many poor I see!
What shall I render to my God
   For all His gifts to me?

Not more than others I deserve,
   Yet God hath given me more;
For I have food, while others starve,
   Or beg from door to door.

How many children in the street
   Half-naked I behold;
While I am cloth'd from head to feet,
   And cover'd from the cold!

While some poor wretches scarce can tell
   Where they may lay their head,
I have a home wherein to dwell,
   And rest upon my bed.

Are these Thy favours, day by day,
   To me above the rest?
Then let me love Thee more than they,
   And try to serve Thee best.

                 ISAAC WATTS.

FIRST SPRING MORNING

   Look! Look! the spring is come;
     O feel the gentle air,
That wanders thro' the boughs to burst
    The thick buds everywhere!
    The birds are glad to see
    The high unclouded sun:
Winter is fled away, they sing,
    The gay time is begun.

Adown the meadows green
Let us go dance and play,
And look for violets in the lane,
And ramble far away
To gather primroses,
That in the woodland grow,
And hunt for oxlips, or if yet
The blades of bluebells show.

There the old woodman gruff
Hath half the coppice cut,
And weaves the hurdles all day long
Beside his willow hut.
We'll steal on him, and then
Startle him, all with glee
Singing our song of winter fled
And summer soon to be.

ROBERT BRIDGES.

GAY ROBIN

Gay Robin is seen no more:
He is gone with the snow,
For winter is o'er
And Robin will go.
In need he was fed, and now he is fled
Away to his secret nest.
No more will he stand
Begging for crumbs,
No longer he comes
Beseeching our hand
And showing his breast
At window and door;
Gay Robin is seen no more.

Blithe Robin is heard no more:
He gave us his song
When summer was o'er
And winter was long:

He sang for his bread and now he is fled
  Away to his secret nest.
  And there in the green
  Early and late
  Alone to his mate
  He pipeth unseen
  And swelleth his breast.
  For us it is o'er,
Blithe Robin is heard no more.

ROBERT BRIDGES.

VALENTINE'S DAY

OH! I wish I were a tiny browny bird from out the south,
  Settled among the alder-holts, and twittering by the stream;
I would put my tiny tail down, and put up my tiny mouth,
  And sing my tiny life away in one melodious dream.

I would sing about the blossoms, and the sunshine and the sky,
  And the tiny wife I mean to have in such a cosy nest;
And if some one came and shot me dead, why then I could but die,
  With my tiny life and tiny song just ended at their best.

CHARLES KINGSLEY.

THE BLACKBIRD

THE blackbird has a mouth of gold, though sombre be his feathers,
The lark is for the summer noon, the blackbird for all weathers;

The lark he sets his heart above all things that are on earth,
But the blackbird in the cherry-tree finds rest and food and mirth.

The blackbird is a bonny bird despite his mourning colour,
He sings but all the merrier when earth and skies grow duller.
He whistles and he sings the while he swings from tree to tree,
For a rare mate and a fair mate in the cherry-boughs has he.

Of all the trees in the orchard the cherry-tree's the best,
For deep amid its branches, like a blithe heart in its breast,
There lilts a hidden blackbird, and he's singing to his dear,
And who would grudge their cherries so sweet a song to hear?

Oh, who would grudge their whitehearts to pay for such a song?
God love the merry blackbird who lifts the years along:
God shield the blackbird's nestlings and the blackbird's brooding wife,
And fill up with sweets full measure the days of the blackbird's life. NORA HOPPER.

GOING INTO BREECHES

Joy to Philip! he this day
Has his long coats cast away,
And (the childish season gone)
Put the manly breeches on.
Officer on gay parade,
Red-coat in his first cockade,

Bridegroom in his wedding-trim,
Birthday beau surpassing him,
Never did with conscious gait
Strut about in half the state
Or the pride (yet free from sin)
Of my little MANIKIN:
Never was there pride or bliss
Half so rational as his.
Sashes, frocks, to those that need 'em,
Philip's limbs have got their freedom—
He can run, or he can ride,
And do twenty things beside,
Which his petticoats forbad;
Is he not a happy lad?
Now he's under other banners
He must leave his former manners;
Bid adieu to female games
And forget their very names;
Puss-in-corners, hide-and-seek,
Sports for girls and punies weak!
Baste-the-bear he now may play at,
Leap-frog, football sport away at;
Show his skill and strength at cricket,
Mark his distance, pitch his wicket;
Run about in winter's snow
Till his cheeks and fingers glow;
Climb a tree or scale a wall
Without any fear to fall.
If he get a hurt or bruise,
To complain he must refuse,
Though the anguish and the smart
Go unto his little heart;
He must have his courage ready,
Keep his voice and visage steady;
Brace his eyeballs stiff as drum,
That a tear may never come;
And his grief must only speak
From the colour in his cheek.

H

This and more he must endure,
Hero he in miniature.
This and more must now be done,
Now the breeches are put on.
CHARLES AND MARY LAMB.

A CHILD'S EVENSONG

The sun is weary, for he ran
  So far and fast to-day;
The birds are weary, for who sang
  So many songs as they?
The bees and butterflies at last
  Are tired out, for just think too
How many gardens through the day
  Their little wings have fluttered through.
  And so, as all tired people do,
They've gone to lay their sleepy heads
Deep deep in warm and happy beds.
The sun has shut his golden eye
And gone to sleep beneath the sky,
The birds and butterflies and bees
Have all crept into flowers and trees,
And all lie quiet, still as mice,
Till morning comes—like father's voice.

So Geoffrey, Owen, Phyllis, you
Must sleep away till morning too.
Close little eyes, down little heads,
And sleep—sleep—sleep in happy beds.
RICHARD LE GALLIENNE.

HUNTING SONG

Waken, lords and ladies gay!
On the mountain dawns the day;
All the jolly chase is here,
With hawk, and horse, and hunting spear!
Hounds are in their couples yelling,
Hawks are whistling, horns are knelling;
Merrily, merrily, mingle they,
'Waken, lords and ladies gay.'

Waken, lords and ladies gay!
The mist has left the mountain grey,
Springlets in the dawn are steaming,
Diamonds on the brake are gleaming;
And foresters have busy been
To track the buck in thicket green;
Now we come to chant our lay,
'Waken, lords and ladies gay.'

Waken, lords and ladies gay!
To the greenwood haste away;
We can show you where he lies,
Fleet of foot, and tall of size;
We can show the marks he made,
When 'gainst the oak his antlers fray'd;
You shall see him brought to bay—
'Waken, lords and ladies gay.'

Louder, louder chant the lay,
Waken, lords and ladies gay!
Tell them youth, and mirth, and glee,
Run a course as well as we;
Time, stern huntsman! who can baulk,
Stanch as hound, and fleet as hawk?
Think of this, and rise with day,
Gentle lords and ladies gay!
     SIR WALTER SCOTT.

SING ON, BLYTHE BIRD

I'VE plucked the berry from the bush, the brown nut from the tree,
But heart of happy little bird ne'er broken was by me;
I saw them in their curious nests, close couching, slyly peer
With their wild eyes, like glittering beads, to note if harm were near:
I passed them by, and blessed them all; I felt that it was good
To leave unmoved the creatures small whose home was in the wood.

And here, even now, above my head, a lusty rogue doth sing,
He pecks his swelling breast and neck, and trims his little wing;
He will not fly; he knows full well, while chirping on that spray,
I would not harm him for a world, or interrupt his lay.
Sing on, sing on, blythe bird! and fill my heart with summer gladness,
It has been aching many a day with measures full of sadness!

WILLIAM MOTHERWELL.

WEE WILLIE WINKIE

WEE Willie Winkie rins through the toon,
Upstairs and downstairs in his nicht-goon,
Tirlin' at the window, crying at the lock,
'Are the weans in their bed, for it's now ten o'clock?'

'Hey, Willie Winkie, are ye comin' ben?
The cat's singing grey thrums to the sleepin' hen,
The dog's speldert on the floor, and disna gie a cheep,
But here's a waukrife laddie that wunna fa' asleep!

'Onything but sleep, you rogue! glow'ring like the moon,
Rattlin' in an airn jug wi' an airn spoon,
Rumblin', tumblin' roon about, crawin' like a cock,
Skirlin' like I kenna what, wauk'nin' sleepin' folk.

'Hey, Willie Winkie—the wean's in a creel!
Wamblin' aff a bodie's knee like a verra eel,
Ruggin' at the cat's lug, and ravelin' a' her thrums—
Hey, Willie Winkie—see, there he comes!'

Wearit is the mither that has a stoorie wean,
A wee stumpie stousie, that canna rin his lane,
That has a battle aye wi' sleep afore he'll close an e'e—
But a kiss frae aff his rosy lips gies strength anew to me.

WILLIAM MILLER.

CREEP AFORE YE GANG

Creep awa, my bairnie,—creep afore ye gang;
Cock ye baith your lugs to your auld Grannie's sang:
Gin ye gang as far ye will think the road lang,
Creep awa, my bairnie,—creep afore ye gang.

Creep awa, my bairnie, ye're ower young to learn
To tot up and down yet, my bonnie wee bairn;
Better creepin' cannie, as fa'in' wi' a bang,
Duntin' a' your wee brow,—creep afore ye gang.

Ye'll creep, an' ye'll hotch, an' ye'll nod to your mither,
Watchin' ilka stap o' your wee donsy brither;
Rest ye on the floor till your wee limbs grow strang,
An' ye'll be a braw chiel yet,—creep afore ye gang.

The wee burdie fa's when it tries ower soon to flee,
Folks are sure to tumble, when they climb ower hie;
They wha dinna walk right, are sure to come to wrang,
Creep awa, my bairnie,—creep afore ye gang.

JAMES BALLANTINE.

AULD DADDY DARKNESS

Auld Daddy Darkness creeps frae his hole,
Black as a blackamoor, blin' as a mole:
Stir the fire till it lowes, let the bairnie sit,
Auld Daddy Darkness is no wantit yet.

See him in the corners hidin' frae the licht,
See him at the window gloomin' at the nicht;
Turn up the gas licht, close the shutters a',
An' Auld Daddy Darkness will flee far awa'.

Awa' to hide the birdie within its cosy nest,
Awa' to lap the wee flooers, on their mither's breast,
Awa' to loosen Gaffer Toil frae his daily ca',
For Auld Daddy Darkness is kindly to a'.

He comes when we're weary to wean's frae oor waes,
He comes when the bairnies are getting aff their claes;
To cover them sae cosy, an' bring bonnie dreams,
So Auld Daddy Darkness is better than he seems.

Steek yer een, my wee tot, ye'll see Daddy then;
He's in below the bed claes, to cuddle ye he's fain;
Noo nestle in his bosie, sleep and dream yer fill,
Till Wee Davie Daylicht comes keekin' ower the hill.

JAMES FERGUSON.

WEE DAVIE DAYLICHT

Wee Davie Daylicht
  Keeks ower the sea
Early in the morning
  Wi' a clear e'e;
Waukens a' the birdies
  That were sleepin' soun'—
Wee Davie Daylicht
  Is nae lazy loon.

Wee Davie Daylicht
  Glowers ower the hill,
Glints through the greenwood,
  Dances on the rill;
Smiles on the wee cot,
  Shines on the ha'—
Wee Davie Daylicht
  Cheers the hearts o' a'.

Come, bonnie bairnie,
  Come awa' to me;
Cuddle in my bosie,
  Sleep upon my knee;—
Wee Davie Daylicht
  Noo has clos'd his e'e
In among the rosy clouds
  Far ayont the sea.

ROBERT TENNANT.

CHANTICLEER

Of all the birds from East to West,
  That tuneful are and dear,
I love that farmyard bird the best,
  They call him Chanticleer.

THE GOLDEN STAIRCASE

Gold plume and copper plume,
  Comb of scarlet gay;
'Tis he that scatters night and gloom,
  And whistles back the day!

He is the sun's brave herald
  That, ringing his blithe horn,
Calls round a world dew-pearled
  The heavenly airs of morn.

O clear gold, shrill and bold!
  He calls through creeping mist
The mountains from the night and cold
  To rose and amethyst.

He sets the birds to singing,
  And calls the flowers to rise;
The morning cometh, bringing
  Sweet sleep to heavy eyes.

Gold plume and silver plume,
  Comb of coral gay;
'Tis he packs off the night and gloom,
  And summons home the day!

Black fear he sends it flying,
  Black care he drives afar;
And creeping shadows sighing
  Before the morning star.

The birds of all the forest
  Have dear and pleasant cheer,
But yet I hold the rarest
  The farmyard Chanticleer.

Red cock or black cock,
  Gold cock or white,
The flower of all the feathered flock,
  He whistles back the light!
                KATHARINE TYNAN-HINKSON.

THE GIRL AND HER FAWN

With sweetest milk and sugar, first
I it at my own fingers nursed;
And as it grew, so every day
It wax'd more white and sweet than they.
It had so sweet a breath! and oft
I blush'd to see its foot more soft
And white,—shall I say,—than my hand?
Nay, any lady's of the land!
It is a wondrous thing how fleet
'Twas on those little silver feet;
With what a pretty skipping grace
It oft would challenge me the race;—
And when 't had left me far away,
'Twould stay, and run again, and stay;
For it was nimbler much than hinds,
And trod as if on the four winds.

I have a garden of my own,
But so with roses overgrown,
And lilies, that you would it guess
To be a little wilderness;
And all the Spring-time of the year
It only lovèd to be there.
Among the bed of lilies, I
Have sought it oft, where it should lie,
Yet could not, till itself would rise,
Find it, although before mine eyes:—
For, in the flaxen lilies' shade,
It like a bank of lilies laid.

Upon the roses it would feed,
Until its lips ev'n seem'd to bleed,
And then to me 'twould boldly trip,
And print those roses on my lip.

But all its chief delight was still
On roses thus itself to fill,
And its pure virgin limbs to fold
In whitest sheets of lilies cold:—
Had it lived long, it would have been
Lilies without,—roses within.

ANDREW MARVELL.

THE IMPS IN THE HEAVENLY MEADOW

To Heaven's Meadows, bright with flowers and sunshine,
    The little children go,
When they have had enough of life's sad dreaming,
    And leave the earth below.

But as they had not time to learn their lessons
    Before they went away,
There is a school, where all the angel children
    Must work four hours a day.

With golden pencils upon silver tablets,
    They copy fairy tales,
And learn to keep their halos bright and shining,
    And sing, and play their scales.

And twice a week they glide with merry laughter
    All down the Milky Way,
And homeward in the evening wander softly
    Upon a sunset ray.

But Sunday is the day they love and long for;
    Then all the children go
And play from morn till night within a meadow
    Where flowers in thousands grow.

THERE IS A SCHOOL, WHERE ALL THE ANGEL CHILDREN MUST WORK FOUR HOURS A DAY.

The meadow is not green, but blue and golden,
    The flowers like dewdrops bright;
When it is night, they burn and glow and glisten—
    Men call them stars of light.

Through Heaven's gate they all must pass to find it,
    Where Peter with the key
Keeps watch and warns the little angels kindly
    How good they all must be.

They must not fly about or run too quickly,
    Nor go too far away,
And when upon his golden key he calls them,
    Then they must all obey.

  .   .   .   .   .   .

One day it was so very hot in Heaven
    That good St. Peter slept,
And when the little angel children saw it,
    Away they quickly crept.

Ah! then they ran and flew about with laughter,
    And fluttered far and wide,
So far they wandered that of Heaven's Meadow
    They reached the other side.

They came to where the strong, tall, wooden paling
    Shuts all that place away,
Where idle, careless, mischief-loving, naughty,
    The Imps of Darkness stray.

And there the angels stopped, devoutly wishing
    Some opening there might be,
So that they might each one in turn peep through it,
    And see what they could see.

But not a chink or hole, for all their seeking,
    No gleam of light pierced through,
So with their little wings outspread and eager,
    Right to the top they flew;

And looking down they saw with awe and wonder,
 Imps all as black as soot;
Each had two horns and each a tail to play with,
 And hoof, instead of foot.

They heard the rustle of the angel feathers,
 They felt the cool sweet air,
And, lifting up their little coal-black faces,
 They saw Heaven's children there.

Then with one voice they cried: 'Oh! angel children,
 You look so good and fair,
We pray you, let us come up into Heaven
 And play a little there.

'We will not tweak nor pull your shining feathers,
 But be so very good;
We will not try and steal your little halos,
 But all do as we should.'

Then quick they flew away for Jacob's ladder,
 (Peter was still asleep,)
And placed it safely, where from Heaven to imp-land
 The way was dark and steep.

Then every little imp, with shouts and laughter,
 Helped by an angel's hand,
Scrambled right over the great wooden paling,
 And stood in Heaven's land.

They all, with air sedate and pious faces,
 Discreetly walked around,
Their tails like trains upon their arms upholding,
 And eyes upon the ground.

The little angels fluttered round in rapture,
 And showed the lovely flowers,
And bade them listen to the thrilling voices
 Of birds in Heaven's bowers.

THE GOLDEN STAIRCASE

And gently led them by the crystal streamlets,
    Bade them on dewdrops feast,
And showed them where the silver moon was rising
    To light them from the east.

Alas! when all the little demons saw her,
    The moon, so large and round,
They all began to roar, and growl, and gibber,
    And leap from off the ground;

And mocked the great white moon with ugly faces,
    Turned somersaults in air,
And when the angels prayed them cease, in terror,
    They vowed they did not care.

They trampled down the grass in Heaven's Meadow,
    They tore the flowers about,
And flung them on the earth beyond the paling,
    With gibe, and jeer, and shout.

They chased the birds that sang among the tree-tops
    And hushed their music sweet,
They pulled the little angels' tender feathers
    And trod upon their feet.

Then to the good St. Peter cried the angels
    To help them in their pain,
And if he would but this one time forgive them,
    They would be good again.

Then rose St. Peter from his peaceful dreaming—
    An angry saint was he—
He wrung his hands and clasped his head in horror,
    And seized his golden key.

Then blew a mighty blast in wrath upon it:
    Back all the angels flew,
And wide he threw the door of Heaven open,
    And thrust the children through.

And then he called two great and powerful angels,
    The strongest of the race,
To chase the little demons out of Heaven,
    And clear the holy place.

They gathered up the little imps in armfuls,
    Bore them with mighty stride,
And flung them over the strong wooden paling
    Down on the other side.

And though they fought and lashed their tails and
    whimpered,
    And kicked with might and main,
To Heaven's Meadow, bright with sun and flowers
    They never came again.

For two long months the little angel-children
    Were not allowed to play
Before the door of Heaven in the meadow,
    But stayed in all the day.

And when again they sought the Heavenly Meadow,
    Each child with humble mind
Must lay aside its little shining halo,
    And leave its wings behind.

    .   .   .   .

But all the flowers that on that day of sorrow,
    Flung out and scattered were,
Took root and bloom again in earth's green meadows,
    As daisies white and fair.

                                KATE E. BUNCE
                            (After Rudolf Baumbach).

THE WRECK OF THE STEAMSHIP PUFFIN

Tell you a story, children? Well, gather round my knee,
And I'll see if I cannot thrill you (though you're torpid after your tea)
With a moving tale of a shipwreck; and—should you refrain from sleep,
For the cake was a trifle heavy—I flatter myself you'll weep!

You all know Kensington Gardens, and some of you, I'll be bound,
Have stood by the level margin of the Pond that's entitled 'Round';
'Tis a pleasant spot on a summer day, when the air is laden with balm,
And the snowy sails are reflected clear in a mirror of flawless calm!

Well, it isn't like that in the winter, when the gardens are shut at four,
And a wind is lashing the water, and driving the ducks ashore.
Ah! the Pond can be black and cruel then, with its waves running inches high,
And a peril lurks for the tautest yacht that pocket-money can buy!

Yet, in weather like this, with a howling blast and a sky of ominous gloom,
Did the good ship Puffin put out to sea, as if trying to tempt her doom!
She was a model steamer, on the latest approved design,
And her powerful 10-slug engines were driven by spirits of wine.

And a smarter crew (they were sixpence each!) never
    shipped on a model bark,
While her Captain, 'Nuremberg Noah,' had once com-
    manded an ark;
Like a fine old salt of the olden school, he had stuck to
    his wooden ship,
But lately he'd been promoted—and this was his trial
    trip.

Off went the Puffin when steam was up, with her crew
    and commander brave!
And her screw was whizzing behind her as she breasted
    the foaming wave;
Danger? each sixpenny seaman smiled at the notion
    of that!
But the face of the skipper looked thoughtful from
    under his broad-brimmed hat.

Was he thinking of his children three—of Japheth, and
    Ham, and Shem?
Or his elephants (both with a trunk unglued!), was he
    sad at the thought of them?
Or the door at the end of his own old ark—did it give
    him a passing pain
To reflect that its unreal knocker might never deceive
    him again?

Nay, children, I cannot answer—he had passed inquiry
    beyond:
He was far away on the billowy waste of the wild and
    heaving Pond,
Battling hard with the angry crests of the waves, that
    were rolling in
And seeking to overwhelm and swamp his staggering
    vessel of tin!

Suddenly, speed she slackened, and seemed of her task
    to tire . . .
Ay! for the seas she had shipped of late had extin-
    guished her engine fire!

And the park-keeper, watching her, shook his head and
  in manner unfeeling cried:
''Twill be nothing short of a miracle now if she makes
  the opposite side!'

Think of it, children—that tiny ship, tossed in the
  boiling froth,
Drifting about at the wild caprice of the elements'
  fitful wrath!
Her screw-propeller was useless now that the flickering
  flame was out,
And the invalids gazed from their snug bath-chairs, till
  they almost forgot the gout.

Help for the gallant vessel! she is overborne by the
  blast!
She is shipping water by spoonfuls now, I tell you, she's
  sinking fast!
'Hi!' cried one of her owners to a spaniel, liver and
  black,
'Good dog, into the water, quick!' . . . But the park-
  keeper held it back!

Yes, spite of indignant pleadings from the eager, ex-
  cited crowd,
He quoted a pedant bye-law: 'In the water no dogs
  allowed.'
Then shame on the regulations that would hinder an
  honest dog
From plunging in to assist a ship that is rolling a helpless log!

Stand by all! for she'll ride it out—though she's left to
  do it alone.
She was drifting in, she was close at hand—when down
  she went like a stone!
A few feet more and they had her safe—and now, it
  was all too late,
For the Puffin had foundered in sight of port, by a
  stroke of ironical Fate!

I

But the other owner was standing by, and, tossing her
    tangled locks,
Down she sat on the nearest seat—and took off her
    shoes and socks!
'One kiss, brother!' she murmured, 'one clutch of your
    strong right hand—
And *I'll* paddle out to the Puffin, and bring her in
    safe to land!'

What can a barefooted child do? More than the pam-
    pered cur,
With his chicken-fed carcase shrinking, afraid from the
    bank to stir!
More than a baffled spaniel—ay, and more than the
    pug-dog pet,
That wrinkles his ebony muzzle, and whines if his paws
    are wet!

'Come back!' the park-keeper shouted—but she merely
    answered, 'I *won't*!'
And into the water she waded—though the invalids
    whimpered 'Don't!'
Ah! but the Pond struck chilly, and the mud at the
    bottom was thick;
But in she paddled, and probed it with the point of a
    borrowed stick!

'Don't let go of me, darling!' 'Keep hold of my fingers
    tight,
And I'll have it out in a minute or two. . . . I haven't
    got up to it quite:
A minute more, and the sunken ship we'll safe to the
    surface bring,
Yes, and the sixpenny sailors, too, that we lashed to
    the funnel with string!'

Up to the knees in water, Ethel and brother Ralph
Groped, till they found the Puffin and her sailors,
    soppy—but *safe*!

All the dear little sailors! . . . but—children—I can't
   go on!
For poor old wooden-faced Noah was—*how* shall I tell
   you?—gone!

He must have fallen over, out of that heeling boat,
Away in the dim grey offing, to rise and to fall like a
   float,
Till the colour deserted his face and form, as it might
   at an infant's suck,
And he sank to his rest in his sailor's tomb—the maw
   of a hungry duck!

You are weeping? I cannot wonder. Mine *is* a pathetic
   style.
Weep for him, children, freely. . . . But, when you
   have finished, smile
With joy for his shipmates, rescued as though by a
   Prospero's wand,
And the Puffin, snatched from the slimy depths of the
   Round but treacherous Pond!

F. ANSTEY.

THE CHOICE

   THERE were dolls in grand confections
      Of satins, silks, and laces,
   And dolls with fine complexions
      Requiring air-tight cases.
   And dumb dolls, and talking dolls,
   And squawking dolls, and walking dolls,
   And dolls that sleep or keep awake,
   And dolls that never, never break,
   And lady dolls with hats on,
   And gentlemen with spats on,
   And rubber, rag, and wood dolls,
   And doubtful, bad, and good dolls—

In fact, they were of all kinds,
Small kinds and tall kinds.
And did you count on fingers, toes,
Eyes, ears, and cheeks, lips, teeth, and nose,
You'd hardly count up any
Of the dolls that were so many—
From a guinea to a penny.

. . . . .

And Florence, lost in fairy-land,
Could only gasp and clutch my hand,
   And feast her pretty eyes.
'And which one would you like?' I said.
But Florence merely shook her head,
   With sundry little sighs.
The shopman kindly showed us round;
And more than once I thought we'd found
   The very doll for Flo.
Yet when I asked, 'Is this your choice?'
I heard a very shy young voice
   Distinctly answer 'No!'
But lo! at last the child espied
A doll that all her want supplied,
   And clasped it to her breast!
And when I cried, 'Oh, put it down! . . .
The shabby thing!' ('twas half a crown)
   She said, 'I like him best!'
And though the doll was plain and poor,
A meagre male of visage dour,
   She would not let it go.
So after much ignored advice
I paid the very modest price—
Nay, more, I had to call it 'nice,'
   To satisfy Miss Flo.

J. J. BELL.

THE ENCHANTED SHIRT

The King was sick. His cheek was red
   And his eye was clear and bright;
He ate and drank with kingly zest,
   And peacefully snored at night.

But he said he was sick, and a King should know,
   And doctors came by the score.
They did not cure him. He cut off their heads
   And sent to the schools for more.

At last two famous doctors came,
   And one was as poor as a rat,
He had passed his life in studious toil,
   And never found time to grow fat.

The other had never looked in a book;
   His patients gave him no trouble,
If they recovered they paid him well,
   If they died their heirs paid double.

Together they looked at the royal tongue,
   As the King on his couch reclined;
In succession they thumped his august chest,
   But no trace of disease could find.

The old sage said, 'You're as sound as a nut.'
   'Hang him up!' roared the King in a gale,
In a ten-knot gale of royal rage;
   The other leech grew a shade pale;

But he pensively rubbed his sagacious nose,
   And thus his prescription ran—
The King will be well if he sleeps one night
   In the Shirt of a Happy Man.

Wide o'er the realm the couriers rode,
    And fast their horses ran,
And many they saw, and to many they spoke,
    But they found no Happy Man.

They found poor men who would fain be rich,
    And rich who thought they were poor;
And men who twisted their waists in stays,
    And women that short-hose wore.

They saw two men by the roadside sit,
    And both bemoaned their lot;
For one had buried his wife, he said,
    And the other one had not.

At last they came to a village gate,
    A beggar lay whistling there;
He whistled and sang and laughed and rolled
    On the grass in the soft June air.

The weary couriers paused and looked
    At the scamp so blithe and gay;
And one of them said, 'Heaven save you, friend
    You seem to be happy to-day.'

'O yes, fair Sirs,' the rascal laughed,
    And his voice rang free and glad,
'An idle man has so much to do
    That he never has time to be sad.'

'This is our man,' the courier said;
    'Our luck has led us aright.
I will give you a hundred ducats, friend,
    For the loan of your shirt to-night.'

The merry blackguard lay back on the grass,
    And laughed till his face was black;
'I would do it, God wot,' and he roared with the fun,
    'But I haven't a shirt to my back.'

Each day to the King the reports came in
    Of his unsuccessful spies,
And the sad panorama of human woes
    Passed daily under his eyes.

And he grew ashamed of his useless life,
    And his maladies hatched in gloom;
He opened his windows and let the air
    Of the free heaven into his room.

And out he went in the world and toiled
    In his own appointed way;
And the people blessed him, the land was glad,
    And the King was well and gay.

JOHN HAY.

THE FAIRIES OF THE CALDON LOW

A MIDSUMMER LEGEND

'AND where have you been, my Mary,
    And where have you been from me?'
'I've been to the top of the Caldon Low,
    The midsummer-night to see!'

'And what did you see, my Mary,
    All up on the Caldon Low?'
'I saw the glad sunshine come down,
    And I heard the merry winds blow.'

'And what did you hear, my Mary,
    All up on the Caldon Hill?'
'I heard the drops of water made,
    And I heard the corn-ears fill.'

'Oh! tell me all, my Mary,
    All, all that ever you know,
For you must have seen the fairies,
    Last night on the Caldon Low.'

'Then take me on your knee, mother;
  And listen, mother of mine.
A hundred fairies danced last night,
  And the harpers they were nine.

'And their harp-strings rung so merrily
  To their dancing feet so small;
But oh! the words of their talking
  Were merrier far than all.'

'And what were the words, my Mary,
  That then you heard them say?'
'I'll tell you all, my mother;
  But let me have my way.

'Some of them played with the water,
  And rolled it down the hill;
"And this," they said, "shall speedily turn
  The poor old miller's mill:

'"For there has been no water
  Ever since the first of May;
And a busy man the miller will be
  At dawning of the day.

'"Oh! the miller, how he will laugh
  When he sees the mill-dam rise!
The jolly old miller, how he will laugh,
  Till the tears fill both his eyes!"

'And some they seized the little winds
  That sounded over the hill;
And each put a horn into his mouth,
  And blew both loud and shrill:

'"And there," they said, "the merry winds go,
  Away from every horn;
And they shall clear the mildew dank
  From the blind old widow's corn.

THE GOLDEN STAIRCASE

'"Oh! the poor blind widow,
  Though she has been blind so long,
She'll be blithe enough when the mildew's gone,
  And the corn stands tall and strong."

'And some they brought the brown lint-seed,
  And flung it down from the Low;
'"And this," they said, "by the sunrise,
  In the weaver's croft shall grow.

'"Oh! the poor lame weaver,
  How he will laugh outright,
When he sees his dwindling flax-field
  All full of flowers by night!"

'And then outspoke a brownie,
  With a long beard on his chin;
"I have spun up all the tow," said he,
  "And I want some more to spin.

'"I've spun a piece of hempen cloth,
  And I want to spin another;
A little sheet for Mary's bed,
  And an apron for her mother."

'With that I could not help but laugh,
  And I laughed out loud and free;
And then on the top of the Caldon Low
  There was no one left but me.

'And all on the top of the Caldon Low
  The mists were cold and grey,
And nothing I saw but the mossy stones
  That round about me lay.

'But coming down from the hill-top,
  I heard afar below,
How busy the jolly miller was,
  And how the wheel did go.

'And I peeped into the widow's field,
 And, sure enough, were seen
The yellow ears of the mildewed corn,
 All standing stout and green.

'And down by the weaver's croft I stole,
 To see if the flax were sprung;
But I met the weaver at his gate,
 With the good news on his tongue.

'Now this is all I heard, mother,
 And all that I did see;
So, pr'ythee, make my bed, mother,
 For I'm tired as I can be.'
MARY HOWITT.

LLEWELLYN AND HIS DOG

The spearman heard the bugle sound,
 And cheerly smiled the morn;
And many a brach, and many a hound,
 Obeyed Llewellyn's horn.

And still he blew a louder blast,
 And gave a louder cheer:
'Come, Gelert, come, wert never last
 Llewellyn's horn to hear!

'Oh, where does faithful Gelert roam?
 The flower of all his race!
So true, so brave—a lamb at home,
 A lion in the chase!'

That day Llewellyn little loved
 The chase of hart or hare;
And scant and small the booty proved,
 For Gelert was not there.

Unpleased Llewellyn homeward hied,
    When, near the portal-seat,
His truant, Gelert, he espied,
    Bounding his lord to greet.

But when he gained his castle-door,
    Aghast the chieftain stood;
The hound all o'er was smeared with gore—
    His lips, his fangs ran blood!

Llewellyn gazed with fierce surprise,
    Unused such looks to meet,
His favourite checked his joyful guise,
    And crouched and licked his feet.

Onward in haste Llewellyn passed—
    And on went Gelert too—
And still, where'er his eyes were cast,
    Fresh blood-gouts shocked his view!

O'erturned his infant's bed he found,
    The bloodstained covert rent,
And all around, the walls and ground,
    With recent blood besprent.

He called his child—no voice replied;
    He searched—with terror wild;
Blood! blood! he found on every side,
    But nowhere found the child!

'Hell-hound! my child's by thee devoured!'
    The frantic father cried;
And, to the hilt, his vengeful sword
    He plunged in Gelert's side!

His suppliant looks, as prone he fell,
    No pity could impart;
But still his Gelert's dying yell,
    Passed heavy o'er his heart.

Aroused by Gelert's dying yell,
    Some slumberer wakened nigh:
What words the parent's joy can tell,
    To hear his infant cry?

Concealed beneath a tumbled heap,
    His hurried search had missed,
All glowing from his rosy sleep
    The cherub-boy he kissed.

Nor scathe had he, nor harm, nor dread—
    But the same couch beneath
Lay a gaunt wolf, all torn and dead—
    Tremendous still in death!

Ah! what was then Llewellyn's pain,
    For now the truth was clear:
The gallant hound the wolf had slain,
    To save Llewellyn's heir.

Vain, vain was all Llewellyn's woe;
    'Best of thy kind, adieu!
The frantic deed which laid thee low
    This heart shall ever rue!'

And now a gallant tomb they raise,
    With costly sculpture decked;
And marbles, storied with his praise,
    Poor Gelert's bones protect.

Here never could the spearman pass,
    Or forester, unmoved;
Here oft the tear-besprinkled grass
    Llewellyn's sorrow proved.

And here he hung his horn and spear,
    And there, as evening fell,
In fancy's ear he oft would hear
    Poor Gelert's dying yell.

THE HON. W. R. SPENCER.

THE BATTLE OF BLENHEIM

It was a summer evening,
   Old Kaspar's work was done,
And he before his cottage door
   Was sitting in the sun,
And by him sported on the green
His little grandchild Wilhelmine.

She saw her brother Peterkin
   Roll something large and round,
Which he beside the rivulet
   In playing there, had found;
He came to ask what he had found,
That was so large, and smooth, and round.

Old Kaspar took it from the boy,
   Who stood expectant by;
And then the old man shook his head,
   And with a natural sigh,
' 'Tis some poor fellow's skull,' said he,
' Who fell in the great victory.

' I find them in the garden,
   For there's many here about;
And often when I go to plough,
   The ploughshare turns them out!
For many thousand men,' said he,
' Were slain in that great victory.'

' Now, tell us what 'twas all about,'
   Young Peterkin, he cries;
And little Wilhelmine looks up
   With wonder-waiting eyes;
' Now tell us all about the war,
And what they fought each other for.'

' It was the English,' Kaspar cried,
   ' Who put the French to rout;

But what they fought each other for,
   I could not well make out;
But everybody said,' quoth he,
' That 'twas a famous victory.

' My father lived at Blenheim then,
   Yon little stream hard by;
They burnt his dwelling to the ground,
   And he was forced to fly;
So with his wife and child he fled,
Nor had he where to rest his head.

' With fire and sword the country round
   Was wasted far and wide,
And many a gentle mother then,
   And new-born baby, died;
But things like that, you know, must be
At every famous victory.

' They say it was a shocking sight,
   After the field was won;
For many thousand bodies here
   Lay rotting in the sun;
But things like that, you know, must be
After a famous victory.

' Great praise the Duke of Marlbro' won,
   And our good Prince Eugene.'
' Why, 'twas a very wicked thing!'
   Said little Wilhelmine.
' Nay—nay—my little girl,' quoth he,
' It was a famous victory.

' And everybody praised the Duke
   Who this great fight did win.'
' But what good came of it at last?'
   Quoth little Peterkin.
' Why, that I cannot tell,' said he,
' But 'twas a famous victory.'

ROBERT SOUTHEY,

THE INCHCAPE ROCK

No stir in the air, no stir in the sea,
The ship was still as she could be,
Her sails from heaven received no motion,
Her keel was steady in the ocean.

Without either sign or sound of their shock
The waves flow'd over the Inchcape Rock;
So little they rose, so little they fell,
They did not move the Inchcape Bell.

The Abbot of Aberbrothok
Had placed that bell on the Inchcape Rock;
On a buoy in the storm it floated and swung,
And over the waves its warning rung.

When the Rock was hid by the surge's swell,
The mariners heard the warning bell;
And then they knew the perilous Rock,
And blest the Abbot of Aberbrothok.

The Sun in heaven was shining gay,
All things were joyful on that day;
The sea-birds scream'd as they wheel'd round,
And there was joyaunce in their sound.

The buoy of the Inchcape Bell was seen
A darker speck on the ocean green;
Sir Ralph the Rover walk'd his deck,
And he fixed his eye on the darker speck.

He felt the cheering power of spring,
It made him whistle, it made him sing;
His heart was mirthful to excess,
But the Rover's mirth was wickedness.

His eye was on the Inchcape float;
Quoth he, 'My men, put out the boat,
And row me to the Inchcape Rock,
And I'll plague the Abbot of Aberbrothok.'

The boat is lower'd, the boatmen row,
And to the Inchcape Rock they go;
Sir Ralph bent over from the boat,
And he cut the Bell from the Inchcape float.

Down sunk the Bell with a gurgling sound,
The bubbles rose and burst around;
Quoth Sir Ralph, 'The next who comes to the Rock
Won't bless the Abbot of Aberbrothok.'

Sir Ralph the Rover sail'd away,
He scour'd the seas for many a day;
And now grown rich with plunder'd store,
He steers his course for Scotland's shore.

So thick a haze o'erspreads the sky,
They cannot see the Sun on high;
The wind hath blown a gale all day,
At evening it hath died away.

On the deck the Rover takes his stand,
So dark it is they see no land.
Quoth Sir Ralph, 'It will be lighter soon,
For there is the dawn of the rising Moon.'

'Canst hear,' said one, 'the breakers roar?
For methinks we should be near the shore.'
'Now where we are I cannot tell,
But I wish I could hear the Inchcape Bell.'

They hear no sound, the swell is strong;
Though the wind hath fallen they drift along,
Till the vessel strikes with a shivering shock,—
'O Christ! it is the Inchcape Rock!'

Sir Ralph the Rover tore his hair;
He cursed himself in his despair;
The waves rushed in on every side,
The ship is sinking beneath the tide.

But even in his dying fear
One dreadful sound could the Rover hear,
A sound as if with the Inchcape Bell,
The Devil below was ringing his knell.

ROBERT SOUTHEY.

THE ARAB'S FAREWELL TO HIS STEED

My beautiful! my beautiful! thou standest meekly by,
With thy proudly arched and glossy neck, and dark and fiery eye;
Fret not to roam the desert now with all thy wingèd speed,—
I may not mount on thee again,—thou 'rt sold, my Arab steed!
Fret not with that impatient hoof,—snuff not the breezy wind;
The furthest that thou fliest now, so far am I behind:
The stranger hath thy bridle rein—thy master hath his gold—
Fleet limbed and beautiful, farewell! thou 'rt sold, my steed—thou 'rt sold!

Farewell! those free untired limbs full many a mile must roam,
To reach the chill and wintry sky which clouds the stranger's home;
Some other hand, less fond, must now thy corn and bread prepare;
The silky mane I braided once must be another's care!

The morning sun shall dawn again, but never more with
    thee
Shall I gallop through the desert paths, where we were
    wont to be:
Evening shall darken on the earth; and o'er the sandy
    plain
Some other steed, with slower step, shall bear me home
    again.

Yes, thou must go! the wild, free breeze, the brilliant
    sun and sky,
Thy master's home—from all of these my exiled one
    must fly:
Thy proud, dark eye will grow less proud, thy step
    become less fleet,
And vainly shalt thou arch thy neck thy master's hand
    to meet.
Only in sleep shall I behold that dark eye glancing
    bright,
Only in sleep shall hear again that step so firm and
    light;
And when I raise my dreaming arm to check or cheer
    thy speed,
Then must I starting wake, to feel—thou'rt sold, my
    Arab steed.

Ah! rudely then, unseen by me, some cruel hand may
    chide,
Till foam-wreaths lie, like crested waves, along thy
    panting side:
And the rich blood that is in thee swells in thy indignant
    pain,
Till careless eyes which rest on thee may count each
    started vein.
Will they ill-use thee? If I thought—but no, it
    cannot be;
Thou art so swift, yet easy curbed; so gentle, yet so
    free:

And yet, if haply, when thou 'rt gone, my lonely heart
    shall yearn,
Can the hand which casts thee from it now command
    thee to return?

Return! alas, my Arab steed! what shall thy master do,
When thou who wert his all of joy hast vanished from
    his view?
When the dim distance cheats mine eye, and through
    the gathering tears
Thy bright form for a moment like the false mirage
    appears?
Slow and unmounted will I roam, with weary feet alone,
Where with fleet step and joyous bound thou oft hast
    borne me on;
And sitting down by the green well, I'll pause and sadly
    think,
''Twas here he bowed his glossy neck when last I saw
    him drink!'

When last I saw thee drink!—away! the fevered dream
    is o'er;
I could not live a day and know that we should meet
    no more.
They tempted me, my beautiful! for hunger's power is
    strong;
They tempted me, my beautiful! but I have loved too
    long.
Who said that I had given thee up? Who said that
    thou wert sold?
'Tis false!—'tis false, my Arab steed! I fling them back
    their gold!
Thus, thus, I leap upon thy back, and scour the distant
    plains;
Away! who overtakes us now shall claim thee for his
    pains!

                THE HON. CAROLINE NORTON.

BERNARDO DEL CARPIO

The warrior bow'd his crested head, and tamed his
  heart of fire,
And sued the haughty king to free his long imprison'd
  sire;
'I bring thee here my fortress keys, I bring my captive
  train,
I pledge thee faith, my liege, my lord!—oh, break my
  father's chain!'

'Rise, rise! even now thy father comes, a ransom'd
  man this day;
Mount thy good horse, and thou and I will meet him
  on his way.'
Then lightly rose that loyal son, and bounded on his
  steed,
And urged, as if with lance in rest, the charger's foamy
  speed.

And lo! from far, as on they press'd, there came a
  glittering band,
With one that 'midst them stately rode, as a leader in
  the land;
'Now haste, Bernardo, haste! for there, in very truth,
  is he,
The father whom thy faithful heart hath yearn'd so
  long to see.'

His dark eyes flash'd, his proud breast heaved, his
  cheek's blood came and went;
He reach'd that grey-hair'd chieftain's side, and there,
  dismounting, bent;
A lowly knee to earth he bent, his father's hand he
  took,—
What was there in its touch that all his fiery spirit
  shook?

That hand was cold—a frozen thing—it dropp'd from
    his like lead,—
He look'd up to the face above—the face was of the
    dead!
A plume waved o'er the noble brow—the brow was
    fix'd and white;—
He met at last his father's eyes—but in them was no
    sight!

Up from the ground he sprang, and gazed, but who
    could paint that gaze?
They hush'd their very hearts, that saw its horror and
    amaze;
They might have chain'd him, as before that stony
    form he stood,
For the power was stricken from his arm, and from his
    lip the blood.

'Father!' at length he murmur'd low—and wept like
    childhood then,—
Talk not of grief till thou hast seen the tears of war-
    like men!—
He thought on all his glorious hopes, and all his young
    renown,—
He flung the falchion from his side, and in the dust sat
    down.

Then covering with his steel-gloved hands his darkly
    mournful brow,
'No more, there is no more,' he said, 'to lift the sword
    for now.—
My king is false, my hope betray'd, my father, oh! the
    worth,
The glory, and the loveliness, are pass'd away from
    earth!

'I thought to stand where banners waved, my sire!
    beside thee yet,
I would that there our kindred blood on Spain's free
    soil had met,—

Thou wouldst have known my spirit then,—for thee
    my fields were won,—
And thou hast perish'd in thy chains, as though thou
    hadst no son!'

Then, starting from the ground once more, he seized
    the monarch's rein,
Amidst the pale and wilder'd looks of all the courtier
    train;
And with a fierce, o'ermastering grasp, the rearing
    war-horse led,
And sternly set them face to face,—the king before
    the dead!

'Came I not forth upon thy pledge, my father's hand
    to kiss?
Be still, and gaze thou on, false king! and tell me what
    is this!
The voice, the glance, the heart I sought—give answer,
    where are they?—
If thou wouldst clear thy perjured soul, send life
    through this cold clay!

'Into these glassy eyes put light—be still! keep down
    thine ire,—
Bid these white lips a blessing speak—this earth is not
    my sire!
Give me back him for whom I strove, for whom my
    blood was shed,—
Thou canst not—and a king! His dust be mountains
    on thy head!'

He loosed the steed; his slack hand fell,—upon the
    silent face
He cast one long, deep, troubled look—then turn'd from
    that sad place:
His hope was crush'd, his after-fate untold in martial
    strain,—
His banner led the spears no more amidst the hills of
    Spain.   FELICIA HEMANS.

BERNARDO AND ALPHONSO

WITH some good ten of his chosen men, Bernardo
    hath appeared,
Before them all, in the palace hall, the lying King to
    beard;
With cap in hand and eye on ground, he came in
    reverent guise,
But ever and anon he frown'd, and flame broke from
    his eyes.

'A curse upon thee,' cries the King, 'who com'st unbid
    to me;
But what from traitor's blood should spring save traitor
    like to thee?
His sire, lords, had a traitor's heart; perchance our
    champion brave
May think it were a pious part to share Don Sancho's
    grave.'

'Whoever told this tale, the King hath rashness to
    repeat,'
Cries Bernard, 'here my gage I fling before the liar's
    feet!
No treason was in Sancho's blood, no stain in mine
    doth lie—
Below the throne, what knight will own the coward
    calumny?

'The blood that I like water shed, when Roland did
    advance,
By secret traitors hired and led, to make us slaves of
    France;—
The life of King Alphonso I saved at Roncesval—
Your words, Lord King, are recompense abundant for
    it all!

'Your horse was down,—your hope was flown,—I saw
  the falchion shine
That soon had drunk your royal blood, had I not ventured mine;
But memory soon of service done deserteth the ingrate,
And you've thank'd the son for life and crown by the
  father's bloody fate.

'You swore upon your kingly faith to set Don Sancho
  free,
But, curse upon your paltering breath! the light he
  ne'er did see;
He died in dungeon cold and dim, by Alphonso's base
  decree,
And visage blind and stiffen'd limb were all they gave
  to me.

'The King that swerveth from his word hath stain'd his
  purple black—
No Spanish lord will draw the sword behind a liar's
  back;
But noble vengeance shall be mine; an open hate I'll
  show—
The King hath injured Carpio's line, and Bernard is his
  foe.'

'Seize—seize him!' loud the King doth scream. 'There
  are a thousand here—
Let his foul blood this instant stream—what! caitiffs,
  do you fear?
Seize—seize the traitor!' But not one to move a finger
  dareth,—
Bernardo standeth by the throne, and calm his sword
  he bareth.

He drew the falchion from the sheath and held it up
  on high,
And all the hall was still as death; cries Bernard, 'Here
  am I;

And here's the sword that owns no lord, excepting
    Heaven and me;
Fain would I know who dares its point—King, Condé,
    or Grandee?'

Then to his mouth the horn he drew—(it hung below
    his cloak)—
His ten true men the signal knew, and through the
    ring they broke;
With helm on head and blade in hand, the knights the
    circle brake;
And back the lordlings 'gan to stand, and the false
    King to quake.

'Ha! Bernard,' quoth Alphonso, 'what means this war-
    like guise?
You know full well I jested—you know your worth I
    prize.'
But Bernard turned upon his heel, and smiling passed
    away;
Long rued Alphonso and Castille the jesting of that
    day.

J. G. LOCKHART.

BERNARDO'S REVENGE

WHAT tents gleam on the green hillside, like snow in
    the sunny beam,
What gloomy warriors gather there, like a surly moun-
    tain stream?
These, for Bernardo's vengeance, have come like a
    stormy blast,
The rage of their long cherished hate on a cruel king
    to cast.

'Smiters of tyranny!' cries their chief, 'see yonder slavish host,
We shall drench the field with their craven blood, or freedom's hopes were lost;
You know I come for a father's death, my filial vow to pay,
Then let the "Murdered Sancho!" be your battle-cry to-day.

'On, on! for the death of the tyrant king!' 'Hurrah!' was the answering cry;
'We follow thee to victory, or follow thee to die!'
The battlefield,—the charge,—the shock,—the quivering struggle now,—
The rout,—the shout!—while lightnings flash from Bernardo's angry brow.

The chieftain's arm has need of rest, his brand drips red with gore,
But one last sacrifice remains, ere his work of toil is o'er.
The King, who looked for victory from his large and well-trained host,
Now flies for safety from the field, where all his hopes are lost;

But full in front, with blood-red sword, a warrior appears,
And the war-cry, 'Murdered Sancho!' rings in the tyrant's ears.
'Ha! noble King, have we met at last?' with scornful lip he cries:
'Don Sancho's son would speak with you once more before he dies;

'Your kindness to my sainted sire is graven on my heart,
And I would show my gratitude once more before we part.

Draw! for the last of Sancho's race is ready for your
    sword;—
Bernardo's blood should flow by him, by whom his
    sire's was poured!

'What wait you for, vile, craven wretch? it was not
    thus you stood
When laying out your fiendish plans to spill my father's
    blood.
Draw! for I will not learn from thee the assassin's
    coward trade,
I scorn the lesson you have taught—unsheath your
    murderous blade!'

Roused by Bernardo's fiery taunts, the King at length
    engaged:
He fought for life, but all in vain; unequal strife he
    waged!
Bernardo's sword has pierced his side,—the tyrant's
    reign is o'er,—
'Father, I have fulfilled my vow, I thirst for blood no
    more.'

UNKNOWN.

LOCHINVAR

O, YOUNG Lochinvar is come out of the west,
Through all the wide Border his steed was the best;
And save his good broadsword he weapons had none,
He rode all unarm'd, and he rode all alone.
So faithful in love, and so dauntless in war,
There never was knight like the young Lochinvar.

He staid not for brake, and he stopp'd not for stone,
He swam the Esk river where ford there was none;

But ere he alighted at Netherby gate,
The bride had consented, the gallant came late:
For a laggard in love, and a dastard in war,
Was to wed the fair Ellen of brave Lochinvar.

So boldly he enter'd the Netherby Hall,
Among bride's-men, and kinsmen, and brothers, and all:
Then spoke the bride's father, his hand on his sword,
(For the poor craven bridegroom said never a word),
'O come ye in peace here, or come ye in war,
Or to dance at our bridal, young Lord Lochinvar?'

'I long woo'd your daughter, my suit you denied;—
Love swells like the Solway, but ebbs like its tide—
And now am I come, with this lost love of mine,
To lead but one measure, drink one cup of wine.
There are maidens in Scotland more lovely by far,
That would gladly be bride to the young Lochinvar.'

The bride kiss'd the goblet: the knight took it up,
He quaff'd off the wine, and he threw down the cup.
She look'd down to blush, and she look'd up to sigh,
With a smile on her lips, and a tear in her eye.
He took her soft hand, ere her mother could bar,—
'Now tread we a measure!' said young Lochinvar.

So stately his form, and so lovely her face,
That never a hall such a galliard did grace;
While her mother did fret, and her father did fume,
And the bridegroom stood dangling his bonnet and plume;
And the bride-maidens whisper'd, ''Twere better by far,
To have match'd our fair cousin with young Lochinvar.'

One touch to her hand, and one word in her ear,
When they reach'd the hall-door, and the charger stood near;
So light to the croupe the fair lady he swung,
So light to the saddle before her he sprung!

HE TOOK HER SOFT HAND, ERE HER MOTHER COULD BAR,—
"NOW TREAD WE A MEASURE!" SAID YOUNG LOCHINVAR.

'She is won! we are gone, over bank, bush, and scaur;
They'll have fleet steeds that follow,' quoth young
    Lochinvar.

There was mounting 'mong Græmes of the Netherby
    clan;
Forsters, Fenwicks, and Musgraves, they rode and they
    ran:
There was racing, and chasing, on Cannobie Lee,
But the lost bride of Netherby ne'er did they see.
So daring in love, and so dauntless in war,
Have ye e'er heard of gallant like young Lochinvar?
SIR WALTER SCOTT.

YE MARINERS OF ENGLAND

I

Ye Mariners of England!
That guard our native seas,
Whose flag has braved a thousand years
The battle and the breeze!
Your glorious standard launch again,
To match another foe!
And sweep through the deep,
While the stormy tempests blow;
While the battle rages loud and long,
And the stormy tempests blow.

II

The spirits of your fathers
Shall start from every wave!
For the deck it was their field of fame,
And Ocean was their grave:
Where Blake and mighty Nelson fell,
Your manly hearts shall glow,

As ye sweep through the deep,
While the stormy tempests blow;
While the battle rages loud and long,
And the stormy tempests blow.

III

Britannia needs no bulwark,
No towers along the steep;
Her march is o'er the mountain-waves,
Her home is on the deep.
With thunders from her native oak,
She quells the floods below—
As they roar on the shore,
When the stormy tempests blow:
When the battle rages loud and long,
And the stormy tempests blow.

IV

The meteor-flag of England
Shall yet terrific burn,
Till danger's troubled night depart,
And the star of peace return.
Then, then, ye ocean-warriors!
Our song and feast shall flow
To the fame of your name,
When the storm has ceased to blow;
When the fiery fight is heard no more,
And the storm has ceased to blow.

THOMAS CAMPBELL.

THE PILGRIM FATHERS

The breaking waves dashed high
 On a stern and rock-bound coast,
And the woods against a stormy sky
 Their giant branches tossed;

THE GOLDEN STAIRCASE

And the heavy night hung dark
   The hills and waters o'er,
When a band of exiles moored their bark
   On the wild New England shore.

Not as the conqueror comes,
   They, the true-hearted, came;
Not with the roll of stirring drums,
   And the trumpet that sings of fame;

Not as the flying come,
   In silence and in fear;—
They shook the depths of the desert gloom
   With their hymns of lofty cheer.

Amidst the storm they sang,
   And the stars heard and the sea;
And the sounding aisles of the dim woods rang
   To the anthem of the free!

The ocean eagle soared
   From his nest by the white wave's foam;
And the rocking pines of the forest roared—
   This was their welcome home!

There were men with hoary hair
   Amidst that pilgrim band;
Why had they come to wither there,
   Away from their childhood's land?

There was woman's fearless eye,
   Lit by her deep love's truth;
There was manhood's brow serenely high,
   And the fiery heart of youth.

What sought they thus afar?
   Bright jewels of the mine?
The wealth of seas, the spoils of war?—
   They sought a faith's pure shrine!

Ay, call it holy ground,
   The soil where first they trod.
They have left unstained what there they
     found—
   Freedom to worship God.

FELICIA HEMANS.

INCIDENT OF THE FRENCH CAMP

I

You know, we French stormed Ratisbon:
   A mile or so away,
On a little mound, Napoleon
   Stood on our storming-day;
With neck out-thrust, you fancy how,
   Legs wide, arms locked behind,
As if to balance the prone brow
   Oppressive with its mind.

II

Just as perhaps he mused, 'My plans
   That soar, to earth may fall,
Let once my army-leader Lannes
   Waver at yonder wall,'—
Out 'twixt the battery-smokes there flew
   A rider, bound on bound
Full-galloping; nor bridle drew
   Until he reached the mound.

III

Then off there flung in smiling joy,
   And held himself erect
By just his horse's mane, a boy:
   You hardly could suspect—

THE GOLDEN STAIRCASE

(So tight he kept his lips compressed,
   Scarce any blood came through)—
You looked twice ere you saw his breast
   Was all but shot in two.

IV

'Well,' cried he, 'Emperor, by God's grace
   We've got you Ratisbon!
The Marshal's in the market-place,
   And you'll be there anon
To see your flag-bird flap his vans
   Where I, to heart's desire,
Perched him!' The chief's eye flashed; his plans
   Soared up again like fire.

V

The chief's eye flashed; but presently
   Softened itself, as sheathes
A film the mother-eagle's eye
   When her bruised eaglet breathes;
'You're wounded!' 'Nay,' the soldier's pride
   Touched to the quick, he said:
'I'm killed, Sire!' And his chief beside
   Smiling the boy fell dead.

ROBERT BROWNING.

HORATIUS

BUT the Consul's brow was sad,
   And the Consul's speech was low,
And darkly looked he at the wall,
   And darkly at the foe.

'Their van will be upon us
  Before the bridge goes down;
And if they once may win the bridge,
  What hope to save the town?'

Then out spake brave Horatius,
  The Captain of the Gate:
'To every man upon this earth
  Death cometh soon or late.
And how can man die better
  Than facing fearful odds,
For the ashes of his fathers,
  And the temples of his Gods.

'Hew down the bridge, Sir Consul,
  With all the speed ye may;
I, with two more to help me,
  Will hold the foe in play.
In yon strait path a thousand
  May well be stopped by three.
Now who will stand on either hand,
  And keep the bridge with me?'

Then out spake Spurius Lartius;
  A Ramnian proud was he:
'Lo, I will stand at thy right hand,
  And keep the bridge with thee.'
And out spake strong Herminius;
  Of Titian blood was he:
'I will abide on thy left side,
  And keep the bridge with thee.'

'Horatius,' quoth the Consul,
  'As thou sayest, so let it be.'
And straight against that great array
  Forth went the dauntless Three.

THE GOLDEN STAIRCASE

For Romans in Rome's quarrel
   Spared neither land nor gold,
Nor son nor wife, nor limb nor life,
   In the brave days of old.

Now while the Three were tightening
   Their harness on their backs,
The Consul was the foremost man
   To take in hand an axe:
And Fathers mixed with Commons,
   Seized hatchet, bar, and crow,
And smote upon the planks above,
   And loosed the props below.

Meanwhile the Tuscan army,
   Right glorious to behold,
Came flashing back the noonday light,
Rank behind rank, like surges bright
   Of a broad sea of gold.
Four hundred trumpets sounded
   A peal of warlike glee,
As that great host, with measured tread,
And spears advanced, and ensigns spread,
Rolled slowly towards the bridge's head,
   Where stood the dauntless Three.

The Three stood calm and silent,
   And looked upon the foes,
And a great shout of laughter
   From all the vanguard rose:
And forth three chiefs came spurring
   Before that deep array;
To earth they sprang, their swords they drew,
And lifted high their shields, and flew
   To win the narrow way.

But meanwhile axe and lever
   Have manfully been plied;
And now the bridge hangs tottering
   Above the boiling tide.
'Come back, come back, Horatius!'
   Loud cried the Fathers all.
'Back, Lartius! back, Herminius!
   Back, ere the ruin fall!'

Back darted Spurius Lartius;
   Herminius darted back:
And, as they passed, beneath their feet
   They felt the timbers crack.
But when they turned their faces,
   And on the farther shore
Saw brave Horatius stand alone,
   They would have crossed once more.

But with a crash like thunder
   Fell every loosened beam,
And, like a dam, the mighty wreck
   Lay right athwart the stream:
And a long shout of triumph
   Rose from the walls of Rome,
As to the highest turret-tops
   Was splashed the yellow foam.

Alone stood brave Horatius,
   But constant still in mind;
Thrice thirty thousand foes before,
   And the broad flood behind.
'Down with him!' cried false Sextus,
   With a smile on his pale face.
'Now yield thee,' cried Lars Porsena,
   'Now yield thee to our grace.'

Round turned he, as not deigning
   Those craven ranks to see;
Nought spake he to Lars Porsena,
   To Sextus nought spake he;
But he saw on Palatinus
   The white porch of his home;
And he spake to the noble river
   That rolls by the towers of Rome.

'O Tiber! father Tiber!
   To whom the Romans pray,
A Roman's life, a Roman's arms,
   Take thou in charge this day!'
So he spake, and speaking sheathed
   The good sword by his side,
And with his harness on his back,
   Plunged headlong in the tide.

No sound of joy or sorrow
   Was heard from either bank;
But friends and foes in dumb surprise,
With parted lips and straining eyes,
   Stood gazing where he sank;
And when above the surges
   They saw his crest appear,
All Rome sent forth a rapturous cry,
And even the ranks of Tuscany
   Could scarce forbear to cheer.

But fiercely ran the current,
   Swollen high by months of rain:
And fast his blood was flowing;
   And he was sore in pain,

And heavy with his armour,
  And spent with changing blows:
And oft they thought him sinking,
  But still again he rose.

Never, I ween, did swimmer,
  In such an evil case,
Struggle through such a raging flood
  Safe to the landing place:
But his limbs were borne up bravely
  By the brave heart within,
And our good father Tiber
  Bore bravely up his chin.

And now he feels the bottom:
  Now on dry earth he stands;
Now round him throng the Fathers
  To press his gory hands;
And now, with shouts and clapping,
  And noise of weeping loud,
He enters through the River-Gate,
  Borne by the joyous crowd.

LORD MACAULAY.

THE SLAVE'S DREAM

Beside the ungathered rice he lay,
  His sickle in his hand;
His breast was bare, his matted hair
  Was buried in the sand.
Again, in the mist and shadow of sleep,
  He saw his Native Land.

Wide through the landscape of his dreams
   The lordly Niger flowed;
Beneath the palm-trees on the plain
   Once more a king he strode;
And heard the tinkling caravans
   Descend the mountain-road.

He saw once more his dark-eyed queen
   Among her children stand;
They clasped his neck, they kissed his cheeks,
   They held him by the hand!—
A tear burst from the sleeper's lids
   And fell into the sand.

And then at furious speed he rode
   Along the Niger's bank;
His bridle-reins were golden chains,
   And, with a martial clank,
At each leap he could feel his scabbard of steel
   Smiting his stallion's flank.

Before him, like a blood-red flag,
   The bright flamingoes flew;
From morn till night he followed their flight,
   O'er plains where the tamarind grew,
Till he saw the roofs of Caffre huts,
   And the ocean rose to view.

At night he heard the lion roar,
   And the hyæna scream,
And the river-horse, as he crushed the reeds
   Beside some hidden stream;
And it passed, like a glorious roll of drums,
   Through the triumph of his dream.

The forests, with their myriad tongues,
   Shouted of liberty;
And the Blast of the Desert cried aloud,
   With a voice so wild and free,
That he started in his sleep and smiled
   At their tempestuous glee.

He did not feel the driver's whip,
    Nor the burning heat of day;
For Death had illumined the Land of Sleep,
    And his lifeless body lay
A worn-out fetter, that the soul
    Had broken and thrown away!

                HENRY W. LONGFELLOW.

THE GLOVE AND THE LIONS

KING FRANCIS was a hearty king, and loved a royal sport,
And one day, as his lions fought, sat looking on the court;
The nobles fill'd the benches, and the ladies in their pride,
And 'mongst them sat the Count de Lorge, with one for whom he sigh'd;
And truly 'twas a gallant thing to see that crowning show—
Valour and love, and a king above, and the royal beasts below.

Ramped and roared the lions, with horrid, laughing jaws;
They bit, they glared, gave blows like beams, a wind went with their paws;
With wallowing might and stifled roar they rolled on one another,
Till all the pit, with sand and mane, was in a thunderous smother;
The bloody foam above the bars came whisking through the air;
Said Francis then, 'Faith, gentlemen, we're better here than there!'

De Lorge's love o'erheard the King, a beauteous, lively
    dame,
With smiling lips, and sharp, bright eyes, which always
    seemed the same;
She thought, 'The Count my lover, is as brave as brave
    can be,
He surely would do wondrous things to show his love
    of me;
King, ladies, lovers, all look on, the occasion is divine;
I'll drop my glove to prove his love; great glory will
    be mine!'

She dropped her glove to prove his love, then looked
    at him and smiled;
He bowed, and in a moment leaped among the lions
    wild:
The leap was quick; return was quick; he has regained
    his place,
Then threw the glove, but not with love, right in the
    lady's face!
'By Heav'n!' said Francis, 'rightly done!' and he rose
    from where he sat;
'No love,' quoth he, 'but vanity, sets love a task like
    that.'
                                    LEIGH HUNT.

LUCY GRAY; OR SOLITUDE

OFT I had heard of Lucy Gray;
    And, when I crossed the wild,
I chanced to see at break of day
    The solitary child.

No mate, no comrade Lucy knew;
    She dwelt on a wide moor,
—The sweetest thing that ever grew
    Beside a human door!

You yet may spy the fawn at play,
　　The hare upon the green;
But the sweet face of Lucy Gray
　　Will never more be seen.

'To-night will be a stormy night—
　　You to the town must go;
And take a lantern, Child, to light
　　Your mother through the snow.'

'That, Father! will I gladly do:
　　'Tis scarcely afternoon—
The minster-clock has just struck two,
　　And yonder is the moon!'

At this the Father raised his hook,
　　And snapped a faggot-band;
He plied his work;—and Lucy took
　　The lantern in her hand.

Not blither is the mountain roe:
　　With many a wanton stroke
Her feet disperse the powdery snow,
　　That rises up like smoke.

The storm came on before its time:
　　She wandered up and down;
And many a hill did Lucy climb,
　　But never reached the town.

The wretched parents all that night
　　Went shouting far and wide;
But there was neither sound nor sight
　　To serve them for a guide.

At day-break on a hill they stood
　　That over-looked the moor;
And thence they saw the bridge of wood,
　　A furlong from their door.

THE STORM CAME ON BEFORE ITS TIME:
SHE WANDERED UP AND DOWN;

They wept—and, turning homeward, cried,
　'In Heaven we all shall meet';
—When in the snow the mother spied
　The print of Lucy's feet.

Then downwards from the steep hill's edge
　They tracked the footmarks small;
And through the broken hawthorn hedge,
　And by the long stone wall;

And then an open field they crossed:
　The marks were still the same;
They tracked them on, nor ever lost;
　And to the bridge they came.

They followed from the snowy bank
　Those footmarks, one by one,
Into the middle of the plank;
　And further there were none!

—Yet some maintain that to this day
　She is a living child;
That you may see sweet Lucy Gray
　Upon the lonesome wild.

O'er rough and smooth she trips along,
　And never looks behind;
And sings a solitary song
　That whistles in the wind.
　　　　　　　　WILLIAM WORDSWORTH.

THE WRECK OF THE HESPERUS

It was the schooner Hesperus,
　That sailed the wintry sea;
And the skipper had taken his little daughter,
　To bear him company.

Blue were her eyes as the fairy-flax,
    Her cheeks like the dawn of day,
And her bosom white as the hawthorn buds,
    That ope in the month of May.

The skipper he stood beside the helm,
    His pipe was in his mouth,
And he watched how the veering flaw did blow
    The smoke now West, now South.

Then up and spake an old Sailor,
    Had sailed the Spanish Main,
'I pray thee, put into yonder port,
    For I fear a hurricane.

'Last night, the moon had a golden ring,
    And to-night no moon we see!'
The skipper he blew a whiff from his pipe,
    And a scornful laugh laughed he.

Colder and louder blew the wind,
    A gale from the North-east;
The snow fell hissing in the brine,
    And the billows frothed like yeast.

Down came the storm, and smote amain
    The vessel in its strength;
She shuddered and paused, like a frighted steed,
    Then leaped her cable's length.

'Come hither! come hither! my little daughter,
    And do not tremble so;
For I can weather the roughest gale,
    That ever wind did blow.'

He wrapped her warm in his seaman's coat,
    Against the stinging blast;
He cut a rope from a broken spar,
    And bound her to the mast.

THE GOLDEN STAIRCASE

'O father! I hear the church-bells ring,
    Oh, say, what may it be?'
''Tis a fog-bell on a rock-bound coast!'—
    And he steered for the open sea.

'O father! I hear the sound of guns,
    Oh, say, what may it be?'
'Some ship in distress, that cannot live
    In such an angry sea!'

'O father, I see a gleaming light,
    Oh, say, what may it be?'
But the father answered never a word,
    A frozen corpse was he.

Lashed to the helm, all stiff and stark,
    With his face turned to the skies,
The lantern gleamed through the gleaming snow
    On his fixed and glassy eyes.

Then the maiden clasped her hands and prayed
    That savèd she might be;
And she thought of Christ, who stilled the wave,
    On the Lake of Galilee.

And fast through the midnight dark and drear,
    Through the whistling sleet and snow,
Like a sheeted ghost, the vessel swept
    Towards the reef of Norman's Woe.

And ever the fitful gusts between
    A sound came from the land;
It was the sound of the trampling surf,
    On the rocks and the hard sea-sand.

The breakers were right beneath her bows,
    She drifted a dreary wreck,
And a whooping billow swept the crew
    Like icicles from her deck.

She struck where the white and fleecy waves
    Looked soft as carded wool,
But the cruel rocks, they gored her side,
    Like the horns of an angry bull.

Her rattling shrouds, all sheathed in ice,
    With the masts, went by the board;
Like a vessel of glass, she stove and sank.
    Ho! ho! the breakers roared!

At daybreak, on the bleak sea-beach,
    A fisherman stood aghast,
To see the form of a maiden fair,
    Lashed close to a drifting mast.

The salt sea was frozen on her breast,
    The salt tears in her eyes;
And he saw her hair, like the brown sea-weed,
    On the billows fall and rise.

Such was the wreck of the Hesperus,
    In the midnight and the snow!
Christ save us all from a death like this,
    On the reef of Norman's Woe!

                  HENRY W. LONGFELLOW.

LORD ULLIN'S DAUGHTER

A CHIEFTAIN, to the Highlands bound,
    Cries, 'Boatman, do not tarry!
And I'll give thee a silver pound
    To row us o'er the ferry.'

'Now who be ye would cross Loch Gyle
    This dark and stormy water?'
'O, I'm the chief of Ulva's Isle,
    And this, Lord Ullin's daughter.

'And fast before her father's men
   Three days we've fled together,
For should he find us in the glen,
   My blood would stain the heather.

'His horsemen hard behind us ride;
   Should they our steps discover,
Then who will cheer my bonny bride
   When they have slain her lover?'

Out spoke the hardy Highland wight,
   'I'll go, my chief—I'm ready;
It is not for your silver bright,
   But for your winsome lady:

'And, by my word! the bonny bird
   In danger shall not tarry;
So, though the waves are raging white,
   I'll row you o'er the ferry.'

By this the storm grew loud apace,
   The water-wraith was shrieking;
And in the scowl of heaven, each face
   Grew dark as they were speaking.

But still, as wilder grew the wind,
   And as the night drew drearer,
Adown the glen rode armèd men,
   Their trampling sounded nearer.

'O haste thee, haste!' the lady cries,
   'Though tempests round us gather;
I'll meet the raging of the skies,
   But not an angry father.'

The boat has left the stormy land,
   A stormy sea before her,—
When, oh! too strong for human hand,
   The tempest gathered o'er her.

And still they rowed amidst the roar
  Of waters fast prevailing:
Lord Ullin reached that fatal shore,—
  His wrath was changed to wailing.

For, sore dismayed, through storm and shade
  His child he did discover;
One lovely hand she stretched for aid,
  And one was round her lover.

'Come back! come back!' he cried in grief,
  'Across this stormy water;
And I'll forgive your Highland chief,
  My daughter!—O my daughter!'

'Twas vain: the loud waves lashed the shore,
  Return or aid preventing;
The waters wild went o'er his child—
  And he was left lamenting.
                    THOMAS CAMPBELL.

EDINBURGH AFTER FLODDEN

News of battle!—news of battle!
  Hark! 'tis ringing down the street:—
And the archways and the pavement
  Bear the clang of hurrying feet.
News of battle! who hath brought it?
  News of triumph? Who should bring
Tidings from our noble army,
  Greetings from our gallant King?
All last night we watched the beacons
  Blazing on the hills afar,
Each one bearing, as it kindled,
  Message of the opened war.
All night long the northern streamers
  Shot across the trembling sky:
Fearful lights that never beckon
  Save when kings or heroes die.

News of battle! Who hath brought it?
   All are thronging to the gate;
'Warder—warder! open quickly!
   Man—is this a time to wait?'
And the heavy gates are opened:
   Then a murmur long and loud,
And a cry of fear and wonder
   Bursts from out the bending crowd.
For they see in battered harness
   Only one hard-stricken man;
And his weary steed is wounded,
   And his cheek is pale and wan:
Spearless hangs a bloody banner
   In his weak and drooping hand—
God! can that be Randolph Murray,
   Captain of the city band?

Round him crush the people, crying,
   'Tell us all—oh, tell us true!
Where are they who went to battle,
   Randolph Murray, sworn to you?
Where are they, our brothers—children?
   Have they met the English foe?
Why art thou alone, unfollowed?
   Is it weal, or is it woe?'
Like a corpse the grisly warrior
   Looks from out his helm of steel;
But no word he speaks in answer—
   Only with his armèd heel
Chides his weary steed, and onward
   Up the city streets they ride;
Fathers, sisters, mothers, children,
   Shrieking, praying by his side.
'By the God that made thee, Randolph!
   Tell us what mischance hath come.'
Then he lifts his riven banner
   And the asker's voice is dumb.

The elders of the city
    Have met within their hall—
The men whom good King James had charged
    To watch the tower and wall.
'Your hands are weak with age,' he said,
    'Your hearts are stout and true;
So bide ye in the Maiden Town,
    While others fight for you.
My trumpet from the Border-side
    Shall send a blast so clear,
That all who wait within the gate
    That stirring sound may hear.
Or, if it be the will of Heaven
    That back I never come,
And if, instead of Scottish shouts,
    Ye hear the English drum,—
Then let the warning bells ring out,
    Then gird you to the fray,
Then man the walls like burghers stout,
    And fight while fight you may.
'Twere better that in fiery flame
    The roofs should thunder down,
Than that the foot of foreign foe
    Should trample in the town!'

Then in came Randolph Murray—
    His step was slow and weak,
And, as he doffed his dinted helm,
    The tears ran down his cheek:
They fell upon his corslet,
    And on his mailèd hand,
As he gazed around him wistfully,
    Leaning sorely on his brand.
And none who then beheld him
    But straight were smote with fear,
For a bolder and a sterner man
    Had never couched a spear.

They knew so sad a messenger
  Some ghastly news must bring;
And all of them were fathers,
  And their sons were with the King.

And up then rose the Provost—
  A brave old man was he,
Of ancient name and knightly fame,
  And chivalrous degree.
He ruled our city like a Lord
  Who brooked no equal here,
And ever for the townsman's rights
  Stood up 'gainst prince and peer.
And he had seen the Scottish host
  March from the Borough-muir,
With music-storm and clamorous shout
And all the din that thunders out,
  When youth's of victory sure.
But yet a dearer thought had he—
  For, with a father's pride,
He saw his last remaining son
  Go forth by Randolph's side,
With casque on head and spur on heel,
  All keen to do and dare;
And proudly did that gallant boy
  Dunedin's banner bear.
Oh! woeful now was the old man's look,
  And he spake right heavily—
'Now, Randolph, tell thy tidings,
  However sharp they be!
Woe is written on thy visage,
  Death is looking from thy face:
Speak! though it be of overthrow—
  It cannot be disgrace!'

Right bitter was the agony
  That wrung that soldier proud:
Thrice did he strive to answer,
  And thrice he groaned aloud.

Then he gave the riven banner
    To the old man's shaking hand,
Saying—' That is all I bring ye
    From the bravest in the land!
Ay! ye may look upon it—
    It was guarded well and long,
By your brothers and your children,
    By the valiant and the strong.
One by one they fell around it,
    As the archers laid them low,
Grimly dying, still unconquered,
    With their faces to the foe.
' Ay! ye well may look upon it—
    There is more than honour there,
Else, be sure, I had not brought it
    From the field of dark despair.
Never yet was royal banner
    Steeped in such a costly dye;
It hath lain upon a bosom
    Where no other shroud shall lie.
Sirs! I charge you, keep it holy,
    Keep it as a sacred thing,
For the stain ye see upon it
    Was the life-blood of your King!'

Woe, woe, and lamentation!
    What a piteous cry was there!
Widows, maidens, mothers, children,
    Shrieking, sobbing in despair!
Through the streets the death-word rushes,
    Spreading terror, sweeping on.
' Jesu Christ! our King has fallen—
    O Great God, King James is gone!
Holy Mother Mary, shield us,
    Thou who erst did lose thy Son!
O the blackest day for Scotland
    That she ever knew before!
O our King—the good, the noble,
    Shall we see him never more?

THE GOLDEN STAIRCASE

Woe to us! and woe to Scotland!
  O our sons, our sons and men!
Surely some have 'scaped the Southron,
  Surely some will come again!'
Till the oak that fell last winter
  Shall uprear its shattered stem—
Wives and mothers of Dunedin—
  Ye may look in vain for them!

But within the Council Chamber
  All was silent as the grave.
Whilst the tempest of their sorrow
  Shook the bosoms of the brave.
Well indeed might they be shaken
  With the weight of such a blow:
He was gone—their prince, their idol,
  Whom they loved and worshipped so!
Like a knell of death and judgment
  Rung from heaven by angel hand,
Fell the words of desolation
  On the elders of the land.
Hoary heads were bowed and trembling,
  Withered hands were clasped and wrung:
God had left the old and feeble,
  He had ta'en away the young.

Then the Provost he uprose,
  And his lip was ashen white.
But a flush was on his brow,
  And his eye was full of light.
'Thou hast spoken, Randolph Murray,
  Like a soldier stout and true,
Thou hast done a deed of daring
  Had been perilled but by few.
For thou hast not shamed to face us,
  Nor to speak thy ghastly tale,
Standing—thou, a knight and captain—
  Here, alive within thy mail!

Now, as my God shall judge me,
  I hold it braver done,
Than hadst thou tarried in thy place,
  And died above my son!
Thou needst not tell it: he is dead.
  God help us all this day!
But speak—how fought the citizens
  Within the furious fray?
For, by the might of Mary!
  'Twere something still to tell,
That no Scottish foot went backward
  When the Royal Lion fell!'

                WILLIAM AYTOUN.

SOLDIER, REST!

(From The Lady of the Lake)

SOLDIER, rest! thy warfare o'er,
  Sleep the sleep that knows not breaking;
Dream of battlefields no more,
  Days of danger, nights of waking.
In our isle's enchanted hall,
  Hands unseen thy couch are strewing,
Fairy strains of music fall,
  Every sense in slumber dewing.
Soldier, rest! thy warfare o'er,
Dream of fighting fields no more:
Sleep the sleep that knows not breaking,
Morn of toil, nor night of waking.

No rude sound shall reach thine ear,
  Armour's clang, or war-steed's champing,
Trump nor pibroch summon here,
  Mustering clan, or squadron tramping.
Yet the lark's shrill fife may come
  At the daybreak, from the fallow,
And the bittern sound his drum,
  Booming from the sedgy shallow.

Ruder sounds shall none be near,
Guards nor warders challenge here,
Here's no war-steed's neigh and champing,
Shouting clans, or squadrons stamping.

SIR WALTER SCOTT.

GATHERING-SONG OF DONALD DHU

PIBROCH of Donuil Dhu,
    Pibroch of Donuil,
Wake thy wild voice anew,
    Summon Clan Conuil.
Come away, come away,
    Hark to the summons!
Come in your war array,
    Gentles and Commons.

Come from deep glen, and
    From mountain so rocky,
The war-pipe and pennon
    Are at Inverlochy.
Come every hill-plaid, and
    True heart that wears one,
Come every steel blade, and
    Strong hand that bears one.

Leave untended the herd,
    The flock without shelter;
Leave the corpse uninterr'd,
    The bride at the altar;
Leave the deer, leave the steer,
    Leave nets and barges:
Come with your fighting gear,
    Broadswords and targes.

Come as the winds come, when
    Forests are rended,
Come as the waves come, when
    Navies are stranded:

Faster come, faster come,
    Faster and faster,
Chief, vassal, page and groom,
    Tenant and master.

Fast they come, fast they come;
    See how they gather!
Wide waves the eagle plume,
    Blended with heather.
Cast your plaids, draw your blades,
    Forward each man set!
Pibroch of Donuil Dhu
    Knell for the onset!

              SIR WALTER SCOTT.

BORDER BALLAD

(From The Monastery)

MARCH, march, Ettrick and Teviotdale,
    Why the deil dinna ye march forward in order?
March, march, Eskdale and Liddesdale,
    All the Blue Bonnets are bound for the Border.
        Many a banner spread,
        Flutters above your head,
Many a crest that is famous in story.
        Mount and make ready then,
        Sons of the mountain glen,
Fight for the Queen and our old Scottish glory.

Come from the hills where your hirsels are grazing,
    Come from the glen of the buck and the roe;
Come to the crag where the beacon is blazing,
    Come with the buckler, the lance, and the bow.

Trumpets are sounding,
War-steeds are bounding,
Stand to your arms, and march in good order,
England shall many a day
Tell of the bloody fray,
When the Blue Bonnets came over the Border.

SIR WALTER SCOTT.

THE CHARGE OF THE LIGHT BRIGADE

Half a league, half a league,
  Half a league onward,
All in the valley of Death
  Rode the six hundred.
'Forward, the Light Brigade!
Charge for the guns!' he said :
Into the valley of Death
  Rode the six hundred.

'Forward, the Light Brigade!'
Was there a man dismay'd?
Not tho' the soldier knew
  Some one had blunder'd :
Their's not to make reply,
Their's not to reason why,
Their's but to do and die :
Into the valley of Death
  Rode the six hundred.

Cannon to right of them,
Cannon to left of them,
Cannon in front of them
  Volley'd and thunder'd;
Storm'd at with shot and shell,
Boldly they rode and well,
Into the jaws of Death,
Into the mouth of Hell
  Rode the six hundred.

Flash'd all their sabres bare,
Flash'd as they turn'd in air
Sabring the gunners there,
Charging an army, while
  All the world wonder'd:
Plunged in the battery-smoke
Right thro' the line they broke;
Cossack and Russian
Reel'd from the sabre-stroke
  Shatter'd and sunder'd.
Then they rode back, but not
  Not the six hundred.

Cannon to right of them,
Cannon to left of them,
Cannon behind them
  Volley'd and thunder'd;
Storm'd at with shot and shell,
While horse and hero fell,
They that had fought so well
Came thro' the jaws of Death,
Back from the mouth of Hell,
All that was left of them,
  Left of six hundred.

When can their glory fade?
O the wild charge they made!
  All the world wonder'd.
Honour the charge they made!
Honour the Light Brigade,
  Noble six hundred!

                LORD TENNYSON.

VITAÏ LAMPADA

There's a breathless hush in the Close to-night—
  Ten to make and the match to win—
A bumping pitch and a blinding light,
  An hour to play and the last man in.

And it's not for the sake of a ribboned coat,
   Or the selfish hope of a season's fame,
But his Captain's hand on his shoulder smote—
   'Play up! play up! and play the game!'

The sand of the desert is sodden red,—
   Red with the wreck of a square that broke;—
The Gatling's jammed and the Colonel dead,
   And the regiment blind with dust and smoke.
The river of death has brimmed his banks,
   And England's far, and Honour a name,
But the voice of a schoolboy rallies the ranks:
   'Play up! play up! and play the game!'

This is the word that year by year,
   While in her place the School is set,
Every one of her sons must hear,
   And none that hears it dare forget.
This they all with a joyful mind
   Bear through life like a torch in flame,
And falling fling to the host behind—
   'Play up! play up! and play the game!'

HENRY NEWBOLT.

ADMIRALS ALL

EFFINGHAM, Grenville, Raleigh, Drake,
   Here's to the bold and free!
Benbow, Collingwood, Byron, Blake,
   Hail to the Kings of the Sea!
Admirals all, for England's sake,
   Honour be yours and fame!
And honour, as long as waves shall break,
   To Nelson's peerless name!
     Admirals all, for England's sake,
       Honour be yours and fame!
     And honour, as long as waves shall break,
       To Nelson's peerless name!

Essex was fretting in Cadiz Bay
  With the galleons fair in sight;
Howard at last must give him his way,
  And the word was passed to fight.
Never was schoolboy gayer than he,
  Since holidays first began:
He tossed his bonnet to wind and sea,
  And under the guns he ran.

Drake nor devil nor Spaniard feared,
  Their cities he put to the sack;
He singed His Catholic Majesty's beard,
  And harried his ships to wrack.
He was playing at Plymouth a rubber of bowls
  When the great Armada came;
But he said, 'They must wait their turn, good souls,'
  And he stooped, and finished the game.

Fifteen sail were the Dutchmen bold,
  Duncan, he had but two:
But he anchored them fast where the Texel shoaled,
  And his colours aloft he flew.
'I've taken the depth to a fathom,' he cried,
  'And I'll sink with a right good will,
For I know when we're all of us under the tide,
  My flag will be fluttering still.'

Splinters were flying above, below,
  When Nelson sailed the Sound:
'Mark you, I wouldn't be elsewhere now,'
  Said he, 'for a thousand pound!'
The Admiral's signal bade him fly,
  But he wickedly wagged his head,
He clapped the glass to his sightless eye,
  And 'I'm damned if I see it!' he said.

Admirals all, they said their say,
  (The echoes are ringing still)
Admirals all, they went their way
  To the haven under the hill.

THE GOLDEN STAIRCASE

But they left us a kingdom none can take,
   The realm of the circling sea,
To be ruled by the rightful sons of Blake
   And the Rodneys yet to be.
      Admirals all, for England's sake,
         Honour be yours and fame!
      And honour, as long as waves shall break,
         To Nelson's peerless name!
HENRY NEWBOLT.

HOW THEY BROUGHT THE GOOD NEWS FROM GHENT TO AIX

I

I SPRANG to the stirrup, and Joris, and he;
I galloped, Dirck galloped, we galloped all three;
'Good speed!' cried the watch, as the gate-bolts undrew;
'Speed!' echoed the wall to us galloping through;
Behind shut the postern, the lights sank to rest,
And into the midnight we galloped abreast.

II

Not a word to each other; we kept the great pace
Neck by neck, stride by stride, never changing our place;
I turned in my saddle and made its girths tight,
Then shortened each stirrup, and set the pique right,
Rebuckled the cheek-strap, chained slacker the bit,
Nor galloped less steadily Roland a whit.

III

'Twas moonset at starting; but while we drew near
Lokeren, the cocks crew, and twilight dawned clear;
At Boom, a great yellow star came out to see;
At Düffeld, 'twas morning as plain as could be;

And from Mecheln church-steeple we heard the half-chime,
So Joris broke silence with, ' Yet there is time!'

IV

At Aershot, up leaped of a sudden the sun,
And against him the cattle stood black every one,
To stare thro' the mist at us galloping past,
And I saw my stout galloper Roland at last,
With resolute shoulders, each butting away
The haze, as some bluff river headland its spray :

V

And his low head and crest, just one sharp ear bent back
For my voice, and the other pricked out on his track ;
And one eye's black intelligence,—ever that glance
O'er its white edge at me, his own master, askance!
And the thick heavy spume-flakes which aye and anon
His fierce lips shook upwards in galloping on.

VI

By Hasselt, Dirck groaned ; and cried Joris, ' Stay spur !
Your Roos galloped bravely, the fault's not in her,
We'll remember at Aix,'—for one heard the quick wheeze
Of her chest, saw the stretched neck and staggering knees,
And sunk tail, and horrible heave of the flank,
As down on her haunches she shuddered and sank.

VII

So we were left galloping, Joris and I,
Past Looz and past Tongres, no cloud in the sky;

The broad sun above laughed a pitiless laugh,
'Neath our feet broke the brittle bright stubble like
　　chaff;
Till over by Dalhem a dome-spire sprang white,
And 'Gallop,' cried Joris, 'for Aix is in sight!'

VIII

'How they'll greet us!'—and all in a moment his roan
Rolled neck and crop over; lay dead as a stone;
And there was my Roland to bear the whole weight
Of the news which alone could save Aix from her fate,
With his nostrils like pits full of blood to the brim,
And with circles of red for his eye-sockets' rim.

IX

Then I cast loose my buff-coat, each holster let fall,
Shook off both my jack-boots, let go belt and all,
Stood up in the stirrup, leaned, patted his ear,
Called my Roland his pet-name, my horse without
　　peer;
Clapped my hands, laughed and sang, any noise, bad or
　　good,
Till at length into Aix Roland galloped and stood.

X

And all I remember is—friends flocking round
As I sat with his head 'twixt my knees on the ground;
And no voice but was praising this Roland of mine,
As I poured down his throat our last measure of wine,
Which (the burgesses voted by common consent)
Was no more than his due who brought good news
　　from Ghent.

　　　　　　　　　　　　　ROBERT BROWNING.

THE LOSS OF THE BIRKENHEAD

RIGHT on our flank the sun was dropping down;
  The deep sea heaved around in bright repose;
When, like the wild shriek from some captured town,
  A cry of women rose.

The stout ship Birkenhead lay hard and fast,
  Caught without hope upon a hidden rock;
Her timbers thrilled as nerves, when through them passed
  The spirit of that shock.

And ever, like base cowards, who leave their ranks
  In danger's hour, before the rush of steel,
Drifted away, disorderly, the planks
  From underneath her keel.

So calm the air—so calm and still the flood,
  That low down in its blue translucent glass
We saw the great fierce fish, that thirst for blood,
  Pass slowly, then repass.

They tarried, the waves tarried, for their prey!
  The sea turned one clear smile! Like things asleep
Those dark shapes in the azure silence lay,
  As quiet as the deep.

Then amidst oath, and prayer, and rush, and wreck,
  Faint screams, faint questions waiting no reply,
Our colonel gave the word, and on the deck
  Form'd us in line to die.

To die!—'twas hard, while the sleek ocean glow'd
  Beneath a sky as fair as summer flowers:—
' All to the boats!' cried one—he was, thank God,
  No officer of ours.

THE GOLDEN STAIRCASE

Our English hearts beat true—we would not stir:
　That base appeal we heard, but heeded not:
On land, on sea, we had our Colours, sir,
　　　To keep without a spot.

They shall not say in England, that we fought
　With shameful strength, unhonour'd life to seek;
Into mean safety, mean deserters, brought
　　　By trampling down the weak.

So we made women with their children go,
　The oars ply back again, and yet again;
Whilst, inch by inch, the drowning ship sank low,
　　　Still, under steadfast men.

—What follows, why recall?—The brave who died,
　Died without flinching in the bloody surf,
They sleep as well beneath that purple tide
　　　As others under turf.

They sleep as well! and, roused from their wild grave,
　Wearing their wounds like stars, shall rise again,
Joint-heirs with Christ, because they bled to save
　　　His weak ones, not in vain.

If that day's work no clasp or medal mark;
　If each proud heart no cross of bronze may press,
Nor cannon thunder loud from Tower or Park,
　　　This feel we none the less:—

That those whom God's high grace there saved from ill,
　Those also left His martyrs in the bay,
Though not by siege, though not in battle, still
　　　Full well had earned their pay.

　　　　　　　　　　SIR FRANCIS H. DOYLE.

THE RED THREAD OF HONOUR

(TOLD TO THE AUTHOR BY THE LATE
SIR CHARLES JAMES NAPIER)

Eleven men of England
   A breast-work charged in vain;
Eleven men of England
   Lie stripped, and gashed, and slain.
Slain; but of foes that guarded
   Their rock-built fortress well,
Some twenty had been mastered,
   When the last soldier fell.

Whilst Napier piloted his wondrous way
   Across the sand-waves of the desert sea,
There flashed at once, on each fierce clan, dismay,
   Lord of their wild Truckee.
These missed the glen to which their steps were bent,
   Mistook a mandate, from afar half heard,
And, in that glorious error, calmly went
   To death without a word.

   The robber-chief mused deeply,
     Above those daring dead;
   'Bring here,' at length he shouted,
     'Bring quick, the battle thread.
   Let Eblis blast for ever
     Their souls, if Allah will:
   But we must keep unbroken
     The old rules of the hill.

   'Before the Ghiznee tiger
     Leapt forth to burn and slay;
   Before the holy Prophet
     Taught our grim tribes to pray;

THE GOLDEN STAIRCASE 195

    Before Secunder's lances
        Pierced through each Indian glen;
    The mountain laws of honour
        Were framed for fearless men.

    'Still, when a chief dies bravely,
        We bind with green ONE wrist—
    Green for the brave, for heroes,
        ONE crimson thread we twist.
    Say ye, oh gallant Hillmen,
        For these, whose life has fled,
    Which is the fitting colour,
        The green one, or the red?'

'Our brethren, laid in honoured graves, may wear
    Their green reward,' each noble savage said;
'To these, whom hawks and hungry wolves shall tear,
    Who dares deny the red?'
Thus conquering hate, and steadfast to the right,
    Fresh from the heart that haughty verdict came;
Beneath a waning moon, each spectral height
    Rolled back its loud acclaim.

    Once more the chief gazed keenly
        Down on those daring dead;
    From his good sword their hearts' blood
        Crept to that crimson thread.
    Once more he cried: 'The judgment,
        Good friends, is wise and true,
    But though the red *be* given,
        Have we not more to do?

    'These were not stirred by anger,
        Nor yet by lust made bold;
    Renown they thought above them,
        Nor did they look for gold.
    To them their leader's signal
        Was as the voice of God:
    Unmoved, and uncomplaining,
        The path it showed, they trod.

'As, without sound or struggle,
   The stars unhurrying march,
Where Allah's finger guides them,
   Through yonder purple arch,
These Franks, sublimely silent,
   Without a quickened breath,
Went in the strength of duty,
   Straight to their goal of death.

'If I were now to ask you
   To name our bravest man,
Ye all at once would answer,
   They called him Mehrab Khan.
He sleeps among his fathers
   Dear to our native land,
With the bright mark he bled for
   Firm round his faithful hand.

'The songs they sing of Roostum
   Fill all the past with light;
If truth be in their music,
   He was a noble knight.
But were those heroes living,
   And strong for battle still,
Would Mehrab Khan or Roostum,
   Have climbed, like these, the Hill?'

And they replied: 'Though Mehrab Khan was brave,
   As chief, he chose himself what risks to run;
Prince Roostum lied, his forfeit life to save,
   Which these had never done.'

'Enough!' he shouted fiercely;
   'Doomed though they be to hell,
Bind fast the crimson trophy
   Round BOTH wrists—bind it well.
Who knows but that great Allah
   May grudge such matchless men,
With none so decked in heaven,
   To the fiends' flaming den?'

Then all those gallant robbers
    Shouted a stern 'Amen!'
They raised the slaughtered sergeant,
    They raised his mangled ten.
And when we found their bodies
    Left bleaching in the wind,
Around BOTH wrists in glory
    That crimson thread was twined.

Then Napier's knightly heart, touched to the core,
   Rung like an echo, to that knightly deed,
He bade its memory live for evermore,
   That those who run may read.
SIR FRANCIS H. DOYLE.

THE BATTLE OF THE BALTIC

Of Nelson and the North,
Sing the glorious day's renown,
When to battle fierce came forth
All the might of Denmark's crown,
And her arms along the deep proudly shone;
By each gun the lighted brand,
In a bold, determined hand,
And the Prince of all the land
Led them on.

Like leviathans afloat,
Lay their bulwarks on the brine;
While the sign of battle flew
On the lofty British line:
It was ten of April morn by the chime;
As they drifted on their path,
There was silence deep as death;
And the boldest held his breath
For a time.

But the might of England flushed
To anticipate the scene;
And her van the fleeter rushed
O'er the deadly space between.
'Hearts of oak!' our captain cried; when
    each gun
From its adamantine lips
Spread a death-shade round the ships,
Like the hurricane eclipse
Of the sun.

Again! again! again!
And the havoc did not slack,
Till a feeble cheer the Dane
To our cheering sent us back—
Their shots along the deep slowly boom—
Then ceased—and all is wail,
As they strike the shattered sail;
Or, in conflagration pale,
Light the gloom.

Out spoke the victor then,
As he hailed them o'er the wave:
'Ye are brothers! ye are men!
And we conquer but to save—
So peace instead of death let us bring;
But yield, proud foe, thy fleet,
With the crews, at England's feet,
And make submission meet
To our King.'

Then Denmark blessed our chief,
That he gave her wounds repose,
And the sounds of joy and grief
From her people wildly rose,
As death withdrew his shades from the day.
While the sun looked smiling bright
O'er a wide and woeful sight,
Where the fires of funeral light
Died away.

Now joy, Old England, raise!
For the tidings of thy might,
By the festal cities' blaze,
While the wine-cup shines in light;
And yet amidst that joy and uproar,
Let us think of them that sleep,
Full many a fathom deep,
By thy wild and stormy steep,
Elsinore.

Brave hearts! to Britain's pride
Once so faithful and so true,
On the deck of fame that died,
With the gallant, good Riou;—
Soft sighs the winds of Heaven o'er their grave!
While the billow mournful rolls,
And the mermaid's song condoles,
Singing glory to the souls
Of the brave! THOMAS CAMPBELL.

NORA'S VOW

Hear what Highland Nora said,—
'The Earlie's son I will not wed,
Should all the race of nature die,
And none be left but he and I.
For all the gold, for all the gear,
And all the lands both far and near,
That ever valour lost or won,
I would not wed the Earlie's son.'

'A maiden's vows,' old Callum spoke,
'Are lightly made, and lightly broke;
The heather on the mountain's height
Begins to bloom in purple light;

The frost-wind soon shall sweep away
That lustre deep from glen and brae;
Yet Nora, ere its bloom be gone,
May blithely wed the Earlie's son.'

'The swan,' she said, 'the lake's clear breast
May barter for the eagle's nest;
The Awe's fierce stream may backward turn,
Ben-Cruachan fall and crush Kilchurn;
Our kilted clans, when blood is high,
Before their foes may turn and fly;
But I, were all these marvels done,
Would never wed the Earlie's son.'

Still in the water-lily's shade
Her wonted nest the wild-swan made;
Ben-Cruachan stands as fast as ever,
Still downward foams the Awe's fierce river;
To shun the clash of foeman's steel
No Highland brogue has turn'd the heel:
But Nora's heart is lost and won,
—She's wedded to the Earlie's son!

SIR WALTER SCOTT.

FROM 'AS YOU LIKE IT'

(ACT IV. SCENE 2)

WHAT shall he have that kill'd the deer?
His leather skin, and horns to wear.
Take thou no scorn, to wear the horn;
It was a crest ere thou wast born,
  Thy father's father wore it,
  And thy father bore it:
The horn, the horn, the lusty horn,
Is not a thing to laugh to scorn.

FROM 'THE WINTER'S TALE'

(ACT IV. SCENE 2)

Jog on, jog on, the footpath way,
   And merrily hent the stile-a:
A merry heart goes all the day,
   Your sad tires in a mile-a.

FROM 'KING HENRY VIII.'

(ACT III. SCENE 1)

Orpheus with his lute made trees,
And the mountain-tops that freeze,
Bow themselves, when he did sing:
To his music, plants and flowers
Ever sprung; as Sun and showers
   There had made a lasting Spring.

Every thing that heard him play,
Even the billows of the sea,
Hung their heads, and then lay by.
In sweet music is such art,
Killing care and grief of heart
   Fall asleep, or, hearing, die.

FROM 'THE TEMPEST'

(ACT V. SCENE 1)

Where the bee sucks, there suck I:
In a cowslip's bell I lie,—
There I couch: when owls do cry,
On the bat's back I do fly
After summer merrily.
Merrily, merrily shall I live now
Under the blossom that hangs on the bough.

               WILLIAM SHAKESPEARE.

LADY CLARE

It was the time when lilies blow,
   And clouds are highest up in air,
Lord Ronald brought a lily-white doe
   To give his cousin, Lady Clare.

I trow they did not part in scorn:
   Lovers long betroth'd were they:
They too will wed the morrow morn:
   God's blessing on the day!

'He does not love me for my birth,
   Nor for my lands so broad and fair;
He loves me for my own true worth,
   And that is well,' said Lady Clare.

In there came old Alice the nurse,
   Said, 'Who was this that went from thee?'
'It was my cousin,' said Lady Clare,
   'To-morrow he weds with me.'

'O God be thank'd!' said Alice the nurse,
   'That all comes round so just and fair:
Lord Ronald is heir of all your lands,
   And you are not the Lady Clare.'

'Are ye out of your mind, my nurse, my nurse?'
   Said Lady Clare, 'that ye speak so wild?'
'As God's above,' said Alice the nurse,
   'I speak the truth: you are my child.

'The old Earl's daughter died at my breast;
   I speak the truth, as I live by bread!
I buried her like my own sweet child,
   And put my child in her stead.'

'Falsely, falsely have ye done,
   O mother,' she said, 'if this be true,
To keep the best man under the sun
   So many years from his due.'

YET HERE'S A KISS FOR MY MOTHER DEAR

THE GOLDEN STAIRCASE

'Nay now, my child,' said Alice the nurse,
  'But keep the secret for your life,
And all you have will be Lord Ronald's,
  When you are man and wife.'

'If I'm a beggar born,' she said,
  'I will speak out, for I dare not lie.
Pull off, pull off, the brooch of gold,
  And fling the diamond necklace by.'

'Nay now, my child,' said Alice the nurse,
  'But keep the secret all ye can.'
She said, 'Not so: but I will know
  If there be any faith in man.'

'Nay now, what faith?' said Alice the nurse,
  'The man will cleave unto his right.'
'And he shall have it,' the lady replied,
  'Tho' I should die to-night.'

'Yet give one kiss to your mother dear!
  Alas! my child, I sinn'd for thee.'
'O mother, mother, mother,' she said,
  'So strange it seems to me.

'Yet here's a kiss for my mother dear,
  My mother dear, if this be so,
And lay your hand upon my head,
  And bless me, mother, ere I go.'

She clad herself in a russet gown,
  She was no longer Lady Clare:
She went by dale, and she went by down,
  With a single rose in her hair.

The lily-white doe Lord Ronald had brought
  Leapt up from where she lay,
Dropt her head in the maiden's hand,
  And follow'd her all the way.

Down stept Lord Ronald from his tower:
  'O Lady Clare, you shame your worth!
Why come you drest like a village maid,
  That are the flower of the earth?'

'If I come drest like a village maid,
  I am but as my fortunes are:
I am a beggar born,' she said,
  'And not the Lady Clare.'

'Play me no tricks,' said Lord Ronald,
  'For I am yours in word and in deed.
Play me no tricks,' said Lord Ronald,
  'Your riddle is hard to read.'

O and proudly stood she up!
  Her heart within her did not fail:
She look'd into Lord Ronald's eyes,
  And told him all her nurse's tale.

He laugh'd a laugh of merry scorn:
  He turn'd and kiss'd her where she stood:
'If you are not the heiress born,
  And I,' said he, 'the next in blood—

'If you are not the heiress born,
  And I,' said he, 'the lawful heir,
We two will wed to-morrow morn,
  And you shall still be Lady Clare.'

                LORD TENNYSON.

THE GREEN GNOME

RING, sing! ring, sing! pleasant Sabbath bells!
Chime, rhyme! chime, rhyme! through the dales and
  dells!
Rhyme, ring! chime, sing! pleasant Sabbath bells!
Chime, sing! rhyme, ring! over fields and fells!

And I gallop'd and I gallop'd on my palfrey white as milk,
My robe was of the sea-green woof, my serk was of the silk,
My hair was golden yellow, and it floated to my shoe,
My eyes were like two harebells bathed in shining drops of dew;
My palfrey, never stopping, made a music sweetly blent
With the leaves of autumn dropping all around me as I went;
And I heard the bells grow fainter, far behind me peal and play,
Fainter, fainter, fainter, fainter, till they seem'd to die away;
And beside a silver runnel, on a lonely heap of sand,
I saw the green Gnome sitting, with his cheek upon his hand;
Then he started up to see me, and he ran with cry and bound,
And drew me from my palfrey white, and set me on the ground:
O crimson, crimson were his locks, his face was green to see,
But he cried, 'O light-hair'd lassie, you are bound to marry me!'
He claspt me round the middle small, he kissed me on the cheek,
He kissed me once, he kissed me twice—I could not stir or speak;
He kissed me twice, he kissed me thrice—but when he kissed again,
I called aloud upon the name of Him who died for men!

Ring, sing! ring, sing! pleasant Sabbath bells!
Chime, rhyme! chime, rhyme! through the dales and dells!
Rhyme, ring! chime, sing! pleasant Sabbath bells!
Chime, sing! rhyme, ring! over fields and fells!

O faintly, faintly, faintly, calling men and maids to pray,
So faintly, faintly, faintly, rang the bells afar away;
And as I named the Blessed Name, as in our need we can,
The ugly green green Gnome became a tall and comely man!
His hands were white, his beard was gold, his eyes were black as sloes,
His tunic was of scarlet woof, and silken were his hose;
A pensive light from Faëryland still linger'd on his cheek,
His voice was like the running brook, when he began to speak:
'O you have cast away the charm my stepdame put on me,
Seven years I dwelt in Faëryland, and you have set me free!
O I will mount thy palfrey white, and ride to kirk with thee,
And by those sweetly shining eyes, we twain will wedded be!'

Back we gallop'd, never stopping, he before and I behind,
And the autumn leaves were dropping, red and yellow, in the wind,
And the sun was shining clearer, and my heart was high and proud,
As nearer, nearer, nearer, rang the kirk-bells sweet and loud,
And we saw the kirk before us, as we trotted down the fells,
And nearer, clearer, o'er us rang the welcome of the bells!

Ring, sing! ring, sing! pleasant Sabbath bells!
Chime, rhyme! chime, rhyme! through the dales and dells!
Rhyme, ring! chime, sing! pleasant Sabbath bells!
Chime, sing! rhyme, ring! over fields and fells!

ROBERT BUCHANAN.

BALLAD OF EARL HALDAN'S DAUGHTER

It was Earl Haldan's daughter,
   She looked across the sea;
She looked across the water,
   And long and loud laughed she:
'The locks of six princesses
   Must be my marriage fee,
So hey bonny boat, and ho bonny boat!
   Who comes a-wooing me?'

It was Earl Haldan's daughter,
   She walked along the sand;
When she was aware of a knight so fair,
   Came sailing to the land.
His sails were all of velvet,
   His mast of beaten gold,
And 'Hey bonny boat, and ho bonny boat!
   Who saileth here so bold?'

'The locks of five princesses
   I won beyond the sea;
I clipt their golden tresses,
   To fringe a cloak for thee.
One handful yet is wanting,
   But one of all the tale;
So hey bonny boat, and ho bonny boat!
   Furl up thy velvet sail!'

He leapt into the water,
   That rover young and bold,
He gript Earl Haldan's daughter,
   He clipt her locks of gold:
'Go weep, go weep, proud maiden,
   The tale is full to-day.
Now hey bonny boat, and ho bonny boat!
   Sail Westward ho! away!'

CHARLES KINGSLEY.

BARBARA FRIETCHIE

Up from the meadows rich with corn,
Clear in the cool September morn,

The clustered spires of Frederick stand
Green-walled by the hills of Maryland.

Round about them orchards sweep,
Apple and peach tree fruited deep,

Fair as the garden of the Lord
To the eyes of the famished rebel horde,

On that pleasant morn of the early fall
When Lee marched over the mountain-wall;

Over the mountains winding down,
Horse and foot, into Frederick town.

Forty flags with their silver stars,
Forty flags with their crimson bars,

Flapped in the morning wind: the sun
Of noon looked down, and saw not one.

Up rose old Barbara Frietchie then,
Bowed with her fourscore years and ten;

Bravest of all in Frederick town,
She took up the flag the men hauled down;

In her attic window the staff she set,
To show that one heart was loyal yet.

Up the street came the rebel tread,
Stonewall Jackson riding ahead.

Under his slouched hat left and right
He glanced; the old flag met his sight.

'Halt!'—the dust-brown ranks stood fast.
'Fire!'—out blazed the rifle-blast.

It shivered the window, pane and sash;
It rent the banner with seam and gash.

Quick, as it fell, from the broken staff
Dame Barbara snatched the silken scarf.

She leaned far out on the window-sill,
And shook it forth with a royal will.

'Shoot, if you must, this old grey head,
But spare your country's flag,' she said.

A shade of sadness, a blush of shame,
Over the face of the leader came;

The nobler nature within him stirred
To life at that woman's deed and word:

'Who touches a hair of yon grey head
Dies like a dog! March on!' he said.

All day long through Frederick street
Sounded the tread of marching feet:

All day long that free flag tost
Over the heads of the rebel host.

Ever its torn folds rose and fell
On the loyal winds that loved it well;

And through the hill-gaps sunset light
Shone over it with a warm good-night.

Barbara Frietchie's work is o'er,
And the Rebel rides on his raids no more.

Honour to her! and let a tear
Fall, for her sake, on Stonewall's bier.

Over Barbara Frietchie's grave,
Flag of Freedom and Union, wave!

Peace and order and beauty draw
Round thy symbol of light and law;

And ever the stars above look down
On thy stars below in Frederick town!

JOHN GREENLEAF WHITTIER.

KING JOHN AND THE ABBOT OF CANTERBURY

An ancient story I'll tell you anon
Of a notable prince that was called King John;
And he ruled England with main and with might,
For he did great wrong, and maintained little right.

And I'll tell you a story, a story so merrie,
Concerning the Abbot of Canterbury;
How for his housekeeping and high renown,
They rode post for him to fair London town.

An hundred men, the king did hear say,
The abbot kept in his house every day;
And fifty gold chains without any doubt,
In velvet coats waited the abbot about.

' How now, father abbot, I hear it of thee,
Thou keepest a far better house than me;
And for thy housekeeping and high renown,
I fear thou work'st treason against my crown.'

' My liege,' quo' the abbot, ' I would it were known
I never spend nothing, but what is my own;
And I trust your grace will do me no deere,
For spending of my own true-gotten gear.'

' Yes, yes, father abbot, thy fault it is high,
And now for the same thou needest must die;

For except thou canst answer me questions three,
Thy head shall be smitten from thy bodie.

'And first,' quo' the king, 'when I'm in this stead,
With my crown of gold so fair on my head
Among all my liege-men so noble of birth,
Thou must tell me to one penny what I am worth.

'Secondlie, tell me, without any doubt,
How soon I may ride the whole world about;
And at the third question thou must not shrink,
But tell me here truly what I do think.'

'Oh, these are hard questions for my shallow wit,
Nor I cannot answer your grace as yet:
But if you will give me but three weeks' space,
I'll do my endeavour to answer your grace.'

'Now three weeks' space to thee will I give,
And that is the longest time thou hast to live;
For if thou dost not answer my questions three,
Thy lands and thy livings are forfeit to me.'

Away rode the abbot all sad at that word,
And he rode to Cambridge and Oxenford,
But never a doctor there was so wise,
That could with his learning an answer devise.

Then home rode the abbot of comfort so cold,
And he met his shepherd a-going to fold;
'How now, my lord abbot, you are welcome home;
What news do you bring us from good King John?'

'Sad news, sad news, shepherd, I must give,
That I have but three days more to live;
For if I do not answer him questions three,
My head will be smitten from my bodie.

'The first is to tell him there in that stead,
With his crown of gold so fair on his head,
Among all his liege-men so noble of birth,
To within one penny of what he is worth.

'The second to tell him, without any doubt,
How soon he may ride this whole world about:
And at the third question I must not shrink,
But tell him there truly what he does think.'

'Now cheer up, sir abbot, did you never hear yet,
That a fool he may learn a wise man wit?
Lend me horse and serving-men, and your apparel,
And I'll ride to London to answer your quarrel.

'Nay, frown not, if it hath been told unto me,
I am like your lordship as ever may be;
And if you will but lend me your gown,
There is none shall know us at fair London town.'

'Now horses and serving-men thou shalt have,
With sumptuous array most gallant and brave,
With crozier and mitre, and rochet and cope,
Fit to appear 'fore our father the pope.'

'Now welcome, sir abbot,' the king he did say,
''Tis well thou 'rt come back to keep thy day:
For and if thou canst answer my questions three,
Thy life and thy living both saved shall be.

'And first, when thou seest me here in this stead,
With my crown of gold so fair on my head,
Among all my liege-men so noble of birth,
Tell me to one penny what I am worth.'

'For thirty pence our Saviour was sold
Among the false Jews, as I have been told:
And twenty-nine is the worth of thee,
For I think thou art one penny worser than he!'

The king he laughed, and swore by St. Bittel,
'I did not think I had been worth so little!
—Now secondly, tell me, without any doubt,
How soon I may ride this whole world about.'

'You must rise with the sun, and ride with the same
Until the next morning he rises again;
And then your grace need not make any doubt
But in twenty-four hours you'll ride it about.'

The king he laughed, and swore by St. John,
'I did not think it could be done so soon!
Now from the third question thou must not shrink,
But tell me here truly what I do think.'

'Yea, that shall I do, and make your grace merrie;
You think I'm the abbot of Canterbury;
But I'm his poor shepherd, as plain you may see,
That am come to beg pardon for him and for me.'

The king he laughed, and swore by the mass,
'I'll make thee lord abbot this day in his place!'
'Now nay, my liege, be not in such speed,
For alack, I can neither write nor read.'

'Four nobles a week, then, I will give thee,
For this merrie jest thou hast shown unto me;
And tell the old abbot when thou comest home,
Thou hast brought him a pardon from good King
    John.'

UNKNOWN.

HIAWATHA'S CHILDHOOD

By the shores of Gitchee Gumee,
By the shining Big-Sea-Water,
Stood the wigwam of Nokomis,
Daughter of the Moon, Nokomis.
Dark behind it rose the forest,
Rose the black and gloomy pine-trees,
Rose the firs with cones upon them;
Bright before it beat the water,
Beat the clear and sunny water,
Beat the shining Big-Sea-Water.

There the wrinkled, old Nokomis
Nursed the little Hiawatha,
Rocked him in his linden cradle,
Bedded soft in moss and rushes,
Safely bound with reindeer sinews;
Stilled his fretful wail by saying,
'Hush! the Naked Bear will get thee!'
Lulled him into slumber singing,
'Ewa-yea! my little owlet!
Who is this that lights the wigwam?
With his great eyes lights the wigwam?
Ewa-yea! my little owlet!'

Many things Nokomis taught him
Of the stars that shine in heaven;
Showed him Ishkoodah, the comet,
Ishkoodah, with fiery tresses;
Showed the Death-Dance of the spirits,
Warriors with their plumes and war-clubs,
Flaring far away to northward
In the frosty nights of Winter;
Showed the broad, white road in heaven,
Pathway of the ghosts, the shadows,
Running straight across the heavens,
Crowded with the ghosts, the shadows.

At the door, on summer evenings
Sat the little Hiawatha;
Heard the whispering of the pine-trees,
Heard the lapping of the water,
Sounds of music, words of wonder;
'Minnie-wawa!' said the pine-trees,
'Mudway aushka!' said the water.
Saw the fire-fly, Wah-wah-taysee,
Flitting through the dusk of evening,
With the twinkle of its candle
Lighting up the brakes and bushes,
And he sang the song of children,
Sang the song Nokomis taught him:

'Wah-wah-taysee, little fire-fly,
Little, flitting, white-fire insect,
Little, dancing, white-fire creature,
Light me with your little candle,
Ere upon my bed I lay me,
Ere in sleep I close my eyelids!'

Saw the moon rise from the water
Rippling, rounding from the water,
Saw the flecks and shadows on it,
Whispered, 'What is that, Nokomis?'
And the good Nokomis answered:
'Once a warrior, very angry,
Seized his grandmother, and threw her
Up into the sky at midnight;
Right against the moon he threw her;
'Tis her body that you see there.'

Saw the rainbow in the heaven,
In the eastern sky, the rainbow,
Whispered, 'What is that, Nokomis?'
And the good Nokomis answered:
''Tis the heaven of flowers you see there:
All the wild-flowers of the forest,
All the lilies of the prairie,
When on earth they fade and perish,
Blossom in that heaven above us.'

When he heard the owls at midnight,
Hooting, laughing in the forest,
'What is that?' he cried in terror;
'What is that,' he said, 'Nokomis?'
And the good Nokomis answered:
'That is but the owl and owlet,
Talking in their native language,
Talking, scolding at each other.'

Then the little Hiawatha
Learned of every bird its language,

Learned their names and all their secrets,
How they built their nests in Summer,
Where they hid themselves in Winter,
Talked with them whene'er he met them,
Called them 'Hiawatha's Chickens.'

Of all beasts he learned the language,
Learned their names and all their secrets,
How the beavers built their lodges,
Where the squirrels hid their acorns,
How the reindeer ran so swiftly,
Why the rabbit was so timid,
Talked with them whene'er he met them,
Called them 'Hiawatha's Brothers.'

HENRY W. LONGFELLOW.

THE PIED PIPER OF HAMELIN

I

HAMELIN Town's in Brunswick,
  By famous Hanover city;
The river Weser, deep and wide,
Washes its walls on the southern side;
A pleasanter spot you never spied;
  But, when begins my ditty,
Almost five hundred years ago,
To see the townsfolk suffer so
  From vermin, was a pity.

II

  Rats!
They fought the dogs, and killed the cats,
  And bit the babies in the cradles,
And ate the cheeses out of the vats,
  And licked the soup from the cooks' own ladles,

Split open the kegs of salted sprats,
Made nests inside men's Sunday hats,
And even spoiled the women's chats
   By drowning their speaking
   With shrieking and squeaking
In fifty different sharps and flats.

III

At last the people in a body
   To the Town Hall came flocking:
''Tis clear,' cried they, 'our Mayor's a noddy;
   And as for our Corporation—shocking
To think we buy gowns lined with ermine
For dolts that can't or won't determine
What's best to rid us of our vermin!
You hope, because you're old and obese,
To find in the furry civic robe ease?
Rouse up, sirs! Give your brains a racking
To find the remedy we're lacking,
Or, sure as fate, we'll send you packing!'
At this the Mayor and Corporation
Quaked with a mighty consternation.

IV

An hour they sat in council,
   At length the Mayor broke silence:
'For a guilder I'd my ermine gown sell;
   I wish I were a mile hence!
It's easy to bid one rack one's brain—
I'm sure my poor head aches again,
I've scratched it so, and all in vain.
Oh for a trap, a trap, a trap!'
Just as he said this, what should hap
At the chamber door but a gentle tap?
'Bless us,' cried the Mayor, 'what's that?'
(With the Corporation as he sat,
Looking little though wondrous fat;

Nor brighter was his eye, nor moister
Than a too-long-opened oyster,
Save when at noon his paunch grew mutinous
For a plate of turtle green and glutinous)
'Only a scraping of shoes on the mat?
Anything like the sound of a rat
Makes my heart go pit-a-pat!'

V

'Come in!'—the Mayor cried, looking bigger:
And in did come the strangest figure!
His queer long coat from heel to head
Was half of yellow and half of red,
And he himself was tall and thin,
With sharp blue eyes, each like a pin,
And light loose hair, yet swarthy skin,
No tuft on cheek nor beard on chin,
But lips where smiles went out and in;
There was no guessing his kith and kin:
And nobody could enough admire
The tall man and his quaint attire.
Quoth one: 'It's as my great-grandsire,
Starting up at the Trump of Doom's tone,
Had walked this way from his painted tombstone!'

VI

He advanced to the council table:
And, 'Please your honours,' said he, 'I'm able,
By means of a secret charm, to draw
   All creatures living beneath the sun,
  That creep, or swim, or fly, or run,
After me so as you never saw!
And I chiefly use my charm
On creatures that do people harm,
The mole, and toad, and newt, and viper;
And people call me the Pied Piper.'

(And here they noticed round his neck
   A scarf of red and yellow stripe,
To match with his coat of the self-same cheque;
   And at the scarf's end hung a pipe;
And his fingers, they noticed, were ever straying
As if impatient to be playing
Upon this pipe, as low it dangled
Over his vesture so old-fangled.)
'Yet,' said he, 'poor piper as I am,
In Tartary I freed the Cham,
   Last June, from his huge swarms of gnats;
I eased in Asia the Nizam
   Of a monstrous brood of vampyre-bats:
And as for what your brain bewilders,
   If I can rid your town of rats
Will you give me a thousand guilders?'
'One? fifty thousand!'—was the exclamation
Of the astonished Mayor and Corporation.

VII

Into the street the Piper stept,
   Smiling first a little smile,
As if he knew what magic slept
   In his quiet pipe the while;
Then, like a musical adept,
To blow the pipe his lips he wrinkled,
And green and blue his sharp eyes twinkled,
Like a candle-flame where salt is sprinkled;
And ere three shrill notes the pipe uttered,
You heard as if an army muttered;
And the muttering grew to a grumbling;
And the grumbling grew to a mighty rumbling;
And out of the houses the rats came tumbling.
Great rats, small rats, lean rats, brawny rats,
Brown rats, black rats, grey rats, tawny rats,
Grave old plodders, gay young friskers,
   Fathers, mothers, uncles, cousins,

Cocking tails and pricking whiskers,
    Families by tens and dozens,
Brothers, sisters, husbands, wives—
Followed the Piper for their lives.
From street to street he piped advancing,
And step for step they followed dancing,
Until they came to the river Weser,
    Wherein all plunged and perished!
—Save one who, stout as Julius Cæsar,
Swam across and lived to carry
    (As he, the manuscript he cherished)
To Rat-land home his commentary:
Which was, 'At the first shrill notes of the pipe,
I heard a sound as of scraping tripe,
And putting apples, wondrous ripe,
Into a cider-press's gripe:
And a moving away of pickle-tub-boards,
And a leaving ajar of conserve-cupboards,
And a drawing the corks of train-oil flasks,
And a breaking the hoops of butter-casks;
And it seemed as if a voice
    (Sweeter far than bý harp or bý psaltery
Is breathed) called out, "Oh rats, rejoice!
    The world is grown to one vast drysaltery!
So munch on, crunch on, take your nuncheon,
Breakfast, supper, dinner, luncheon!"
And just as a bulky sugar-puncheon,
All ready staved, like a great sun shone
Glorious scarce an inch before me,
Just as methought it said: "Come, bore me!"
—I found the Weser rolling o'er me.'

VIII

You should have heard the Hamelin people
Ringing the bells till they rocked the steeple.
'Go,' cried the Mayor, 'and get long poles,
Poke out the nests and block up the holes!

THE GOLDEN STAIRCASE

Consult with carpenters and builders,
And leave in our town not even a trace
Of the rats!'—when suddenly, up the face
Of the Piper perked in the market-place,
With a, 'First, if you please, my thousand guilders!'

IX

A thousand guilders! The Mayor looked blue;
So did the Corporation too.
For council dinners made rare havoc
With Claret, Moselle, Vin-de-Grave, Hock;
And half the money would replenish
Their cellar's biggest butt with Rhenish.
To pay this sum to a wandering fellow
With a gipsy coat of red and yellow!
'Beside,' quoth the Mayor, with a knowing wink,
'Our business was done at the river's brink;
We saw with our eyes the vermin sink,
And what's dead can't come to life, I think.
So, friend, we're not the folks to shrink
From the duty of giving you something for drink,
And a matter of money to put in your poke;
But, as for the guilders, what we spoke
Of them, as you very well know, was in joke.
Beside, our losses have made us thrifty.
A thousand guilders! Come, take fifty!'

X

The Piper's face fell, and he cried:
'No trifling! I can't wait, beside!
I've promised to visit by dinner time
Bagdat, and accept the prime
Of the Head Cook's pottage, all he's rich in,
For having left, in the Caliph's kitchen,
Of a nest of scorpions no survivor:
With him I proved no bargain-driver,
With you, don't think I'll bate a stiver!
And folks who put me in a passion
May find me pipe after another fashion.'

XI

'How?' cried the Mayor, 'd'ye think I brook
Being worse treated than a Cook?
Insulted by a lazy ribald
With idle pipe and vesture piebald?
You threaten us, fellow? Do your worst,
Blow your pipe there till you burst!'

XII

Once more he stept into the street,
    And to his lips again
    Laid his long pipe of smooth straight cane;
And ere he blew three notes (such sweet
Soft notes as yet musician's cunning
    Never gave the enraptured air)
There was a rustling, that seemed like a bustling
Of merry crowds justling at pitching and hustling,
Small feet were pattering, wooden shoes clattering,
Little hands clapping, and little tongues chattering,
And, like fowls in a farm-yard when barley is
    scattering,
Out came the children running.
All the little boys and girls,
With rosy cheeks and flaxen curls,
And sparkling eyes and teeth like pearls,
Tripping and skipping, ran merrily after
The wonderful music with shouting and laughter.

XIII

The Mayor was dumb, and the Council stood
As if they were changed into blocks of wood,
Unable to move a step, or cry
To the children merrily skipping by,
—Could only follow with the eye
That joyous crowd at the Piper's back.
But how the Mayor was on the rack,
And the wretched Council's bosoms beat,
As the Piper turned from the High Street

TRIPPING AND SKIPPING, RAN MERRILY AFTER
THE WONDERFUL MUSIC WITH SHOUTING AND LAUGHTER.

To where the Weser rolled its waters
Right in the way of their sons and daughters!
However he turned from South to West,
And to Koppelberg Hill his steps addressed,
And after him the children pressed;
Great was the joy in every breast.
'He never can cross that mighty top!
He's forced to let the piping drop,
And we shall see our children stop!'
When, lo, as they reached the mountain-side,
A wondrous portal opened wide,
As if a cavern was suddenly hollowed;
And the Piper advanced and the children followed,
And when all were in to the very last,
The door in the mountain-side shut fast.
Did I say all? No! One was lame,
   And could not dance the whole of the way;
And in after years, if you would blame
   His sadness, he was used to say,—
'It's dull in our town since my playmates left!
I can't forget that I'm bereft
Of all the pleasant sights they see,
Which the Piper also promised me.
For he led us, he said, to a joyous land,
Joining the town and just at hand,
Where waters gushed and fruit-trees grew,
And flowers put forth a fairer hue,
And everything was strange and new;
The sparrows were brighter than peacocks here,
And their dogs outran our fallow deer,
And honey-bees had lost their stings,
And horses were born with eagles' wings:
And just as I became assured
My lame foot would be speedily cured,
The music stopped and I stood still,
And found myself outside the hill,
Left alone against my will,
To go now limping as before,
And never hear of that country more!'

XIV

Alas, alas for Hamelin!
   There came into many a burgher's pate
   A text which says that heaven's gate
   Opes to the rich at as easy rate
As the needle's eye takes a camel in!
The Mayor sent East, West, North, and South,
To offer the Piper, by word of mouth,
   Wherever it was men's lot to find him,
Silver and gold to his heart's content,
If he'd only return the way he went,
   And bring the children behind him.
But when he saw 'twas a lost endeavour,
And Piper and dancers were gone for ever,
They made a decree that lawyers never
   Should think their records dated duly
If, after the day of the month and year,
These words did not as well appear,
'And so long after what happened here
   On the Twenty-second of Júly,
Thirteen hundred and seventy-six':
And the better in memory to fix
The place of the children's last retreat,
They called it, the Pied Piper's Street—
Where any one playing on pipe or tabor
Was sure for the future to lose his labour.
Nor suffered they hostelry or tavern
   To shock with mirth a street so solemn;
But opposite the place of the cavern
   They wrote the story on a column,
And on the great church-window painted
The same, to make the world acquainted
How their children were stolen away,
And there it stands to this very day.
And I must not omit to say
That in Transylvania there's a tribe
Of alien people who ascribe

THE GOLDEN STAIRCASE

The outlandish ways and dress
On which their neighbours lay such stress,
To their fathers and mothers having risen
Out of some subterraneous prison
Into which they were trepanned
Long time ago in a mighty band
Out of Hamelin town in Brunswick land,
But how or why, they don't understand.

XV

So, Willy, let me and you be wipers
Of scores out with all men—especially pipers!
And, whether they pipe us free fróm rats or fróm mice,
If we've promised them aught, let us keep our promise!

ROBERT BROWNING.

THE PRIEST AND THE MULBERRY TREE

Did you hear of the curate who mounted his mare,
And merrily trotted along to the fair?
Of creature more tractable none ever heard:
In the height of her speed she would stop at a word;
But again with a word, when the curate said 'Hey,'
She put forth her mettle and gallop'd away.

As near to the gates of the city he rode,
While the sun of September all brilliantly glow'd,
The good priest discover'd, with eyes of desire,
A mulberry tree in a hedge of wild brier;
On boughs long and lofty, in many a green shoot,
Hung, large, black, and glossy, the beautiful fruit.

The curate was hungry and thirsty to boot;
He shrank from the thorns, though he longed for the
    fruit;
With a word he arrested his courser's keen speed,
And he stood up erect on the back of his steed;
On the saddle he stood while the creature stood still,
And he gather'd the fruit till he took his good fill.

'Sure never,' he thought, 'was a creature so rare,
So docile, so true, as my excellent mare;
Lo, here now I stand,' and he gazed all around,
'As safe and as steady as if on the ground;
Yet how had it been, if some traveller this way,
Had, dreaming no mischief, but chanced to cry,
    "Hey"?'

He stood with his head in the mulberry tree,
And he spoke out aloud in his fond revery;
At the sound of the word the good mare made a push,
And down went the priest in the wild-brier bush.
He remember'd too late, on his thorny green bed,
Much that well may be thought cannot wisely be said.

      THOMAS LOVE PEACOCK.

TO-DAY

So here hath been dawning
Another blue Day:
Think wilt thou let it
Slip useless away.

Out of Eternity
This new Day is born;
Into Eternity,
At night, will return.

Behold it aforetime
No eye ever did:
So soon it forever
From all eyes is hid.

Here hath been dawning
Another blue Day:
Think wilt thou let it
Slip useless away.

THOMAS CARLYLE.

A BOY'S PRAYER

God who created me
  Nimble and light of limb,
In three elements free,
  To run, to ride, to swim:
  Not when the sense is dim,
But now from the heart of joy,
  I would remember Him:
Take the thanks of a boy.

H. C. BEECHING.

A FAREWELL

My fairest child, I have no song to give you;
  No lark could pipe to skies so dull and grey;
Yet, ere we part, one lesson I can leave you
    For every day.

Be good, sweet maid, and let who will be clever,
  Do noble things, not dream them, all day long;
And so make life, death, and that vast for-ever
    One grand, sweet song.

CHARLES KINGSLEY.

SHEPHERD BOY'S SONG

He that is down, needs fear no fall;
    He that is low, no pride:
He that is humble, ever shall
    Have God to be his guide.

I am content with what I have,
    Little be it or much;
And, Lord, contentment still I crave,
    Because Thou savest such.

Fulness to such a burden is,
    That go on pilgrimage;
Here little, and hereafter bliss,
    Is best from age to age.

                    JOHN BUNYAN.

PIPPA'S SONG

(From *Pippa Passes*)

The year's at the spring
And day's at the morn;
Morning's at seven;
The hill-side's dew-pearled;
The lark's on the wing;
The snail's on the thorn:
God's in His heaven—
All's right with the world!

                    ROBERT BROWNING.

THE TIGER

Tiger, tiger, burning bright
In the forests of the night,
What immortal hand or eye
Could frame thy fearful symmetry?

In what distant deeps or skies
Burnt the fire of thine eyes?
On what wings dare he aspire?
What the hand dare seize the fire?

And what shoulder and what art,
Could twist the sinews of thy heart?
And when thy heart began to beat,
What dread hand, and what dread feet?

What the hammer? what the chain?
In what furnace was thy brain?
What the anvil? what dread grasp
Dares its deadly terrors clasp?

When the stars threw down their spears,
And watered heaven with their tears,
Did He smile His work to see?
Did He who made the lamb make thee?

Tiger, tiger, burning bright
In the forests of the night,
What immortal hand or eye
Dare frame thy fearful symmetry?
WILLIAM BLAKE.

NURSE'S SONG

When the voices of children are heard on the green,
    And laughing is heard on the hill,
My heart is at rest within my breast,
    And everything else is still.

'Then come home, my children, the sun is gone down,
    And the dews of night arise;
Come, come, leave off play, and let us away,
    Till the morning appears in the skies.'

'No, no, let us play, for it is yet day,
   And we cannot go to sleep;
Besides, in the sky the little birds fly,
   And the hills are all cover'd with sheep.'

'Well, well, go and play till the light fades away,
   And then go home to bed.'
The little ones leaped, and shouted, and laughed,
   And all the hills echoèd.

WILLIAM BLAKE.

THE SANDPIPER

Across the narrow beach we flit,
   One little sandpiper and I,
And fast I gather, bit by bit,
   The scattered driftwood bleached and dry.
The wild waves reach their hands for it,
   The wild wind raves, the tide runs high,
As up and down the beach we flit,—
   One little sandpiper and I.

Above our heads the sullen clouds
   Scud black and swift across the sky;
Like silent ghosts in misty shrouds
   Stand out the white lighthouses high.
Almost as far as eye can reach
   I see the close-reefed vessels fly,
As fast we flit along the beach,—
   One little sandpiper and I.

I watch him as he skims along
   Uttering his sweet and mournful cry;
He starts not at my fitful song,
   Or flash of fluttering drapery.
He has no thought of any wrong,
   He scans me with a fearless eye.
Staunch friends are we, well tried and strong,
   The little sandpiper and I.

Comrade, where wilt thou be to-night,
　　When the loosed storm breaks furiously?
My driftwood fire will burn so bright!
　　To what warm shelter canst thou fly?
I do not fear for thee, though wroth
　　The tempest rushes through the sky:
For are we not God's children both,
　　Thou, little sandpiper, and I?

CELIA THAXTER.

MODEREEN RUE

(*i.e.* THE LITTLE RED ROGUE—THE FOX)

Och, Modereen Rue, you little red rover,
By the glint of the moon you stole out of your cover,
And now there is never an egg to be got,
Nor a handsome fat chicken to put in the pot.
　　　　Och, Modereen Rue!

With your nose to the earth and your ear on the listen,
You slunk through the stubble with frost-drops a-glisten,
With my lovely fat drake in your teeth as you went,
That your red roguish children should breakfast content.
　　　　Och, Modereen Rue!

Och, Modereen Rue, hear the horn for a warning,
They are looking for red roguish foxes this morning;
But let them come my way, you little red rogue,
'Tis I will betray you to huntsman and dog.
　　　　Och, Modereen Rue!

The little red rogue, he's the colour of bracken,
O'er mountains, o'er valleys, his pace will not slacken.
Tantara! tantara! he is off now, and, faith!
'Tis a race 'twixt the little red rogue and his death.
　　　　Och, Modereen Rue!

Och, Modereen Rue, I've no cause to be grieving
For little red rogues with their tricks and their
 thieving.
The hounds they give tongue, and the quarry's in sight,
The hens on the roost may sleep easy to-night.
      Och, Modereen Rue!

But my blessing be on him. He made the hounds follow
Through the woods, through the dales, over hill, over
 hollow,
It was Modereen Rue led them fast, led them far,
From the glint of the morning till eve's silver star.
      Och, Modereen Rue!

And he saved his red brush for his own future wearing,
He slipped into a drain, and he left the hounds swearing.
Good luck, my fine fellow, and long may you show
Such a clean pair of heels to the hounds as they go.
      Och, Modereen Rue!
          KATHARINE TYNAN-HINKSON.

THE SHIPS

FOR many a year I've watched the ships a-sailing to
 and fro,
The mighty ships, the little ships, the speedy and the
 slow;
And many a time I've told myself that some day I
 would go
  Around the world that is so full of wonders.

The swift and stately liners, how they run without a
 rest!
The great three-masters, they have touched the East
 and told the West!
The monster burden-bearers—oh, they all have plunged
 and pressed
  Around the world that is so full of wonders!

The cruiser and the battleship that loom as dark as doubt,
The devilish destroyer and the hateful, hideous scout—
These deathly things may also rush, with roar and snarl and shout,
   Around the world that is so full of wonders!

My lord he owns a grand white yacht, most beautiful and fine,
But seldom does she leave the firth lest he should fail to dine.
I'd find a thousand richer feasts than his—if she were mine—
   Around the world that is so full of wonders.

The shabby tramp that like a wedge is hammered through the seas,
The little brown-sailed brigantine that traps the lightest breeze—
Oh, I'd be well content to fare aboard the least of these
   Around the world that is so full of wonders.

The things I've heard, the things I've read, the things I've dreamed might be,
The boyish tales, the old men's yarns—they will not pass from me.
I've heard, I've read, I've dreamed . . . But all the time I've longed to *see*—
   Around the world that is so full of wonders.

So year by year I watch the ships a-sailing to and fro,
The ships that come as strangers and the ships I've learned to know.
. . . Folk smile to hear an old man say that *some* day he will go
   Around the world that is so full of wonders.

                        J. J. BELL.

ON THE QUAY

I've never travelled for more'n a day,
  I never was one to roam,
    But I likes to sit on the busy quay,
    Watchin' the ships that says to me—
'Always somebody goin' away,
  Somebody gettin' home.'

I likes to think that the world's so wide—
  'Tis grand to be livin' there,
    Takin' a part in its goin's on. . . .
    Ah, now ye're laughin' at poor old John,
Talkin' o' works o' the world wi' pride
  As if he was doin' his share!

But laugh if ye will! When ye're old as me
  Ye'll find 'tis a rare good plan
    To look at the world—an' love it too!—
    Tho' never a job are ye fit to do. . . .
Oh! 'tisn't all sorrow an' pain to see
  The work o' another man.

'Tis good when the heart grows big at last,
  Too big for trouble to fill—
    Wi' room for the things that was only stuff
    When workin' an' winnin' seemed more'n
      enough—
Room for the world, the world so vast,
  Wi' its peoples an' all their skill.

That's what I'm thinkin' on all the days
  I'm loafin' an' smokin' here,
    An' the ships do make me think the most
    (Of readin' in books 'tis little I'd boast),—
But the ships, they carries me long, long ways,
  An' draws far places near.

THE GOLDEN STAIRCASE

I sees the things that a sailor brings,
  I hears the stories he tells. . . .
    'Tis surely a wonderful world, indeed!
    'Tis more 'n the peoples can ever need!
An' I praises the Lord—to myself I sings—
  For the world in which I dwells.

An' I loves the ships more every day,
  Tho' I never was one to roam.
    Oh! the ships is comfortin' sights to see,
    An' they means a lot when they says to me—
'Always somebody goin' away,
  Somebody gettin' home.'   J. J. BELL.

THE DIVERTING HISTORY OF JOHN GILPIN

JOHN GILPIN was a citizen
  Of credit and renown,
A train-band captain eke was he,
  Of famous London town.

John Gilpin's spouse said to her dear,
  'Though wedded we have been
These twice ten tedious years, yet we
  No holiday have seen.

'To-morrow is our wedding-day,
  And we will then repair
Unto the Bell at Edmonton,
  All in a chaise and pair.

'My sister, and my sister's child,
  Myself and children three
Will fill the chaise; so you must ride
  On horseback after we.'

He soon replied: 'I do admire
  Of womankind but one,
And you are she, my dearest dear,
  Therefore it shall be done.

'I am a linen-draper bold,
 As all the world doth know,
And my good friend the calender
 Will lend his horse to go.'

Quoth Mrs. Gilpin: 'That's well said;
 And for that wine is dear,
We will be furnished with our own,
 Which is both bright and clear.'

John Gilpin kissed his loving wife;
 O'erjoyed was he to find
That, though on pleasure she was bent,
 She had a frugal mind.

The morning came, the chaise was brought,
 But yet was not allowed
To drive up to the door, lest all
 Should say that she was proud.

So three doors off the chaise was stayed,
 Where they did all get in;
Six precious souls, and all agog
 To dash through thick and thin.

Smack went the whip, round went the wheels,
 Were never folk so glad,
The stones did rattle underneath,
 As if Cheapside were mad.

John Gilpin at his horse's side
 Seized fast the flowing mane,
And up he got, in haste to ride,
 But soon came down again;

For saddle-tree scarce reach'd had he,
 His journey to begin,
When turning round his head, he saw
 Three customers come in.

THE GOLDEN STAIRCASE

So down he came; for loss of time,
   Although it grieved him sore,
Yet loss of pence, full well he knew,
   Would trouble him much more.

'Twas long before the customers
   Were suited to their mind,
When Betty screaming came down stairs—
   'The wine is left behind!'

'Good lack!' quoth he, 'yet bring it me,
   My leathern belt likewise,
In which I bear my trusty sword,
   When I do exercise.'

Now, Mistress Gilpin (careful soul!)
   Had two stone bottles found,
To hold the liquor that she loved,
   And keep it safe and sound.

Each bottle had a curling ear,
   Through which the belt he drew,
And hung a bottle on each side,
   To make his balance true.

Then over all, that he might be
   Equipped from top to toe,
His long red cloak, well brushed and neat,
   He manfully did throw.

Now see him mounted once again
   Upon his nimble steed,
Full slowly pacing o'er the stones
   With caution and good heed.

But finding soon a smoother road
   Beneath his well-shod feet,
The snorting beast began to trot,
   Which galled him in his seat.

So, 'Fair and softly,' John he cried,
   But John he cried in vain;
That trot became a gallop soon,
   In spite of curb and rein.

So stooping down, as needs he must,
   Who cannot sit upright,
He grasped the mane with both his hands,
   And eke with all his might.

His horse, who never in that sort
   Had handled been before,
What thing upon his back had got
   Did wonder more and more.

Away went Gilpin, neck or naught;
   Away went hat and wig;
He little dreamt, when he set out
   Of running such a rig.

The wind did blow, the cloak did fly
   Like streamer long and gay,
Till, loop and button, failing both,
   At last it flew away.

Then might all people well discern
   The bottles he had slung;
A bottle swinging at each side,
   As hath been said or sung.

The dogs did bark, the children screamed,
   Up flew the windows all;
And every soul cried out, 'Well done!'
   As loud as he could bawl.

Away went Gilpin—who but he?
   His fame soon spread around;
He carries weight! He rides a race!
   'Tis for a thousand pound!

THE GOLDEN STAIRCASE

And still, as fast as he drew near,
   'Twas wonderful to view,
How in a trice the turnpike men
   Their gates wide open threw.

And now, as he went bowing down
   His reeking head full low,
The bottles twain behind his back
   Were shatter'd at a blow.

Down ran the wine into the road,
   Most piteous to be seen,
Which made his horse's flanks to smoke,
   As they had basted been.

But still he seemed to carry weight
   With leathern girdle braced,
For all might see the bottle-necks,
   Still dangling at his waist.

Thus all through merry Islington
   Those gambols he did play,
Until he came unto the Wash
   Of Edmonton so gay;

And there he threw the Wash about
   On both sides of the way,
Just like unto a trundling mop,
   Or a wild goose at play.

At Edmonton, his loving wife
   From the balcony espied
Her tender husband, wondering much
   To see how he did ride.

'Stop, stop, John Gilpin! here's the house!'
   They all at once did cry;
'The dinner waits, and we are tired';
   Said Gilpin—'So am I!'

But yet his horse was not a whit
   Inclined to tarry there;
For why?—his owner had a house
   Full ten miles off, at Ware.

So, like an arrow swift he flew,
   Shot by an archer strong;
So did he fly—which brings me to
   The middle of my song.

Away went Gilpin, out of breath,
   And sore against his will,
Till at his friend the calender's,
   His horse at last stood still.

The calender, amazed to see
   His neighbour in such trim,
Laid down his pipe, flew to the gate,
   And thus accosted him:

'What news? what news? your tidings tell!
   Tell me you must and shall—
Say why bareheaded you are come,
   Or why you come at all?'

Now Gilpin had a pleasant wit,
   And loved a timely joke;
And thus unto the calender
   In merry guise he spoke:

'I came because your horse would come;
   And, if I will forbode,
My hat and wig will soon be here,—
   They are upon the road.'

The calender, right glad to find
   His friend in merry pin,
Returned him not a single word,
   But to the house went in;

THE GOLDEN STAIRCASE 241

Whence straight he came with hat and wig,
    A wig that flowed behind;
A hat not much the worse for wear,
    Each comely in its kind.

He held them up, and in his turn
    Thus showed his ready wit:
'My head is twice as big as yours,
    They therefore needs must fit.

'But let me scrape the dirt away
    That hangs upon your face;
And stop and eat, for well you may
    Be in a hungry case.'

Said John: 'It is my wedding-day,
    And all the world would stare,
If wife should dine at Edmonton,
    And I should dine at Ware.'

So turning to his horse, he said:
    'I am in haste to dine;
'Twas for your pleasure you came here,
    You shall go back for mine.'

Ah! luckless speech, and bootless boast,
    For which he paid full dear;
For, while he spake, a braying ass
    Did sing most loud and clear;

Whereat his horse did snort, as he
    Had heard a lion roar,
And galloped off with all his might,
    As he had done before.

Away went Gilpin, and away
    Went Gilpin's hat and wig!
He lost them sooner than the first;
    For why?—they were too big.

Q

THE GOLDEN STAIRCASE

Now Mistress Gilpin, when she saw
   Her husband posting down
Into the country far away,
   She pulled out half-a-crown;

And thus unto the youth she said,
   That drove them to the Bell,
'This shall be yours, when you bring back
   My husband safe and well.'

The youth did ride, and soon did meet
   John coming back amain;
Whom in a trice he tried to stop
   By catching at his rein;

But not performing what he meant,
   And gladly would have done,
The frighted steed he frighted more,
   And made him faster run.

Away went Gilpin, and away
   Went postboy at his heels;
The postboy's horse right glad to miss
   The lumbering of the wheels.

Six gentlemen upon the road,
   Thus seeing Gilpin fly,
With postboy scampering in the rear,
   They raised the hue and cry:—

'Stop thief! stop thief!—a highwayman!'
   Not one of them was mute;
And all and each that pass'd that way
   Did join in the pursuit.

And now the turnpike-gates again
   Flew open in short space;
The toll-men thinking as before
   That Gilpin rode a race.

And so he did, and won it too,
    For he got first to town;
Nor stopped till where he had got up
    He did again get down.

Now let us sing, long live the King!
    And Gilpin, long live he!
And, when he next doth ride abroad,
    May I be there to see!

WILLIAM COWPER.

THE OLD NAVY

The captain stood on the carronade: 'First lieutenant,' says he,
'Send all my merry men aft here, for they must list to me;
I haven't the gift of the gab, my sons—because I'm bred to the sea;
That ship there is a Frenchman, who means to fight with we.
    And odds bobs, hammer and tongs, long as I've been to sea,
      I've fought 'gainst every odds—but I've gained the victory!

'That ship there is a Frenchman, and if we don't take *she*,
'Tis a thousand bullets to one, that she will capture *we*;
I haven't the gift of the gab, my boys; so each man to his gun;
If she's not mine in half an hour, I'll flog each mother's son.
    For odds bobs, hammer and tongs, long as I've been to sea,
      I've fought 'gainst every odds—and I've gained the victory!'

We fought for twenty minutes, when the Frenchman
    had enough;
'I little thought,' said he, 'that your men were of such
    stuff';
Our captain took the Frenchman's sword, a low bow
    made to *he*;
'I haven't the gift of the gab, monsieur, but polite I
    wish to be.
    And odds bobs, hammer and tongs, long as I've
        been to sea,
    I've fought 'gainst every odds—and I've gained
        the victory!'

Our captain sent for all of us: 'My merry men,' said he,
'I haven't the gift of the gab, my lads, but yet I
    thankful be:
You've done your duty handsomely, each man stood to
    his gun;
If you hadn't, you villains, as sure as day, I'd have
    flogged each mother's son.
    For odds bobs, hammer and tongs, as long as
        I'm at sea,
    I'll fight 'gainst every odds—and I'll gain the
        victory!'

CAPTAIN MARRYAT.

O CAPTAIN! MY CAPTAIN!

O CAPTAIN! my Captain! our fearful trip is done,
The ship has weather'd every rack, the prize we sought
    is won;
The port is near, the bells I hear, the people all exulting,
While follow eyes the steady keel, the vessel grim and
    daring;
        But, O heart! heart! heart!
          O the bleeding drops of red,
        Where on the deck my Captain lies,
          Fallen cold and dead.

O Captain! my Captain! rise up and hear the bells;
Rise up—for you the flag is flung—for you the bugle
    trills,
For you bouquets and ribbon'd wreaths—for you the
    shores a-crowding,
For you they call, the swaying mass, their eager faces
    turning;
        Here, Captain! dear father!
        This arm beneath your head!
        It is some dream that on the deck,
          You've fallen cold and dead.

My Captain does not answer, his lips are pale and still,
My father does not feel my arm, he has no pulse nor
    will,
The ship is anchor'd safe and sound, its voyage closed
    and done,
From fearful trip the victor ship comes in with object
    won;
        Exult, O shores, and ring, O bells!
        But I with mournful tread,
    Walk the deck my Captain lies,
        Fallen cold and dead.
                    WALT WHITMAN.

THE BURIAL OF SIR JOHN MOORE

NOT a drum was heard, not a funeral note,
    As his corse to the rampart we hurried;
Not a soldier discharged his farewell shot
    O'er the grave where our hero we buried.

We buried him darkly, at dead of night,
    The sods with our bayonets turning;
By the struggling moonbeam's misty light,
    And the lantern dimly burning.

No useless coffin enclosed his breast,
    Not in sheet nor in shroud we wound him;
But he lay like a warrior taking his rest,
    With his martial cloak around him.

Few and short were the prayers we said,
    And we spoke not a word of sorrow;
But we steadfastly gazed on the face that was dead,
    And we bitterly thought of the morrow.

We thought as we hollowed his narrow bed,
    And smoothed down his lonely pillow,
That the foe and the stranger would tread o'er his head,
    And we far away on the billow!

Lightly they'll talk of the spirit that's gone,
    And o'er his cold ashes upbraid him,—
But little he'll reck, if they let him sleep on
    In the grave where a Briton has laid him.

But half of our weary task was done
    When the clock struck the hour for retiring;
And we heard the distant and random gun
    That the foe was sullenly firing.

Slowly and sadly we laid him down,
    From the field of his fame fresh and gory;
We carved not a line, and we raised not a stone—
    But we left him alone with his glory.

CHARLES WOLFE.

THE EVE OF WATERLOO

(From *Childe Harold*)

There was a sound of revelry by night,
And Belgium's Capital had gathered then
Her Beauty and her Chivalry—and bright
The lamps shone o'er fair women and brave men;

THE GOLDEN STAIRCASE

A thousand hearts beat happily; and when
Music arose with its voluptuous swell,
Soft eyes looked love to eyes which spake again,
And all went merry as a marriage bell;
But hush! hark! a deep sound strikes like a rising knell!

Did ye not hear it?—No—'twas but the wind,
Or the car rattling o'er the stony street;
On with the dance! let joy be unconfined;
No sleep till morn, when Youth and Pleasure meet
To chase the glowing hours with flying feet.—
But hark!—that heavy sound breaks in once more,
As if the clouds its echo would repeat;
And nearer—clearer—deadlier than before!
Arm! Arm! it is—it is—the cannon's opening roar!

Within a windowed niche of that high hall
Sate Brunswick's fated Chieftain; he did hear
That sound the first amidst the festival,
And caught its tone with Death's prophetic ear;
And when they smiled because he deemed it near,
His heart more truly knew that peal too well
Which stretched his father on a bloody bier,
And roused the vengeance blood alone could quell;
He rushed into the field, and, foremost fighting, fell.

Ah! then and there was hurrying to and fro—
And gathering tears, and tremblings of distress,
And cheeks all pale, which but an hour ago
Blushed at the praise of their own loveliness—
And there were sudden partings, such as press
The life from out young hearts, and choking sighs
Which ne'er might be repeated; who could guess
If ever more should meet those mutual eyes,
Since upon night so sweet such awful morn could rise!

And there was mounting in hot haste—the steed,
The mustering squadron, and the clattering car,
Went pouring forward with impetuous speed,
And swiftly forming in the ranks of war—

And the deep thunder peal on peal afar;
And near, the beat of the alarming drum
Roused up the soldier ere the Morning Star;
While thronged the citizens with terror dumb,
Or whispering, with white lips—'The foe! They come!
    They come!'

And wild and high the 'Cameron's Gathering' rose!
The war-note of Lochiel, which Albyn's hills
Have heard, and heard, too, have her Saxon foes:
How in the noon of night that pibroch thrills
Savage and shrill! But with the breath which fills
Their mountain-pipe, so fill the mountaineers
With the fierce native daring which instils
The stirring memory of a thousand years,
And Evan's—Donald's fame rings in each clansman's
    ears!

And Ardennes waves above them her green leaves,
Dewy with Nature's tear-drops, as they pass—
Grieving, if aught inanimate e'er grieves,
Over the unreturning brave,—alas!
Ere evening to be trodden like the grass
Which now beneath them, but above shall grow
In its next verdure, when the fiery mass
Of living Valour, rolling on the foe,
And burning with high Hope, shall moulder cold and
    low.

Last Noon beheld them full of lusty life;—
Last Eve in Beauty's circle proudly gay;
The Midnight brought the signal-sound of strife,
The Morn the marshalling in arms,—the Day
Battle's magnificently-stern array!
The thunder-clouds close o'er it, which when rent
The earth is covered thick with other clay
Which her own clay shall cover, heaped and pent,
Rider and horse,—friend,—foe,—in one red burial blent!
                               LORD BYRON.

THE OLIVE TREE

Said an ancient hermit, bending
   Half in prayer upon his knee,
'Oil I need for midnight watching,
   I desire an olive tree.'

Then he took a tender sapling,
   Planted it before his cave,
Spread his trembling hands above it,
   As his benison he gave.

But he thought, The rain it needeth,
   That the root may drink and swell;
'God! I pray Thee send Thy showers!'
   So a gentle shower fell.

'Lord! I ask for beams of summer
   Cherishing this little child.'
Then the dripping clouds divided,
   And the sun looked down and smiled.

'Send it frost to brace its tissues,
   O my God!' the hermit cried.
Then the plant was bright and hoary,
   But at evensong it died.

Went the hermit to a brother
   Sitting in his rocky cell:
'Thou an olive tree possessest;
   How is this, my brother, tell?

'I have planted one, and prayed,
   Now for sunshine, now for rain;
God hath granted each petition,
   Yet my olive tree hath slain!'

Said the other, 'I intrusted
　　To its God my little tree;
He who made knew what it needed
　　Better than a man like me.

'Laid I on Him no condition,
　　Fixed no ways and means; so I
Wonder not my olive thriveth,
　　Whilst thy olive tree did die.'
S. BARING-GOULD.

ABOU BEN ADHEM

Abou Ben Adhem (may his tribe increase!)
Awoke one night from a deep dream of peace,
And saw, within the moonlight in his room,
Making it rich, and like a lily in bloom,
An angel writing in a book of gold.
Exceeding peace had made Ben Adhem bold,
And to the presence in the room he said:
'What writest thou?'—The vision raised its head,
And with a look made of all sweet accord,
Answered: 'The names of those who love the Lord.'

'And is mine one?' said Abou. 'Nay, not so,'
Replied the angel. Abou spoke more low,
But cheerly still, and said: 'I pray thee, then,
Write me as one that loves his fellow-men.'
The angel wrote, and vanished. The next night
It came again with a great wakening light,
And showed the names whom love of God had
　　bless'd,
And lo! Ben Adhem's name led all the rest!
LEIGH HUNT.

CONTENTMENT

My mind to me a kingdom is;
   Such present joys therein I find,
That it excels all other bliss
   That earth affords or grows by kind:
Though much I want which most would have,
Yet still my mind forbids to crave.

No princely pomp, no wealthy store,
   No force to win the victory,
No wily wit to salve a sore,
   No shape to feed a loving eye;
To none of these I yield as thrall:
For why? My mind doth serve for all.

I see how plenty suffers oft,
   And hasty climbers soon do fall;
I see that those which are aloft
   Mishap doth threaten most of all;
They get with toil, they keep with fear:
Such cares my mind could never bear.

Content I live, this is my stay;
   I seek no more than may suffice;
I press to bear no haughty sway;
   Look—what I lack, my mind supplies:
Lo! thus I triumph like a king,
Content with that my mind doth bring.

Some have too much, yet still do crave;
   I little have, and seek no more.
They are but poor though much they have,
   And I am rich with little store;
They poor, I rich; they beg, I give;
They lack, I leave; they pine, I live.

I laugh not at another's loss,
   I grudge not at another's gain;
No worldly woes my mind can toss:
   My state at one doth still remain:
I fear no foe, I faun no friend:
I loath not life, nor dread my end.

    .   .   .   .   .

SIR E. DYER.

THE HITCHIN MAY-DAY SONG

Remember us poor Mayers all,
   And thus we do begin
To lead our lives in righteousness,
   Or else we die in sin.

We have been rambling all this night,
   And almost all this day,
And now returnèd back again
   We have brought you a branch of May.

A branch of May we have brought you,
   And at your door it stands,
It is but a sprout, but it's well budded out
   By the work of our Lord's hands.

The hedges and trees they are so green,
   As green as any leek,
Our heavenly Father He watered them
   With His heavenly dew so sweet.

The heavenly gates are open wide,
   Our paths are beaten plain,
And if a man be not too far gone,
   He may return again.

The life of man is but a span,
   It flourishes like a flower,
We are here to-day, and gone to-morrow,
   And we are dead in an hour.

The moon shines bright, and the stars give
    a light,
  A little before it is day,
So God bless you all, both great and small,
  And send you a joyful May!

UNKNOWN.

LITTLE BOY BLUE

The little toy dog is covered with dust,
  But sturdy and staunch he stands;
And the little toy soldier is red with rust,
  And his musket moulds in his hands.

Time was when the little toy dog was new,
  And the soldier was passing fair;
And that was the time when our Little Boy Blue
  Kissed them and put them there.

'Now, don't you go till I come,' he said,
  'And don't you make any noise!'
So toddling off to his trundle-bed,
  He dreamt of the pretty toys;

And, as he was dreaming, an angel song
  Awakened our Little Boy Blue—
Oh! the years are many, the years are long,
  But the little toy friends are true!

Ay faithful to Little Boy Blue they stand,
  Each in the same old place—
Awaiting the touch of a little hand,
  The smile of a little face;

And they wonder, as waiting the long years
    through
  In the dust of that little chair,
What has become of our Little Boy Blue,
  Since he kissed them and put them there.

EUGENE FIELD.

THE SANDS OF DEE

'O MARY, go and call the cattle home,
   And call the cattle home,
   And call the cattle home
  Across the sands of Dee';
The western wind was wild and dank with foam,
  And all alone went she.

The western tide crept up along the sand,
   And o'er and o'er the sand,
   And round and round the sand,
  As far as eye could see.
The rolling mist came down and hid the land:
  And never home came she.

'Oh! is it weed, or fish, or floating hair—
   A tress of golden hair,
   A drownèd maiden's hair
  Above the nets at sea?
Was never salmon yet that shone so fair
  Among the stakes on Dee.'

They rowed her in across the rolling foam,
   The cruel crawling foam,
   The cruel hungry foam,
  To her grave beside the sea:
But still the boatmen hear her call the cattle home
  Across the sands of Dee.

                CHARLES KINGSLEY.

THE SKYLARK

  BIRD of the wilderness,
  Blithesome and cumberless,
Sweet be thy matin o'er moorland and lea!
  Emblem of happiness,
  Blest is thy dwelling-place—
Oh to abide in the desert with thee!

Wild is thy lay and loud,
Far in the downy cloud,
Loves gives it energy, love gave it birth.
Where, on thy dewy wing,
Where art thou journeying?
Thy lay is in heaven, thy love is on earth.

O'er fell and fountain sheen,
O'er moor and mountain green,
O'er the red streamer that heralds the day,
Over the cloudlet dim,
Over the rainbow's rim,
Musical cherub, soar, singing, away!

Then, when the gloaming comes,
Low in the heather blooms
Sweet will thy welcome and bed of love be!
Emblem of happiness,
Blest is thy dwelling-place—
Oh to abide in the desert with thee!

JAMES HOGG.

FROM 'TWO GENTLEMEN OF VERONA'

(ACT IV. SCENE 2)

Who is Silvia? What is she,
  That all our swains commend her?
Holy, fair, and wise is she;
  The heaven such grace did lend her,
That she might admirèd be.

Is she kind as she is fair,—
  For beauty lives with kindness?
Love doth to her eyes repair,
  To help him of his blindness;
And, being helped, inhabits there.

Then to Silvia let us sing
   That Silvia is excelling;
She excels each mortal thing
   Upon the dull earth dwelling;
To her let us garlands bring.

FROM 'AS YOU LIKE IT'

(ACT II. SCENE 5)

UNDER the greenwood tree,
Who loves to lie with me,
And turn his merry note
Unto the sweet bird's throat,
Come hither, come hither, come hither:
   Here shall he see no enemy,
But Winter and rough weather.

Who doth ambition shun,
And loves to live i' the sun,
Seeking the food he eats,
And pleased with what he gets,
Come hither, come hither, come hither:
   Here shall he see no enemy,
But Winter and rough weather.

FROM 'A MIDSUMMER-NIGHT'S DREAM'

(ACT II. SCENE 2)

You spotted snakes with double tongue,
   Thorny hedgehogs, be not seen;
Newts and blind-worms, do no wrong,
   Come not near our fairy Queen!

Philomel, with melody
Sing in our sweet lullaby;
Lulla, lulla, lullaby; lulla, lulla, lullaby:

NEWTS, AND BLIND-WORMS, DO NO WRONG; COME NOT NEAR OUR FAIRY QUEEN.

Never harm, nor spell nor charm,
Come our lovely lady nigh;
So, good-night, with lullaby.

Weaving spiders, come not here;
   Hence, you long-legg'd spinners, hence!
Beetles black, approach not near;
   Worm nor snail, do no offence.

Philomel, with melody
Sing in our sweet lullaby;
Lulla, lulla, lullaby; lulla, lulla, lullaby;
Never harm, nor spell nor charm,
Come our lovely lady nigh;
So, good-night, with lullaby.

FROM 'LOVE'S LABOUR'S LOST'

(ACT V. SCENE 2)

WHEN icicles hang by the wall,
   And Dick the shepherd blows his nail,
And Tom bears logs into the hall,
   And milk comes frozen home in pail,
When blood is nipp'd, and ways be foul,
Then nightly sings the staring owl,
        Tu-who;
Tu-whit, tu-who—a merry note,
While greasy Joan doth keel the pot.

When all aloud the wind doth blow,
   And coughing drowns the parson's saw,
And birds sit brooding in the snow,
   And Marian's nose looks red and raw,
When roasted crabs hiss in the bowl,
Then nightly sings the staring owl,
        Tu-who;
Tu-whit, tu-who,—a merry note,
While greasy Joan doth keel the pot.

              WILLIAM SHAKESPEARE.

BE TRUE

Thou must be true thyself
  If thou the truth wouldst teach;
Thy soul must overflow, if thou
  Another's soul wouldst reach!
It needs the overflow of heart
  To give the lips full speech.

Think truly, and thy thoughts
  Shall the world's famine feed;
Speak truly, and each word of thine
  Shall be a fruitful seed;
Live truly, and thy life shall be
  A great and noble creed.

HORATIO BONAR.

THE PERFECT LIFE

(From An Ode)

· · · · · ·

It is not growing like a tree
In bulk, doth make man better be;
Or standing long an oak, three hundred year,
To fall a log at last, dry, bald, and sere:
  A lily of a day
  Is fairer far in May,
Although it fall and die that night;
It was the plant, and flower of light.
In small proportions we just beauties see;
And in short measures, life may perfect be.

· · · · · ·

BEN JONSON.

JOHN GRUMLIE

John Grumlie swore by the licht o' the moon,
  And the green leaves on the tree,
That he could do mair wark in a day,
  Than his wife could do in three.
His wife rose up in the morning
  Wi' cares and troubles enow;
'John Grumlie, bide at hame, John,
  And I'll gae haud the plow.

'First ye maun dress your children fair,
  And put them a' in their gear,
And ye maun turn the malt, John,
  Or else ye'll spoil the beer.
And ye maun reel the tweel, John,
  That I span yesterday;
And ye maun ca' in the hens, John,
  Else they'll a' lay away.'

Oh he did dress his children fair,
  And he put them a' in their gear;
But he forgot to turn the malt,
  And so he spoil'd the beer.
And he sang aloud as he reel'd the tweel
  That his wife span yesterday;
But he forgot to ca' in the hens,
  And the hens a' laid away.

The hawkit crummie loot down nae milk;
  He kirned, nor butter gat;
And a' gaed wrang, and nought gaed right;
  He danced wi' rage, and grat.
Then up he ran to the head o' the knowe,
  Wi' mony a wave and shout—
She heard him as she heard him not,
  And steered the stots about.

John Grumlie's wife cam hame at e'en,
   And laugh'd as she 'd been mad,
When she saw the house in siccan a plight,
   And John sae glum and sad.
Quoth he, 'I gie up my housewife-skep,
   I'll be nae mair guidwife.'
'Indeed,' quo' she, 'I'm weel content,
   Ye may keep it the rest o' your life.'

'The deil be in that!' quo' surly John,
   'I'll do as I've done before.'
Wi' that the guidwife took up a stout rung,
   And John made aff to the door.
'Stop, stop, guidwife, I'll haud my tongue,
   I ken I'm sair to blame,
But henceforth I maun mind the plow,
   And ye maun bide at hame.'

UNKNOWN.

SIR PATRICK SPENS

The king sits in Dunfermline toun,
   Drinking the blude-red wine;
'O whaur will I get a skeely skipper,
   To sail this ship o' mine?'

Then up and spake an eldern knight
   Sat at the king's right knee:
'Sir Patrick Spens is the best sailor
   That ever sail'd the sea.'

The king has written a braid letter,
   And seal'd it wi' his hand,
And sent it to Sir Patrick Spens
   Was walking on the strand.

'To Noroway, to Noroway,
   To Noroway owre the faem;
The king's daughter to Noroway,
   'Tis thou maun tak her hame.'

The first line that Sir Patrick read,
   A loud laugh laughed he;
The neist line that Sir Patrick read,
   The tear blindit his e'e.

'O wha is this has done this deed,
   Has tauld the king o' me,
To send us out at this time o' the year
   To sail upon the sea?

'Be 't wind or weet, be 't hail or sleet,
   Our ship maun sail the faem;
The king's daughter to Noroway
   'Tis we maun tak her hame.'

They hoisted their sails on Monenday morn,
   Wi' a' the haste they may;
And they hae landed in Noroway
   Upon a Wodensday.

They hadna been a week, a week,
   In Noroway but twae,
When that the lords o' Noroway
   Began aloud to say—

'Ye Scotsmen spend a' our king's gowd,
   And a' our queenis fee.'
'Ye lee, ye lee, ye leears loud,
   Sae loud's I hear ye lee!

'For I brought as much o' the white monie
   As gane my men and me,
And a half-fou o' the gude red gowd,
   Out owre the sea wi' me.

'Mak ready, mak ready, my merry men a',
  Our gude ship sails the morn,'
'Now ever alake, my master dear,
  I fear a deidly storm.

'I saw the new moon late yestreen,
  Wi' the auld moon in her arm;
And if we gang to sea, master,
  I fear we'll come to harm!'

They hadna sail'd a league, a league,
  A league but barely three,
When the lift grew dark, and the wind blew loud,
  And gurly grew the sea.

The ankers brak, and the tap-masts lap,
  It was sic a deidly storm;
And the waves cam owre the broken ship,
  Till a' her sides were torn.

'O whaur will I get a gude sailor
  Will tak the helm in hand,
Till I get up to the tall tap-mast
  To see if I can spy land.'

'O here am I, a sailor gude,
  To tak the helm in hand,
Till ye get up to the tall tap-mast—
  But I fear ye'll ne'er spy land.'

He hadna tane a step, a step,
  A step but barely ane,
When a bout flew out o' the gude ship's side,
  And the saut sea it cam in.

'Gae fetch a wab o' the silken claith,
  Anither o' the twine,
And wap them into our gude ship's side,
  And let na the sea come in.'

They fetched a wab o' the silken claith,
 Anither o' the twine,
And they wapp'd them into the gude ship's side,
 But aye the sea cam in.

'Ye 'll pick her weel, an' span her weel,
 And mak her hale an' soun','
But ere he had the words weel spoke
 The bonnie ship was doun.

O laith, laith were our Scots lords' sons
 To weet their coal-black shoon,
But lang ere a' the play was owre,
 They wat their hats abune.

And mony was the feather-bed
 That fluttered on the faem,
And mony was the gude lord's son
 That never mair cam hame.

O lang, lang may the ladies sit,
 Wi' their fans into their hand,
Before they see Sir Patrick Spens
 Come sailing to the strand.

And lang, lang may the maidens sit,
 Wi' the gowd kaims in their hair,
A' waiting for their ain dear loves,
 For them they 'll see nae mair.

Half owre, half owre to Aberdour,
 It 's fifty fathom deep,
And there lies gude Sir Patrick Spens,
 Wi' the Scots lords at his feet.

UNKNOWN.

THE PILGRIM

Who would true valour see,
   Let him come hither;
One here will constant be,
   Come wind, come weather:
There's no discouragement
   Shall make him once relent
His first-avow'd intent
   To be a Pilgrim.

Whoso beset him round
   With dismal stories,
Do but themselves confound—
   His strength the more is.
No lion can him fright;
   He'll with a giant fight;
But he will have a right
   To be a Pilgrim.

Nor enemy, nor fiend,
   Can daunt his spirit;
He knows he at the end
   Shall Life inherit:—
Then, fancies, fly away;
   He'll not fear what men say;
He'll labour night and day,
   To be a Pilgrim.

JOHN BUNYAN.

TO DAFFODILS

Fair daffodils, we weep to see
   You haste away so soon:
As yet the early-rising Sun
   Has not attained his noon;

THE GOLDEN STAIRCASE

Stay, stay,
Until the hasting day
Has run
But to the Even-song;
And, having prayed together, we
Will go with you along.

We have short time to stay, as you,
We have as short a Spring;
As quick a growth to meet Decay,
As you, or any thing.
We die,
As your hours do, and dry
Away,
Like to the Summer's rain;
Or as the pearls of Morning's dew,
Ne'er to be found again.

ROBERT HERRICK.

THE SHEPHERD TO HIS LOVE

Come live with me, and be my love,
And we will all the pleasures prove,
That hills and valleys, dales and fields,
Woods or steepy mountain yields.

And we will sit upon the rocks,
Seeing the shepherds feed their flocks
By shallow rivers, to whose falls
Melodious birds sing madrigals.

And I will make thee beds of roses,
And a thousand fragrant posies;
A cap of flowers, and a kirtle,
Embroider'd all with leaves of myrtle;

A gown made of the finest wool,
Which from our pretty lambs we pull;
Fair-linèd slippers for the cold,
With buckles of the purest gold;

A belt of straw and ivy-buds,
With coral clasps and amber studs:
And if these pleasures may thee move,
Come live with me, and be my love.

Thy silver dishes, for thy meat,
As precious as the gods do eat,
Shall on an ivory table be
Prepared each day for thee and me.

The shepherd-swains shall dance and sing
For thy delight each May morning:
If these delights thy mind may move,
Then live with me, and be my love.
CHRISTOPHER MARLOWE.

SONG

(From The Princess)

THE splendour falls on castle walls
    And snowy summits old in story:
The long light shakes across the lakes,
    And the wild cataract leaps in glory.
Blow, bugle, blow, set the wild echoes flying,
Blow, bugle; answer, echoes, dying, dying, dying.

O hark, O hear! how thin and clear,
    And thinner, clearer, farther going!
O sweet and far from cliff and scar
    The horns of Elfland faintly blowing!
Blow, let us hear the purple glens replying:
Blow, bugle; answer, echoes, dying, dying, dying.

THE GOLDEN STAIRCASE

    O love, they die in yon rich sky,
      They faint on hill or field or river:
    Our echoes roll from soul to soul,
      And grow for ever and for ever.
Blow, bugle, blow, set the wild echoes flying,
And answer, echoes, answer, dying, dying, dying.
LORD TENNYSON.

SHIV AND THE GRASSHOPPER

(From The Jungle Book)

SHIV, who poured the harvest and made the winds to blow,
Sitting at the doorways of a day of long ago,
Gave to each his portion, food and toil and fate,
From the King upon the guddee to the Beggar at the gate.
    All things made he—Shiva the Preserver.
    Mahadeo! Mahadeo! he made all,—
    Thorn for the camel, fodder for the kine,
    And mother's heart for sleepy head, O little son of mine!

Wheat he gave to rich folk, millet to the poor,
Broken scraps for holy men that beg from door to door.
Cattle to the tiger, carrion to the kite,
And rags and bones to wicked wolves without the wall at night.
Naught he found too lofty, none he saw too low—
Parbati beside him watched them come and go,
Thought to cheat her husband, turning Shiv to jest,
Stole the little grasshopper and hid it in her breast!

So she tricked him, Shiva the Preserver.
Mahadeo! Mahadeo! turn and see.
Tall are the camels, heavy are the kine,
But this was Least of Little Things, O little son of
    mine!

When the dole was ended, laughingly she said,
'Master of a million mouths, is not one unfed?'
Laughing, Shiv made answer, 'All have had their
    part,
Even he, the little one, hidden 'neath thy heart.'

From her breast she plucked it, Parbati the thief,
Saw the Least of Little Things gnawed a new-grown
    leaf.
Saw and feared and wondered, making prayer to Shiv,
Who hath surely given meat to all that live.
    All things made he—Shiva the Preserver.
    Mahadeo! Mahadeo! he made all—
    Thorn for the camel, fodder for the kine,
    And mother's heart for sleepy head, O little son of
        mine!

RUDYARD KIPLING.

ST. MOLIOS IN ARRAN

The rhyme of the monk Molios
    For Christ who counted all things loss,
In heath-clad Arran springing free,
    The wild flower of the Northern Sea.

'O Lord, Thy works are manifold,'
    The wondering Psalmist sang of old:
Be mine his music, 'Great and small,
    In wisdom hast Thou made them all.'

Indeed I breathe a blessed air
   Within this island grown so dear;
Each rushing stream, each flower and tree
   Attunes my heart to psalmody.

For iron, lo! He giveth gold.
   Day follows day, new dawns unfold
New glories in the sea and sky;
   I watch the clouds go sailing by,

I watch the changing shadows fall
   On braeside and on mountain wall,
The rainbow's curve, the mist that fills
   The purple hollows of the hills.

And the wild creatures, dear to Him
   Who made them 'good'—white gulls that swim
In quiet pools, the browsing sheep,
   The red deer couched in bracken deep;

I watch them all, and to my eyes
   The happy tears unbidden rise.
Dear Lord, who giveth all things birth,
   How fair, how wonderful Thine earth!

. . . .

My rocky cell is rude and bare,
   Yet when at eve the hour of prayer
Draws round, it somehow grows to me
   Like that dear home of Bethany

Where Christ of old would sit at meat
   With Mary listening at His feet.
His Presence seems to fill the room,
   And banish loneliness and gloom.

A light shines round me as I pray,
   My cell, the world all fade away,
In silent awe I raise my eyes
   And gaze into God's Paradise.

I hear angelic music swell,
   I see the fields of asphodel,
The gates of pearl, and ramparts bright
   With sapphire stone and chrysolite;

And angel faces grave and sweet
   Look into mine; I hear the beat
Of silver wings; I seem to feel
   Christ's hand in blessing as I kneel.

It is as though my spirit trod
   The very tablelands of God,
And saw the Vision that makes blest,
   Like him who leaned on Jesus' breast.

And so the nights and days go by,
   And so my daily round I ply
Of prayer and praise, content to wait
   The Judge's summons at the Gate.

The rhyme of the Monk Molios
   For Christ who counted all things loss.
God shield us from the stormy blast,
   And bring us to His Peace at last!

C. M. STEEDMAN.

LANGLEY LANE

In all the land, range up, range down,
   Is there ever a place so pleasant and sweet,
As Langley Lane, in London town,
   Just out of the bustle of square and street?
Little white cottages, all in a row,
Gardens, where bachelors'-buttons grow,
   Swallows' nests in roof and wall,
And up above the still blue sky,
Where the woolly-white clouds go sailing by,
   I seem to be able to see it all!

THE GOLDEN STAIRCASE

For now in summer, I take my chair,
   And sit outside in the sun, and hear
The distant murmur of street and square,
   And the swallows and sparrows chirping near;
And Fanny, who lives just over the way,
Comes running many a time each day,
   With her little hand's-touch so warm and kind;
And I smile and talk, with the sun on my cheek,
And the little live hand seems to stir and speak,—
   For Fanny is dumb and I am blind.

Fanny is sweet thirteen, and she
   Has fine black ringlets, and dark eyes clear,
And I am older by summers three—
   Why should we hold one another so dear?
Because she cannot utter a word,
Nor hear the music of bee or bird,
   The water-cart's splash, or the milkman's call.
Because I have never seen the sky,
Nor the little singers that hum and fly,—
   Yet know she is gazing upon them all.

For the sun is shining, the swallows fly,
   The bees and the blue-flies murmur low,
And I hear the water-cart go by,
   With its cool splash-splash down the dusty row;
And the little one, close at my side, perceives
Mine eyes upraised to the cottage eaves,
   Where birds are chirping in summer shine,
And I hear, though I cannot look, and she,
Though she cannot hear, can the singers see,—
   And the little soft fingers flutter in mine.

Hath not the dear little hand a tongue,
   When it stirs on my palm for the love of me?
Do I not know she is pretty and young?
   Hath not my soul an eye to see?
'Tis pleasure to make one's bosom stir,
To wonder how things appear to her,

That I only hear as they pass around;
And as long as we sit in the music and light,
 She is happy to keep God's sight,
 And *I* am happy to keep God's sound.

Why, I know her face, though I am blind—
 I made it of music long ago:
Strange large eyes, and dark hair twined
 Round the pensive light of a brow of snow;
And when I sit by my little one,
And hold her hand, and talk in the sun,
 And hear the music that haunts the place,
I know she is raising her eyes to me,
And guessing how gentle my voice must be,
 And *seeing* the music upon my face.

Though, if ever Lord God should grant me a prayer,
 (I know the fancy is only vain),
I should pray: Just once, when the weather is fair,
 To see little Fanny and Langley Lane;
Though Fanny, perhaps, would pray to hear
The voice of the friend that she holds so dear,
 The song of the birds, the hum of the street,—
It is better to be as we have been,—
Each keeping up something, unheard, unseen,
 To make God's heaven more strange and sweet.

Ah! life is pleasant in Langley Lane!
 There is always something sweet to hear;
Chirping of birds, or patter of rain;
 And Fanny, my little one, always near;
And though I am weak, and cannot live long,
And Fanny, my darling, is far from strong,
 And though we can never married be,—
What then?—since we hold one another so dear,
For the sake of the pleasure one cannot hear,
 And the pleasure that only one can see?

ROBERT BUCHANAN.

JOCK O' HAZLEDEAN

'Why weep ye by the tide, ladie?
    Why weep ye by the tide?
I'll wed ye to my youngest son,
    And ye sall be his bride:
And ye sall be his bride, ladie,
    Sae comely to be seen'—
But aye she loot the tears down fa'
    For Jock o' Hazledean.

'Now let this wilfu' grief be done,
    And dry that cheek so pale;
Young Frank is chief of Errington,
    And lord of Langley-dale;
His step is first in peaceful ha',
    His sword in battle keen'—
But aye she loot the tears down fa'
    For Jock o' Hazledean.

'A chain of gold ye sall not lack,
    Nor braid to bind your hair;
Nor mettled hound, nor managed hawk,
    Nor palfrey fresh and fair;
And you, the foremost o' them a',
    Shall ride our forest queen'—
But aye she loot the tears down fa'
    For Jock o' Hazledean.

The kirk was deck'd at morning-tide,
    The tapers glimmer'd fair;
The priest and bridegroom wait the bride,
    And dame and knight are there.
They sought her baith by bower and ha':
    The ladie was not seen!
She's o'er the border and awa'
    Wi' Jock o' Hazledean!

              SIR WALTER SCOTT.

A DAY IN JUNE

(From The Vision of Sir Launfal*)*

For a cap and bells our lives we pay,
Bubbles we buy with a whole soul's tasking:
   'Tis heaven alone that is given away,
'Tis only God may be had for the asking;
No price is set on the lavish summer;
June may be had by the poorest comer.
And what is so rare as a day in June?
   Then, if ever, come perfect days;
Then Heaven tries earth if it be in tune,
   And over it softly her warm ear lays;
Whether we look, or whether we listen,
We hear life murmur, or see it glisten;
Every clod feels a stir of might,
   An instinct within it that reaches and towers,
And, groping blindly above it for light,
   Climbs to a soul in grass and flowers;
The flush of life may well be seen
   Thrilling back over hills and valleys;
The cowslip startles in meadows green,
   The buttercup catches the sun in its chalice,
And there's never a leaf nor a blade too mean
   To be some happy creature's palace;
The little bird sits at his door in the sun,
   Atilt like a blossom among the leaves,
And lets his illumined being o'errun
   With the deluge of summer it receives;
His mate feels the eggs beneath her wings,
And the heart in her dumb breast flutters and sings;
He sings to the wide world, and she to her nest,—
In the nice ear of Nature which song is the best?

                     JAMES RUSSELL LOWELL.

AN ODE

How sleep the brave, who sink to rest
By all their country's wishes bless'd!
When Spring, with dewy fingers cold,
Returns to deck their hallow'd mould,
She there shall dress a sweeter sod
Than Fancy's feet have ever trod.

By fairy hands their knell is rung;
By forms unseen their dirge is sung;
There Honour comes, a pilgrim gray,
To bless the turf that wraps their clay;
And Freedom shall a while repair,
To dwell a weeping hermit there.

WILLIAM COLLINS.

BE USEFUL

(From *The Church*)

BE useful where thou livest, that they may
  Both want and wish thy pleasing presence still.
Kindness, good parts, great places, are the way
  To compass this. Find out men's wants and will,
    And meet them there. All worldly joys go less
    To the one joy of doing kindnesses.

GEORGE HERBERT.

LOVE OF FATHERLAND

(From *The Lay of the Last Minstrel*)

BREATHES there the man, with soul so dead,
Who never to himself hath said,
  This is my own, my native land!

Whose heart hath ne'er within him burn'd,
As home his footsteps he hath turn'd,
   From wandering on a foreign strand!
If such there breathe, go, mark him well;
For him no Minstrel raptures swell;
High though his titles, proud his name,
Boundless his wealth as wish can claim;
Despite those titles, power, and pelf,
The wretch, concentred all in self,
Living, shall forfeit fair renown,
And, doubly dying, shall go down
To the vile dust, from whence he sprung,
Unwept, unhonour'd, and unsung.

O Caledonia! stern and wild,
Meet nurse for a poetic child!
Land of brown heath and shaggy wood,
Land of the mountain and the flood,
Land of my sires! what mortal hand
Can e'er untie the filial band,
That knits me to thy rugged strand!
                SIR WALTER SCOTT.

ENGLAND, MY ENGLAND

I

WHAT have I done for you,
   England, my England?
What is there I would not do,
   England, my own?
With your glorious eyes austere,
As the Lord were walking near,
Whispering terrible things and dear
     As the Song on your bugles blown,
  England—
  Round the world on your bugles blown!

II

Where shall the watchful Sun,
    England, my England,
Match the master-work you 've done,
    England, my own?
When shall he rejoice agen
Such a breed of mighty men
As come forward, one to ten,
    To the Song on your bugles blown,
    England—
    Down the years on your bugles blown?

III

Ever the faith endures,
    England, my England:—
'Take and break us: we are yours,
    England, my own!
Life is good, and joy runs high
Between English earth and sky:
Death is death; but we shall die
    To the Song on your bugles blown,
    England—
    To the stars on your bugles blown!'

IV

They call you proud and hard,
    England, my England:
You with worlds to watch and ward,
    England, my own!
You whose mailed hand keeps the keys
Of such teeming destinies,
You could know nor dread nor ease
    Were the Song on your bugles blown,
    England,
    Round the Pit on your bugles blown!

THE GOLDEN STAIRCASE

v

Mother of Ships whose might,
    England, my England,
Is the fierce old Sea's delight,
    England, my own,
Chosen daughter of the Lord,
Spouse-in-Chief of the ancient sword,
There's the menace of the Word
    In the Song on your bugles blown,
    England—
    Out of heaven on your bugles blown!

W. E. HENLEY.

THE MOON-CHILD

A LITTLE lonely child am I
    That have not any soul:
God made me but a homeless wave,
    Without a goal.

A seal my father was, a seal
    That once was man:
My mother loved him tho' he was
    'Neath mortal ban.

He took a wave and drownèd her,
    She took a wave and lifted him:
And I was born where shadows are
    I' the sea-depths dim.

All through the sunny blue-sweet hours
    I swim and glide in waters green:
Never by day the mournful shores
    By me are seen.

THE GOLDEN STAIRCASE

But when the gloom is on the wave,
    A shell unto the shore I bring:
And then upon the rocks I sit
    And plaintive sing.

O what is this wild song I sing,
    With meanings strange and dim?
No soul am I, a wave am I,
    And sing the Moon-Child's hymn.

FIONA MACLEOD.

THE FORSAKEN MERMAN

Come, dear children, let us away;
Down and away below!
Now my brothers call from the bay,
Now the great winds shoreward blow,
Now the salt tides seaward flow,
Now the wild white horses play,
Champ and chafe and toss in the spray.
Children dear, let us away!
This way, this way!

Call her once before you go—
Call once yet!
In a voice that she will know:
'Margaret! Margaret!'
Children's voices should be dear
(Call once more) to a mother's ear;
Children's voices, wild with pain—
Surely she will come again!
Call her once, and come away;
This way, this way!
'Mother dear, we cannot stay!
The wild white horses foam and fret.'
Margaret! Margaret!

Come, dear children, come away down;
Call no more!
One last look at the white-wall'd town,
And the little grey church on the windy shore;
Then come down!
She will not come though you call all day;
Come away, come away!

Children dear, was it yesterday
We heard the sweet bells over the bay?
In the caverns where we lay,
Through the surf and through the swell,
The far-off sound of a silver bell?
Sand-strewn caverns, cool and deep,
Where the winds are all asleep;
Where the spent lights quiver and gleam,
Where the salt weed sways in the stream,
Where the sea-beasts, ranged all round,
Feed in the ooze of their pasture-ground;
Where the sea-snakes coil and twine,
Dry their mail and bask in the brine;
Where great whales come sailing by,
Sail and sail, with unshut eye,
Round the world for ever and aye?
When did music come this way?
Children dear, was it yesterday?

Children dear, was it yesterday
(Call yet once) that she went away?
Once she sate with you and me,
On a red gold throne in the heart of the sea,
And the youngest sate on her knee.
She combed its bright hair, and she tended it well,
When down swung the sound of a far-off bell.
She sigh'd, she look'd up through the clear green
    sea;
She said: 'I must go, for my kinsfolk pray
In the little grey church on the shore to-day.

"Come, dear children, let us away; Do can and away below!"

THE GOLDEN STAIRCASE

'Twill be Easter-time in the world—ah me!
And I lose my poor soul, Merman! here with thee.'
I said: 'Go up, dear heart, through the waves;
Say thy prayer, and come back to the kind sea-caves!'
She smiled, she went up through the surf in the bay.
Children dear, was it yesterday?

Children dear, were we long alone?
The sea grows stormy, the little ones moan;
'Long prayers,' I said, 'in the world they say;
Come!' I said; and we rose through the surf in the bay.
We went up the beach, by the sandy down
Where the sea-stocks bloom, to the white-wall'd town;
Through the narrow paved streets, where all was still,
To the little grey church on the windy hill.
From the church came a murmur of folk at their prayers,
But we stood without in the cold blowing airs.
We climb'd on the graves, on the stones worn with rains,
And we gazed up the aisle through the small leaded panes.
She sate by the pillar; we saw her clear:
'Margaret, hist! come quick, we are here!
Dear heart,' I said, 'we are long alone;
The sea grows stormy, the little ones moan.'
But, ah, she gave me never a look,
For her eyes were seal'd to the holy book!
Loud prays the priest; shut stands the door.
Come away, children, call no more!
Come away, come down, call no more!

Down, down, down!
Down to the depths of the sea!
She sits at her wheel in the humming town,
Singing most joyfully.

Hark what she sings: 'O joy, O joy,
For the humming street, and the child with its toy!
For the priest, and the bell, and the holy well;
For the wheel where I spun,
And the blessed light of the sun!'
And so she sings her fill,
Singing most joyfully,
Till the spindle drops from her hand,
And the whizzing wheel stands still.
She steals to the window, and looks at the sand,
And over the sand at the sea;
And her eyes are set in a stare;
And anon there breaks a sigh,
And anon there drops a tear,
From a sorrow-clouded eye,
And a heart sorrow-laden,
A long, long sigh;
For the cold strange eyes of a little Mermaiden
And the gleam of her golden hair.

Come away, away children;
Come, children, come down!
The hoarse wind blows coldly;
Lights shine in the town.
She will start from her slumber
When gusts shake the door;
She will hear the winds howling,
Will hear the waves roar.
We shall see, while above us
The waves roar and whirl,
A ceiling of amber,
A pavement of pearl.
Singing: 'Here came a mortal,
But faithless was she!
And alone dwell for ever
The kings of the sea.'

But, children, at midnight,
When soft the winds blow,
When clear falls the moonlight,
When spring-tides are low;
When sweet airs come seaward
From heaths starr'd with broom,
And high rocks throw mildly
On the blanch'd sands a gloom;
Up the still, glistening beaches,
Up the creeks we will hie,
Over banks of bright seaweed
The ebb-tide leaves dry.
We will gaze, from the sand-hills,
At the white, sleeping town;
At the church on the hillside—
And then come back down;
Singing: 'There dwells a loved one,
But cruel is she!
She left lonely for ever
The kings of the sea.'

MATTHEW ARNOLD.

THE GAY GOSHAWK

'O WELL is me, my gay goshawk,
  That you can speak and flee;
For you can carry a love-letter
  To my true love frae me.'

'O how can I carry a letter to her,
  Or how should I her know?
I bear a tongue ne'er wi' her spak',
  And eyes that ne'er her saw.'

'The white o' my love's skin is white
  As down o' dove or maw;
The red o' my love's cheek is red
  As blood that's spilt on snaw.

'When ye come to the castle,
   Light on the tree of ash,
And sit you there and sing our loves
   As she comes frae the mass.

'Four and twenty fair ladies
   Will to the mass repair;
And weel may ye my lady ken,
   The fairest lady there.'

When the goshawk flew to that castle,
   He lighted on the ash;
And there he sat and sang their loves
   As she cam' frae the mass.

'Stay where ye be, my maidens a',
   And sip red wine anon,
Till I go to my west window
   And hear a birdie's moan.'

She's gane unto her west window,
   The bolt she fainly drew;
And unto that lady's white, white neck
   The bird a letter threw.

'Ye're bidden to send your love a send,
   For he has sent you twa;
And tell him where he may see you soon,
   Or he cannot live ava.'

'I send him the ring from my finger,
   The garland off my hair,
I send him the heart that's in my breast;
   What would my love have mair?
And at the fourth kirk in fair Scotland,
   Ye'll bid him wait for me there!'

She hied her to her father dear
   As fast as gang could she;

'I'm sick at the heart, my father dear;
   An asking grant you me!'
'Ask me na for that Scottish lord,
   For him ye'll never see!'

'An asking, an asking, dear father!' she says,
   'An asking grant you me;
That if I die in fair England,
   In Scotland ye'll bury me.

'At the first kirk o' fair Scotland,
   You cause the bells be rung;
At the second kirk o' fair Scotland,
   You cause the mass be sung;

'At the third kirk o' fair Scotland,
   You deal gold for my sake;
At the fourth kirk o' fair Scotland,
   O there you'll bury me at!

'This is all my asking, father,
   I pray you grant it me!'
'Your asking is but small,' he said;
   'Weel granted it shall be.
But why do ye talk o' suchlike things?
   For ye arena going to dee.'

The lady's gane to her chamber,
   And a moanfu' woman was she,
As gin she had ta'en a sudden brash,
   And were about to dee.

The lady's gane to her chamber,
   As fast as she could fare;
And she has drunk a sleepy draught,
   She mix'd it wi' mickle care.

She's fallen into a heavy trance,
   And pale and cold was she;
She seemed to be as surely dead
   As ony corpse could be.

Out and spak' an auld witch-wife,
    At the fireside sat she:
'Gin she has killed herself for love,
    I wot it weel may be:

'But drap the het lead on her cheek,
    And drap it on her chin,
And drap it on her bosom white,
    And she'll maybe speak again.
'Tis much that a young lady will do
    To her true love to win.'

They drapped the het lead on her cheek,
    They drapped it on her chin,
They drapped it on her bosom white,
    But she spake none again.

Her brothers they went to a room,
    To make to her a bier;
The boards were a' o' the cedar wood,
    The edges o' silver clear.

Her sisters they went to a room,
    To make to her a sark;
The cloth was a' o' the satin fine,
    And the stitching silken-wark.

'Now well is me, my gay goshawk,
    That ye can speak and flee!
Come show me any love-tokens
    That you have brought to me.'

'She sends you the ring frae her white finger,
    The garland frae her hair;
She sends you the heart within her breast;
    And what would you have mair?
And at the fourth kirk o' fair Scotland,
    She bids you wait for her there.'

THE GOLDEN STAIRCASE 287

'Come hither, all my merry young men!
    And drink the good red wine;
For we must on towards fair England
    To free my love frae pine.'

The funeral came into fair Scotland,
    And they gart the bells be rung;
And when it came to the second kirk,
    They gart the mass be sung.

And when it came to the third kirk,
    They dealt gold for her sake;
And when it came to the fourth kirk,
    Her love was waiting thereat.

At the fourth kirk in fair Scotland
    Stood spearmen in a row;
And up and started her ain true love,
    The chieftain over them a'.

'Set down, set down the bier,' he says,
    'Till I look upon the dead:
The last time that I saw her face,
    Its colour was warm and red.'

He stripped the sheet from aff her face
    A little below the chin:
The lady then she open'd her eyes,
    And lookèd full on him.

'O give me a shive o' your bread, love,
    O give me a cup o' your wine!
Long have I fasted for your sake,
    And now I fain would dine.

'Gae hame, gae hame, my seven brothers,
    Gae hame and blaw the horn!
And ye may say that ye sought my skaith,
    And that I hae gi'en you the scorn.

'I cam' na here to bonny Scotland
  To lie down in the clay;
But I cam' here to bonny Scotland
  To wear the silks sae gay!

'I cam' na here to bonny Scotland
  Amang the dead to rest;
But I cam' here to bonny Scotland
  To the man that I lo'e best!'

UNKNOWN.

HYNDE ETIN

MAY MARGARET stood in her bower-door,
  Sewing at her silken seam;
She heard a note in Elmond wood,
  And wished she there had been.

She loot the seam fa' frae her side,
  The needle to her tae,
And she's awa' to Elmond wood
  As fast as she could gae.

She hadna pu'd a nut, a nut,
  A nut but barely ane,
Till up started the Hynde Etin,
  Says, 'Lady, lat alane!

'Oh why pu' ye the nut, the nut,
  Or why brak ye the tree?
For I am forester o' this wood—
  Ye sould speir leave o' me.'

But aye she pu'd the ither berry,
  Nae thinking o' the skaith,
And said, 'To wrang ye, Hynde Etin,
  I wad be unco laith.'

But he has ta'en her by the yellow locks,
    And tied her till a tree;
And said, 'For slichting my commands,
    An ill death ye shall dree.'

He pu'd a tree out o' the wood,
    The biggest that was there;
And he houkit a cave monie fathoms deep,
    And put May Margaret there.

'Now rest ye there, ye saucy May!
    My woods are free for thee;
And gif I tak' ye to mysel',
    The better ye'll like me!'

Nae rest, nae rest May Margaret took,
    Sleep gat she never nane;
Her back lay on the cauld, cauld floor,
    Her head upon a stane.

'Oh tak' me out,' May Margaret cried;
    'Oh tak' me hame to thee;
And I shall be your bounden wife
    Until the day I dee.'

He took her out o' the dungeon deep,
    And awa' wi' him she's gane;
But sad was the day an Earl's dauchter
    Gaed hame wi' Hynde Etin.

Oh they hae lived in Elmond wood
    For nine lang years and one;
Till six prettie sons to him she bore,
    And the seventh she's brocht home.

These seven bairns, sae fair and fine,
    That she did to him bring,
They never were in good church door,
    Nor ever got good kirking.

And aye at nicht, wi' harp in hand,
    She harpèd them asleep;
And she sat down at their bedside,
    And bitterlie did weep.

Said, 'Ten lang years now have I lived
    Within this cave o' stane;
And never was at gude kirk-door,
    Nor heard the kirk-bell ring.'

It fell out ance upon a day,
    Hynde Etin went frae hame;
And he's ta'en wi' him his eldest son,
    To gang alang wi' him.

'A question I wad ask, father,
    An' ye wadna angry be!'
'Say on, say on, my bonnie boy,
    Ye'se nae be quarrell'd by me.'

'I see my mither's cheeks aye weet,
    Alas! they are seldom dry';
'Nae wonder, nae wonder, my bonnie boy,
    Though she should brast and die.

'Your mother was an earl's dauchter,
    Sprung frae a high degree,
And she might hae wed the first in the land,
    Had she nae been stown by me.

'But we'll shoot the laverock in the lift,
    The buntin' on the tree,
And ye'll carry them hame to your mither,
    See if she'll merrier be.'

It fell upon another day,
    Hynde Etin he thocht lang;
And he is to the hunting gane,
    As fast as he could gang.

THE GOLDEN STAIRCASE

'Oh, I will tell to you, mither,
   An' ye wadna angry be'—
'Speak on, speak on, my bonnie boy,
   Ask onything at me!'

'As we cam' frae the hind hunting,
   I heard the kirk bells ring.'
'My blessings on you, my bonnie boy!
   I wish I'd been there alane.

'My blessing on your heart, my boy,
   Oh were I there alane!
I hae na been in the haly kirk,
   Sin' twelve lang years are gane!'

He's ta'en his mither by the hand,
   His six brithers also;
And they are on through Elmond wood
   As fast as they could go.

They wist na weel whaur they were gaen,
   Wi' the strattlins o' their feet;
They wist na weel whaur they were gaen,
   Till at her father's yett.

'I hae nae money in my pocket,
   But royal rings hae three:
I'll gie them you, my eldest son,
   And ye'll walk there for me.

'Ye'll gie the first to the proud porter,
   And he will let you in;
Ye'll gie the neist to the butler boy,
   And he will show you ben;

'Ye'll gie the third to the minstrel
   That's harping in the ha':
He'll play success to the bonnie boy,
   That comes frae greenwood shaw.'

He gied the first to the proud porter,
   And he opened and loot him in,
He gied the neist to the butler boy,
   And he has showed him ben;

He gied the third to the minstrel,
   That was harping in the ha',
And he played success to the bonnie boy,
   That cam' frae greenwood shaw.

Now when he came before the Earl,
   He fell low on his knee;
The Earl he turned him round about,
   And the saut tear blint his e'e.

'Win up, win up, my bonnie boy,
   Gang frae my companie;
Ye look sae like my dear dauchter,
   My heart will burst in three.'

'If I look like your dear dauchter,
   A wonder it is nane;
If I look like your dear dauchter,
   For I am her eldest son.'

'Oh tell me now, my little wee boy,
   Where may my Margaret be?'
'She's just now standing at your yetts,
   And my six brithers her wi'.'

'Oh where are a' my porter boys,
   That I pay meat and fee,
To open my yetts baith wide and braid,
   Let her come in to me?'

When she cam' in before the Earl,
   She fell low on her knee;
'Win up, win up, my dauchter dear,
   This day ye'll dine wi' me!'

'Nae, but I canna eat, father,
　　Nor ae drop can I drink,
Till I see my mother and sister dear,
　　For lang for them I think.

'Ae bit I canna eat, father,
　　Nor ae drop can I drink,
Until I see my dear husband,
　　For lang on him I think.'

'Oh where are a' my rangers bauld,
　　That I pay meat and fee,
To search the forest far and wide,
　　And bring Etin to me?'

They searched the country wide and broad,
　　The forests far and near;
Till they found him into Elmond,
　　Tearing his yellow hair.

'Win up, win up now, Hynde Etin,
　　Win up and boun with me,
We're messengers come frae our lord
　　The Earl wants you to see.'

'Oh lat him tak frae me the head,
　　Or hang me on a tree,
For since I've lost my dear ladie,
　　Life's nae pleasure to me.'

'Your head will nae be touch'd, Etin,
　　Nor hanged upon a tree:
Your ladie's in her father's ha',
　　And a' he wants is thee.'

When he cam' in before the Earl,
　　He fell low on his knee:
'Arise, arise now, Hynde Etin,
　　This day ye'se dine wi' me.'

As they were at the dinner set,
  The young boy thus spak' he,
'I wish we were at haly kirk,
  To get our Christendie!'

'Your asking's nae sae great, my boy,
  But granted it shall be;
This day to gude kirk ye shall gang,
  Your mither shall gang you wi'.'

When into the gude kirk they cam',
  She at the door did stan',
She was sae sair sunk down wi' shame,
  She wadna come far'er ben.

Then out and spak' the parish priest,
  And a sweet smile gae he—
'Come ben, come ben, my lilie flower,
  Present your babes to me.'

And he has ta'en and sained them a',
  And gi'en them Christendie;
And they staid in her father's ha',
  And lived wi' mirth and glee.

UNKNOWN.

CRADLE SONGS

CRADLE SONG

Hush-a-bye, baby, on the tree top,
When the wind blows the cradle will rock;
When the bough breaks the cradle will fall,
Down will come baby and cradle and all.

UNKNOWN.

GOOD-NIGHT

Little baby, lay your head
On your pretty cradle-bed;
Shut your eye-peeps, now the day
And the light are gone away;
All the clothes are tucked in tight;
Little baby dear, good-night.

Yes, my darling, well I know
How the bitter wind doth blow;
And the winter's snow and rain
Patter on the window-pane:
But they cannot come in here,
To my little baby dear;

For the window shutteth fast,
Till the stormy night is past;
And the curtains warm are spread
Round about her cradle-bed:
So till morning shineth bright,
Little baby dear, good-night.

JANE TAYLOR.

BABY

(From At the Back of the North Wind)

Where did you come from, baby dear?
'Out of the everywhere into here.'

Where did you get those eyes so blue?
'Out of the sky as I came through.'

What makes the light in them sparkle and spin?
'Some of the starry spikes left in.'

Where did you get that little tear?
'I found it waiting when I got here.'

What makes your forehead so smooth and high?
'A soft hand stroked it as I went by.'

What makes your cheek like a warm white rose?
'I saw something better than any one knows.'

Whence that three-cornered smile of bliss?
'Three angels gave me at once a kiss.'

Where did you get this pearly ear?
'God spoke, and it came out to hear.'

Where did you get those arms and hands?
'Love made itself into hooks and bands.'

Feet, whence did you come, you darling things?
'From the same box as the cherubs' wings.'

How did they all just come to be you?
'God thought about me, and so I grew.'

But how did you come to us, you dear?
'God thought about you, and so I am here.'

GEORGE MACDONALD.

WHERE DID YOU COME FROM BABY DEAR

LITTLE BIRDIE

(From *Sea Dreams*)

What does little birdie say
In her nest at peep of day?
Let me fly, says little birdie,
   Mother, let me fly away.
Birdie, rest a little longer,
Till the little wings are stronger.
So she rests a little longer,
   Then she flies away.

What does little baby say,
In her bed at peep of day?
Baby says, like little birdie,
   Let me rise and fly away.
Baby, sleep a little longer,
Till the little limbs are stronger.
If she sleeps a little longer,
   Baby too shall fly away.

LORD TENNYSON.

JOHNEEN

Sure, he's five months old, an' he's two foot long,
      Baby Johneen;
Watch yerself now, for he's terrible sthrong,
      Baby Johneen.
An' his fists 'ill be up if ye make any slips,
He has finger-ends like the daisy-tips,
But he'll have ye attend to the words of his lips,
      Will Johneen.

There's nobody can rightly tell the colour of his eyes,
    This Johneen;
For they're partly o' the earth an' still they're partly o' the skies,
    Like Johneen.
So far as he's thravelled he's been laughin' all the way,
For the little soul is grave an' wise, the little heart is gay;
An' he likes the merry daffodils, he thinks they'd do to play
    With Johneen.

He'll sail a boat yet, if he only has his luck,
    Young Johneen,
For he takes to the wather like any little duck,
    Boy Johneen.
Sure, them are the hands now to pull on a rope,
An' nate feet for walkin' the deck on a slope,
But the ship she must wait a wee while yet, I hope,
    For Johneen.

For we couldn't do wantin' him, not just yet,
    Och, Johneen!
'Tis you that are the daisy, an' you that are the pet,
    Wee Johneen.
Here's to your health, an' we'll dhrink it to-night.
Slainte gal, avic machree! live and do right,
Slainte gal avourneen! may your days be bright,
    Johneen!

                                MOIRA O'NEILL.

BARTHOLOMEW

    Bartholomew
    Is very sweet,
    From sandy hair
    To rosy feet.

Bartholomew
  Is six months old,
And dearer far
  Than pearls or gold.

Bartholomew
  Has deep blue eyes,
Round pieces dropped
  From out the skies.

Bartholomew
  Is hugged and kissed!
He loves a flower
  In either fist.

Bartholomew's
  My saucy son:
No mother has
  A sweeter one!

NORMAN GALE.

A LULLABY

Baby, baby, hush-a-bye,
  Must you be awake now?
Sweet my lamb, come, close your eye,
  Sleep for mother's sake now.

All the babies in the world
  Lie asleep but you now:
Nigger-babies, brown and curled,
  In the sand dream too now.

Baby mice are safe from harm
  In their downy holes now:
Baby squirrels lie all warm
  In the hollow boles now.

Baby buds are fast asleep
   Rocking on the trees now:
Baby fishes, far and deep,
   Slumber in the seas now.

All the baby stars above
   Dream in cloudy bed now:
Mother moon, for all her love,
   Sleeping hides her head now.

Baby, baby, hush-a-bye,
   Cradled on my breast now,
Sweet my lamb, come, close your eye,
   Let your mother rest now.
LAURENCE ALMA TADEMA.

CHRISTMAS EVE

Oh hush thee, little Dear-my-soul,
   The evening shades are falling,—
Hush thee, my dear, dost thou not hear
   The voice of the Master calling?

Deep lies the snow upon the earth,
   But all the sky is ringing
With joyous song, and all night long
   The stars shall dance with singing.

Oh hush thee, little Dear-my-soul,
   And close thine eyes in dreaming,
And angels fair shall lead thee where
   The singing stars are beaming.

A Shepherd calls His little lambs,
   And He longeth to caress them;
He bids them rest upon His breast,
   That His tender love may bless them.

So hush thee, little Dear-my-soul,
    Whilst evening shades are falling,
And above the song of the heavenly throng
    Thou shalt hear the Master calling.
EUGENE FIELD.

AN IRISH LULLABY

I'VE found my bonny babe a nest
    On Slumber Tree,
I'll rock you there to rosy rest,
    Asthore Machree!
Oh, lulla lo! sing all the leaves
    On Slumber Tree,
Till everything that hurts or grieves
    Afar must flee.

I'd put my pretty child to float
    Away from me,
Within the new moon's silver boat
    On Slumber Sea.
And when your starry sail is o'er
    From Slumber Sea,
My precious one, you'll step to shore
    On Mother's knee.
ALFRED PERCEVAL GRAVES.

LULLABY OF AN INFANT CHIEF

O, HUSH thee, my babie, thy sire was a knight,
Thy mother a lady, both lovely and bright;
The woods and the glens, from the towers which we see,
They all are belonging, dear babie, to thee.

O, fear not the bugle, though loudly it blows,
It calls but the warders that guard thy repose;
Their bows would be bended, their blades would be red,
Ere the step of a foeman draws near to thy bed.

O, hush thee, my babie, the time soon will come,
When thy sleep shall be broken by trumpet and drum;
Then hush thee, my darling, take rest while you may,
For strife comes with manhood, and waking with day.

SIR WALTER SCOTT.

THE ROCK-A-BY LADY

The Rock-a-By Lady from Hushaby Street
   Comes stealing; comes creeping;
The poppies they hang from her head to her feet,
And each hath a dream that is tiny and fleet—
She bringeth her poppies to you, my sweet,
   When she findeth you sleeping!

There is one little dream of a beautiful drum—
   'Rub-a-dub!' it goeth;
There is one little dream of a big sugar-plum,
And lo! thick and fast the other dreams come
Of pop-guns that bang, and tin tops that hum,
   And a trumpet that bloweth!

And dollies peep out of those wee little dreams
   With laughter and singing;
And boats go a-floating on silvery streams,
And the stars peek-a-boo with their own misty gleams,
And up, up, and up, where the Mother Moon beams,
   The fairies go winging!

Would you dream all these dreams that are tiny and
   fleet?
   They'll come to you sleeping;

So shut the two eyes that are weary, my sweet,
For the Rock-a-By Lady from Hushaby Street,
With poppies that hang from her head to her feet,
  Comes stealing; comes creeping.

EUGENE FIELD.

SONG

(From The Princess)

SWEET and low, sweet and low,
Wind of the western sea,
Low, low, breathe and blow,
Wind of the western sea!
Over the rolling waters go,
Come from the dying moon, and blow,
Blow him again to me;
While my little one, while my pretty one,
    sleeps.

Sleep and rest, sleep and rest,
Father will come to thee soon;
Rest, rest, on mother's breast,
Father will come to thee soon;
Father will come to his babe in the nest,
Silver sails all out of the west
Under the silver moon:
Sleep, my little one, sleep, my pretty one,
    sleep.

LORD TENNYSON.

INFANT JOY

'I HAVE no name;
I am but two days old.'
What shall I call thee?
'I happy am,
Joy is my name.'
Sweet joy befall thee!

Pretty joy!
Sweet joy, but two days old.
Sweet joy I call thee;
Thou dost smile,
I sing the while;
Sweet joy befall thee!

WILLIAM BLAKE.

THE COTTAGER TO HER INFANT

The days are cold, the nights are long,
The north-wind sings a doleful song;
Then hush again upon my breast;
All merry things are now at rest
   Save thee, my pretty Love!

The kitten sleeps upon the hearth,
The crickets long have ceased their mirth;
There's nothing stirring in the house
Save one wee, hungry nibbling mouse,
   Then why so busy thou?

Nay! start not at that sparkling light,
'Tis but the moon that shines so bright
On the window-pane bedropped with rain;
There, little darling! sleep again,
   And wake when it is day.

DOROTHY WORDSWORTH.

LULLABY

The wind whistled loud at the window-pane—
   Go away, wind, and let me sleep!
Ruffle the green grass billowy plain,
   Ruffle the billowy deep!

'Hush-a-bye, hush! the wind is fled,
The wind cannot ruffle the soft, smooth bed,—
   Hush thee, darling, sleep!'

The ivy tapped at the window-pane,—
   Silence, ivy! and let me sleep!
Why do you patter like drops of rain,
   And then play creepity-creep?
'Hush-a-bye, hush! the leaves shall lie still,
The moon is walking over the hill,—
   Hush thee, darling, sleep!'

A dream-show rode in on a moonbeam white,—
   Go away, dreams, and let me sleep!
The show may be gay and golden bright,
   But I do not care to peep.
'Hush-a-bye, hush! the dream is fled,
A shining angel guards thy bed,
   Hush thee, darling, sleep!'

                W. B. RANDS.

LULLABY

The rooks' nests do rock on the tree-top,
   Where few foes can stand;
The martin's is high and is deep
   In the steep clift of sand;
But thou, love, a-sleeping where footsteps
   Might come to thy bed,
Hast father and mother to watch thee
   And shelter thy head.
      Lullaby, Lilybrow, lie asleep;
      Blest be thy rest.

And some birds do keep under roofing
   Their young from the storm:
And some wi' nest-hoodings o' moss
   And o' wool, do lie warm.

And we will look well to the house-roof
    That o'er thee might leak,
And the beast that might beat on thy window
    Shall not smite thy cheek.
        Lullaby, Lilybrow, lie asleep;
        Blest be thy rest.

WILLIAM BARNES.

TO A SLEEPING CHILD

Lips, lips, open!
Up comes a little bird that lives inside—
Up comes a little bird, and peeps, and out he flies.

All the day he sits inside, and sometimes he sings,
Up he comes, and out he goes at night to spread his wings.

Little bird, little bird, whither will you go?
Round about the world, while nobody can know.

Little bird, little bird, whither do you flee?
Far away around the world, while nobody can see.

Little bird, little bird, how long will you roam?
All round the world and around again home;

Round the round world, and back through the air,
When the morning comes, the little bird is there.

Back comes the little bird and looks, and in he flies,
Up wakes the little boy, and opens both his eyes.

Sleep, sleep, little boy, little bird's away,
Little bird will come again, by the peep of day;

Sleep, little boy, the little bird must go
Round about the world while nobody can know.

Sleep, sleep sound, little bird goes round,
Round and round he goes; sleep, sleep sound.

ARTHUR HUGH CLOUGH.

A CRADLE HYMN

Hush! my dear, lie still and slumber;
  Holy angels guard thy bed!
Heavenly blessings without number
  Gently falling on thy head.

Sleep, my babe; thy food and raiment,
  House and home, thy friends provide;
All without thy care or payment,
  All thy wants are well supplied.

How much better thou 'rt attended
  Than the Son of God could be,
When from heaven He descended,
  And became a child like thee!

Soft and easy is thy cradle:
  Coarse and hard thy Saviour lay,
When His birthplace was a stable,
  And His softest bed was hay.

． ． ． ．

See the kindly shepherds round Him,
  Telling wonders from the sky!
Where they sought Him, there they found Him,
  With His Virgin-Mother by.

See the lovely babe a-dressing:
  Lovely infant, how He smiled!
When He wept, the mother's blessing
  Sooth'd and hush'd the holy Child.

Lo, He slumbers in His manger,
  Where the hornèd oxen fed!
—Peace, my darling! here's no danger!
  There's no ox a-near thy bed!

． ． ． ．

May'st thou live to know and fear Him,
  Trust and love Him all thy days:
Then go dwell for ever near Him;
  See His face, and sing His praise.

I could give thee thousand kisses,
  Hoping what I most desire:
Not a mother's fondest wishes
  Can to greater joys aspire.

ISAAC WATTS.

HUSHING SONG

Eilidh,[1] Eilidh,
My bonnie wee lass:
The winds blow,
And the hours pass.

But never a wind
Can do thee wrong,
Brown Birdeen, singing
Thy bird-heart song.

And never an hour
But has for thee
Blue of the heaven
And green of the sea:

Blue for the hope of thee,
Eilidh, Eilidh;
Green for the joy of thee,
Eilidh, Eilidh.

Swing in thy nest, then,
Here on my heart,
Birdeen, Birdeen,
Here on my heart,
Here on my heart!

FIONA MACLEOD.

[1] Pronounce *Eily*.

A BLESSING FOR THE BLESSED

When the sun has left the hilltop,
   And the daisy-fringe is furled,
When the birds from wood and meadow
   In their hidden nests are curled,
Then I think of all the babies
   That are sleeping in the world. . . .

There are babies in the high lands
   And babies in the low,
There are pale ones wrapped in furry skins
   On the margin of the snow,
And brown ones naked in the isles
   Where all the spices grow.

And some are in the palace,
   On a white and downy bed,
And some are in the garret
   With a clout beneath their head,
And some are on the cold, hard earth,
   Whose mothers have no bread.

O little men and women,
   Dear flowers yet unblown—
O little kings and beggars
   Of the pageant yet unshown—
Sleep soft and dream pale dreams now,
   To-morrow is your own.

                    LAURENCE ALMA TADEMA.

CAROLS, HYMNS, AND
SACRED VERSE

CRADLE HYMN

Away in a manger, no crib for a bed,
The little Lord Jesus laid down His sweet head.
The stars in the bright sky looked down where He
    lay—
The little Lord Jesus asleep on the hay.

The cattle are lowing, the baby awakes,
But little Lord Jesus, no crying He makes.
I love thee, Lord Jesus! look down from the sky,
And stay by my cradle till morning is nigh.
MARTIN LUTHER.

MARY'S MANGER-SONG

Sleep, my little Jesus,
  On Thy bed of hay,
While the shepherds homeward
  Journey on the way!
Mother is Thy shepherd,
  And will vigil keep;
Oh, did the angels wake Thee?
  Sleep, my Jesus, sleep!

Sleep, my little Jesus,
  While Thou art my own!
Ox and ass thy neighbours,
  Shalt Thou have a throne?
Will they call me blessed?
  Shall I stand and weep?
Oh, be it far, Jehovah!
  Sleep, my Jesus, sleep!

Sleep, my little Jesus,
    Wonder-baby mine!
Well the singing angels
    Greet Thee as divine.
Through my heart, as heaven,
    Low the echoes sweep
Of glory to Jehovah!
    Sleep, my Jesus, sleep!

WILLIAM CHANNING GANNETT.

AS JOSEPH WAS A-WALKING

As Joseph was a-walking
    He heard Angels sing,
'This night there shall be born
    Our heavenly King.'

'He neither shall be born
    In house nor in hall,
Nor in the place of paradise,
    But in an ox-stall.'

'He shall not be clothèd
    In purple nor pall;
But all in fair linen,
    As wear babies all.'

'He shall not be rockèd
    In silver nor gold,
But in a wooden cradle
    That rocks on the mould.'

'He neither shall be christened
    In milk nor in wine,
But in pure spring-well water,
    Fresh sprung from Bethine.'

Mary took her baby,
   She dressed Him so sweet,
She laid Him in a manger,
   All there for to sleep.

As she stood over Him
   She heard Angels sing,
'O bless our dear Saviour,
   Our heavenly King!'

UNKNOWN.

CAROL

MARY, the mother, sits on the hill,
And cradles Child Jesu, that lies so still;
She cradles Child Jesu, that sleeps so sound,
And the little wind blows the song around.

The little wind blows the mother's words,
'Ei, Jesu, ei,' like the song of birds;
'Ei, Jesu, ei,' I heard it still,
As I lay asleep at the foot of the hill.

'Sleep, Babe, sleep, mother watch doth keep,
Ox shall not hurt Thee, nor ass, nor sheep;
Dew falls sweet from Thy Father's sky,
Sleep, Jesu, sleep! ei, Jesu, ei.'

LANGDON E. MITCHELL.

A CHRISTMAS CAROL

WHERE are you going, my little children,
   Soft-eyed Zillah, and brown-faced Seth,
Little David with cheeks so ruddy,
   Dark-haired, slender Elizabeth?

What are the burdens you carry with you,
    Poised on the head and swung in the hand;
What is the song from your red lips ringing,
    What is your errand, you little band?

'Sirs, as you know, we are Hebrew children,
    I am Zillah and this is Seth;
Here is David, our little brother,
    And this our sister Elizabeth.

'Our father's sheep are on yonder hillside,
    He cares for us and he watches them;
We left our home in the early morning,
    And go our way into Bethlehem.

'Surely you know that the Blessèd Baby,
    Greeted by angels with songs of joy,
Is lying there with His gentle mother,
    And we are going to see the Boy.

'Here in our baskets are gifts we bring Him,
    All to lay at His little feet;
Amber honey our bees have gathered,
    Milk from our goats so white and sweet;

'Cakes of our figs, and grapes that are purple,
    Olives plucked from our own old trees,
Savoury herbs, and fragrant spices,
    All we bring on our bended knees.

'See, this is wool so soft and so fleecy,
    Purple dyes that a king might wear;
Skins of the goat, and the ram, and the badger,
    All for the Baby that's sleeping there.

'Here are shells from the Red Sea brought us,
    Here are feathers all light and gay;
Tell us, good sirs, had ever a baby
    Fairer gifts than we bring to-day?

'Seth gives his dove, though he loves it dearly;
    David these shells for the Holy Boy;
Elizabeth wove Him this pretty basket,
    But I have only this little toy,—

'Two sticks of olive-wood, carved by my father,
    One standing up and one crossing it—so;
We have little to offer, we poor little children,
    But we give all we can, and we sing as we go.'

Singing they went with their simple treasures,
    Sweet rang their voices o'er valley and hill,
'Glory, oh, glory to God in the highest,
    Peace upon earth, and to men good will!'

Still they went singing, these Hebrew children,
    Soft-eyed Zillah and brown-faced Seth;
Little David with cheek so ruddy,
    Dark-haired, slender Elizabeth.

ANNIE SLOSSON.

GOD REST YOU MERRY, GENTLEMEN

GOD rest you merry, gentlemen,
    Let nothing you dismay,
Remember Christ our Saviour
    Was born on Christmas Day,
To save us all from Satan's pow'r
    When we were gone astray;
        O tidings of comfort and joy!

In Bethlehem, in Jewry,
    This blessed Babe was born,
And laid within a manger,
    Upon this blessed morn;
The which His mother, Mary,
    Did nothing take in scorn.
        O tidings of comfort and joy!

From God our heavenly Father
　　A blessed angel came,
And unto certain shepherds
　　Brought tidings of the same:
How that in Bethlehem was born
　　The Son of God by name.
　　　　O tidings of comfort and joy!

Fear not, then said the angel,
　　Let nothing you affright,
This day is born a Saviour
　　Of a pure Virgin bright,
To free all those who trust in Him
　　From Satan's power and might.
　　　　O tidings of comfort and joy!

The shepherds at those tidings
　　Rejoicèd much in mind,
And left their flocks a-feeding
　　In tempest, storm, and wind,
And went to Bethlehem straightway
　　The Son of God to find.
　　　　O tidings of comfort and joy!

And when they came to Bethlehem,
　　Where our dear Saviour lay,
They found Him in a manger,
　　Where oxen feed on hay;
His mother Mary kneeling down,
　　Unto the Lord did pray.
　　　　O tidings of comfort and joy!

Now to the Lord sing praises,
　　All you within this place,
And with true love and brotherhood
　　Each other now embrace;
This holy tide of Christmas
　　All other doth deface.
　　　　O tidings of comfort and joy!

　　　　　　　　　　　　UNKNOWN.

THE FIRST NOWELL

The first Nowell the angel did say,
Was to certain poor shepherds in fields as they lay;
In fields where they lay keeping their sheep,
On a cold winter's night that was so deep.
    Nowell, Nowell, Nowell, Nowell,
    Born is the King of Israel.

They looked up and saw a Star
Shining in the East, beyond them far,
And to the earth it gave great light,
And so it continued both day and night.
    Nowell, Nowell, Nowell, Nowell,
    Born is the King of Israel.

And by the light of that same Star,
Three Wise Men came from country far;
To seek for a King was their intent,
And to follow the Star wherever it went.
    Nowell, Nowell, Nowell, Nowell,
    Born is the King of Israel.

This Star drew nigh to the north-west,
O'er Bethlehem it took its rest,
And there it did both stop and stay,
Right over the place where Jesus lay.
    Nowell, Nowell, Nowell, Nowell,
    Born is the King of Israel.

Then entered in those Wise Men three,
Full reverently upon their knee,
And offered there, in His presence,
Their gold, and myrrh, and frankincense.
    Nowell, Nowell, Nowell, Nowell,
    Born is the King of Israel.

Then let us all with one accord
Sing praises to our heavenly Lord,
That hath made heaven and earth of nought,
And with His Blood mankind hath bought.
    Nowell, Nowell, Nowell, Nowell,
    Born is the King of Israel.

UNKNOWN.

THE SON OF GOD IS BORN

THE Son of God is born for all,
At Bethlem in a cattle-stall
He lieth in a crib full small,
And wrapt in swaddling-clothes withal.

Rejoice to-day for Jesu's sake,
Within your hearts His cradle make:
A shrine, wherein the Babe may take
His rest, in slumber or awake.

Beneath Him set His crib, of tree;
Let Hope the little mattress be,
His pillow Faith, full fair to see
With coverlet of Charity.

In bodies pure and undefil'd
Prepare a chamber for the Child:
To Him give incense, myrrh and gold,
Nor raiment, meat, and drink withhold.

Draw nigh, the Son of God to kiss,
Greet Mary's Child (the Lord He is)
Upon those lovely lips of His:
Jesus, your heart's desire and bliss.

Come, rock His cradle cheerily,
As doth His mother, so do ye,
Who nurs'd Him sweetly on her knee,
As told it was by prophecy.

THE GOLDEN STAIRCASE

By, by, lullay before Him sing;
Go, wind the horn, and pluck the string,
Till all the place with music ring;
And bid one prayer to Christ the King.

Thus, Babe, I minister to Thee,
E'en as Thine angels wait on me:
Thy ruddy countenance I see,
And tiny hands outstretched to me.

Sleep, in my soul enshrinèd rest;
Here find Thy cradle neatly drest:
Forsake me not, when sore distrest,
Emmanuel, my Brother blest.

Now chant we merrily *io*
With such as play *in organo*:
And with the singers *in choro*
Benedicamus Domino

UNKNOWN.

GOOD KING WENCESLAS

Good King Wenceslas looked out
  On the Feast of Stephen,
When the snow lay round about,
  Deep, and crisp, and even.

Brightly shone the moon that night,
  Though the frost was cruel,
When a poor man came in sight,
  Gath'ring winter fuel.

'Hither, page, and stand by me,
  If thou know'st it, telling,
Yonder peasant, who is he?
  Where and what his dwelling?'

'Sire, he lives a good league hence,
  Underneath the mountain;
Right against the forest fence,
  By Saint Agnes' fountain.'

'Bring me flesh, and bring me wine,
  Bring me pine-logs hither;
Thou and I will see him dine,
  When we bear them thither.'

Page and monarch, forth they went,
  Forth they went together;
Through the rude wind's wild lament
  And the bitter weather.

'Sire, the night is darker now,
  And the wind blows stronger;
Fails my heart, I know not how,
  I can go no longer.'

'Mark my footsteps, good my page;
  Tread thou in them boldly:
Thou shalt find the winter rage
  Freeze thy blood less coldly.'

In his master's steps he trod,
  Where the snow lay dinted;
Heat was in the very sod
  Which the saint had printed.

Therefore, Christian men, be sure,
  Wealth or rank possessing,
Ye who now will bless the poor,
  Shall yourselves find blessing.

                              UNKNOWN.

A CHRISTMAS CAROL

'WHAT means this glory round our feet,'
   The Magi mused, 'more bright than morn?'
And voices chanted clear and sweet,
   'To-day the Prince of Peace is born.'

'What means that star,' the shepherds said,
   'That brightens through the rocky glen?'
And angels, answering overhead,
   Sang 'Peace on earth, good-will to men.'

'Tis eighteen hundred years and more
   Since those sweet oracles were dumb;
We wait for Him, like them of yore;
   Alas! He seems so slow to come.

But it was said in words of gold,
   No time or sorrow e'er shall dim,
That little children might be bold,
   In perfect trust to come to Him.

All round about our feet shall shine
   A light like that the wise men saw,
If we our willing hearts incline
   To that sweet Life which is the Law.

So shall we learn to understand
   The simple faith of shepherds then,
And, kindly clasping hand in hand,
   Sing, 'Peace on earth, good-will to men.'

For they who to their childhood cling,
   And keep their natures fresh as morn,
Once more shall hear the angels sing,
   'To-day the Prince of Peace is born.'

                JAMES RUSSELL LOWELL.

A CHRISTMAS CAROL

In the bleak mid-winter
   Frosty wind made moan,
Earth stood hard as iron,
   Water like a stone;
Snow had fallen, snow on snow,
   Snow on snow,
In the bleak mid-winter
   Long ago.

Our God, Heaven cannot hold Him,
   Nor earth sustain;
Heaven and earth shall flee away
   When He comes to reign:
In the bleak mid-winter
   A stable-place sufficed
The Lord God Almighty,
   Jesus Christ.

Enough for Him whom cherubim
   Worship night and day,
A breastful of milk
   And a mangerful of hay;
Enough for Him whom angels
   Fall down before,
The ox and ass and camel
   Which adore.

Angels and archangels
   May have gathered there,
Cherubim and Seraphim
   Throng'd the air;
But only His mother
   In her maiden bliss
Worshipped the Beloved
   With a kiss.

What can I give Him,
  Poor as I am?
If I were a shepherd
  I would bring a lamb,
If I were a wise man
  I would do my part,—
Yet what I can I give Him,
  Give my heart.

CHRISTINA G. ROSSETTI.

THE THREE KINGS OF COLOGNE

From out Cologne there came three kings
  To worship Jesus Christ their King.
To Him they sought, fine herbs they brought,
  And many a beauteous golden thing;
They brought their gifts to Bethlehem town,
And in that manger set them down.

Then spake the first king, and he said:
  'O Child, most heavenly, bright and fair!
I bring this crown to Bethlehem town
  For Thee, and only Thee, to wear;
So give a heavenly crown to me
When I shall come at last to Thee!'

The second then: 'I bring Thee here
  This royal robe, O Child!' he cried;
'Of silk 'tis spun, and such an one
  There is not in the world beside;
So in the day of Doom requite
Me with a heavenly robe of white!'

The third king gave his gift and quoth:
  'Spikenard and myrrh to Thee I bring,
And with these twain would I most fain
  Anoint the body of my King;
So may their incense sometime rise
To plead for me in yonder skies!'

Thus spake the three kings of Cologne,
  That gave their gifts and went their way;
And now kneel I in prayer hard by
  The cradle of the Child to-day;
Nor crown, nor robe, nor spice I bring
As offering unto Christ, my King.

Yet have I brought a gift this Child
  May not despise, however small;
For here I lay my heart to-day,
  And it is full of love to all.
Take, then, this poor but loyal thing,
My only tribute, Christ, my King.

EUGENE FIELD.

A CHRISTMAS HYMN

ONCE in royal David's city
  Stood a lowly cattle-shed
Where a mother laid her Baby,
  In a manger for His bed.
Mary was that mother mild,
Jesus Christ her little Child.

He came down to earth from heaven,
  Who is God and Lord of all,
And His shelter was a stable,
  And His cradle was a stall.
With the poor, and mean, and lowly
Lived on earth our Saviour holy.

And through all His wondrous childhood,
  He would honour and obey,
Love and watch the lowly mother
  In whose gentle arms He lay.
Christian children, all must be
Mild, obedient, good as He.

For He is our childhood's Pattern,
  Day by day like us He grew;
He was little, weak, and helpless,
  Tears and smiles like us He knew;
And He feeleth for our sadness,
And He shareth in our gladness.

And our eyes at last shall see Him,
  Through His own redeeming love,
For that Child so dear and gentle
  Is our Lord in Heaven above;
And He leads His children on
To the place where He is gone.

Not in that poor lowly stable,
  With the oxen standing by,
We shall see Him; but in Heaven,
  Set at God's right hand on high;
When like stars His children crowned,
All in white shall wait around.
              C. FRANCES ALEXANDER.

THE CHILD OF BETHLEHEM

O LITTLE town of Bethlehem,
  How still we see thee lie!
Above thy deep and dreamless sleep
  The silent stars go by;
Yet in thy dark streets shineth
  The everlasting light;
The hopes and fears of all the years
  Are met in thee to-night!

For Christ is born of Mary;
  And gathered all above,
While mortals sleep, the angels keep
  Their watch of wondering love.

O morning stars! together
　　Proclaim the holy birth,
And praises sing to God the King,
　　And peace to men on earth!

How silently, how silently,
　　The wondrous gift is given!
So God imparts to human hearts
　　The blessings of His heaven.
No ear may hear His coming;
　　But in this world of sin,
Where meek souls will receive Him, still
　　The dear Christ enters in.

O holy Child of Bethlehem!
　　Descend to us, we pray;
Cast out our sin and enter in—
　　Be born in us to-day!
We hear the Christmas angels
　　The great glad tidings tell;
Oh, come to us, abide with us,
　　Our Lord Emmanuel!

PHILLIPS BROOKS.

CHRISTMAS DAY

A BABY is a harmless thing,
　　And wins our heart with one accord,
And Flower of Babies was their King,
　　Jesus Christ our Lord:
Lily of lilies He
　　Upon His Mother's knee;
Rose of roses, soon to be
　　Crowned with thorns on leafless tree.

A lamb is innocent and mild,
　　And merry on the soft green sod;
And Jesus Christ, the Undefiled,
　　Is the Lamb of God:

Only spotless He
  Upon His Mother's knee;
White and ruddy, soon to be
  Sacrificed for you and me.

Nay, lamb is not so sweet a word,
  Nor lily half so pure a name;
Another name our hearts hath stirred,
  Kindling them to flame:
'Jesus' certainly
  Is music and melody:
Heart with heart in harmony
  Carol we and worship we.

CHRISTINA ROSSETTI.

NEW PRINCE, NEW POMP

Behold a silly[1] tender Babe,
  In freezing winter night,
In homely manger trembling lies;
  Alas, a piteous sight!

The inns are full, no man will yield
  This little Pilgrim bed;
But forc'd He is with silly beasts
  In crib to shroud His head.

Despise not Him for lying there,
  First what He is enquire;
An orient pearl is often found
  In depth of dirty mire.

Weigh not His crib, His wooden dish,
  Nor beasts that by Him feed;
Weigh not His mother's poor attire,
  Nor Joseph's simple weed.

[1] 'Silly' here means 'innocent.'

This stable is a Prince's court,
　　The crib His chair of State;
The beasts are parcel of His pomp,
　　The wooden dish His plate.

The persons in that poor attire
　　His royal liveries wear;
The Prince Himself is come from heaven,
　　This pomp is prizèd there.

With joy approach, O Christian wight,
　　Do homage to thy King;
And highly prize His humble pomp,
　　Which He from heaven doth bring.
　　　　　　　　　　ROBERT SOUTHWELL.

A HYMN OF THE NATIVITY

．　．　．　．　．　．

Gloomy night embraced the place
　　Where the noble Infant lay.
The Babe look'd up and show'd His face;
　　In spite of darkness, it was day.
It was Thy day, Sweet! and did rise
Not from the East, but from Thine eyes.

Winter chid aloud, and sent
　　The angry North to wage his wars.
The North forgot his fierce intent,
　　And left perfumes instead of scars.
By those sweet eyes' persuasive powers,
Where he meant frost, he scatter'd flowers.

We saw Thee in Thy balmy nest,
　　Young dawn of our Eternal Day;
We saw Thine eyes break from their East
　　And chase the trembling shades away.
We saw Thee; and we blest the sight,
We saw Thee by Thine own sweet light.

Poor world, said I, what wilt thou do
  To entertain this Starry Stranger?
Is this the best thou canst bestow?
  A cold, and not too cleanly, manger?
Contend, the powers of Heaven and Earth,
To fit a bed for this huge birth?

 . . . . .

I saw the curl'd drops, soft and slow,
  Come hov'ring o'er the place's head;
Off'ring their whitest sheets of snow
  To furnish the fair Infant's bed:
Forbear, said I; be not too bold,
Your fleece is white, but 'tis too cold.

I saw the obsequious Seraphims
  Their rosy fleece of fire bestow,
For well they now can spare their wing,
  Since Heaven itself lies here below.
Well done, said I; but are you sure
Your down so warm, will pass for pure?

No, no! your King's not yet to seek
  Where to repose His royal head;
See, see! how soon His new-bloom'd cheek
  'Twixt's mother's breasts is gone to bed.
Sweet choice! said we, no way but so
Not to lie cold, yet sleep in snow.

 . . . . .

Welcome, all wonders in one sight!
  Eternity shut in a span!
Summer in Winter, Day in Night!
  Heaven in Earth, and God in man!
Great little One! whose all-embracing birth
Lifts Earth to Heaven, stoops Heaven to Earth.

      RICHARD CRASHAW.

HOW CHRISTMAS CAME

Heaven's fairest star
Trembled a moment in the gold-flecked blue;
  Then, earthward dropped,
Was in an empty cradle lost to view,
  Till angel came,
And softly parting back the curtains, smiled,
  While hosts proclaimed
The birth of Bethlehem's King in new-born child.
CALLIE L. BONNEY.

TO HIS SAVIOUR, A CHILD; A PRESENT, BY A CHILD

Go, prettie child, and beare this Flower
Unto thy little Saviour;
And tell Him, by that Bud now blown,
He is the *Rose of Sharon* known:
When thou hast said so, stick it there
Upon His Bibb, or Stomacher:
And tell Him (for good handsell too)
That thou hast brought a Whistle new,
Made of a clean strait oaten reed,
To charme His cries (at time of need:)
Tell Him, for Corall, thou hast none;
But if thou hadst, He sho'd have one;
But poore thou art, and knowne to be
Even as monilesse, as He.
Lastly, if thou canst win a kisse
From those mellifluous lips of His;
Then never take a second on,
To spoile the first impression.
ROBERT HERRICK.

THE STAR SONG: A CAROLL TO THE KING

Tell us, thou cleere and heavenly Tongue,
Where is the Babe but lately sprung?
Lies He the Lillie-banks among?

Or say, if this new Birth of ours
Sleeps, laid within some Ark of Flowers,
Spangled with deaw-light; thou canst cleere
All doubts, and manifest the where.

Declare to us, bright Star, if we shall seek
Him in the Morning's blushing cheek,
Or search the beds of Spices through,
To find Him out?

STAR

No, this ye need not do;
But only come, and see Him rest
A Princely Babe in 's Mother's Brest.

. . . . . .

CHORUS

Come then, come then, and let us bring
Unto our prettie Twelfth-Tide King,
Each one his severall offering;

And when night comes, we 'll give Him wassailing;
And that His treble Honours may be seen,
We 'll chuse Him King, and make His Mother Queen.
ROBERT HERRICK.

A CAROL FOR CHRISTMAS EVE

Listen, lordlings, unto me, a tale I will you tell,
Which, as on this night of glee, in David's town befell.

Joseph came from Nazareth, with Mary, that sweet
    maid:
Weary were they, nigh to death; and for a lodging
    pray'd.
      Sing high, sing low, sing to and fro,
        Go tell it out with speed,
      Cry out and shout all round about,
        That Christ is born indeed.

In the inn they found no room; a scanty bed they
    made:
Soon a Babe from Heaven high was in the manger laid.
Forth He came, maid Mary's Son: He came to save
    us all.
In the stable, ox and ass before their Maker fall.
      Sing high, sing low, sing to and fro,
        Go tell it out with speed,
      Cry out and shout all round about,
        That Christ is born indeed.

Shepherds lay afield that night, to keep the silly sheep,
Hosts of Angels in their sight came down from heaven's
    high steep.
Tidings! Tidings! unto you: to you a Child is born,
Purer than the drops of dew, and brighter than the
    morn.
      Sing high, sing low, sing to and fro,
        Go tell it out with speed,
      Cry out and shout all round about,
        That Christ is born indeed.

Onward then the Angels sped, the shepherds onward
    went,
God was in His manger-bed, in worship low they bent.
In the morning, see ye mind, my masters one and all,
At the Altar Him to find who lay within the stall.
      Sing high, sing low, sing to and fro,
        Go tell it out with speed,
      Cry out and shout all round about,
        That Christ is born indeed.   UNKNOWN.

"IN WORSHIP LOW THEY BENT"

THE NEW-YEERE'S GIFT

Let others looke for Pearle and Gold,
Tissues, or Tabbies manifold:
One onely lock of that sweet Hay
Whereon the blessed Babie lay,
Or one poore Swadling-clout, shall be
The richest New-Yeere's Gift to me.

ROBERT HERRICK.

A LITTLE CHILD'S HYMN

Thou that once, on mother's knee,
Wert a little one like me,
When I wake or go to bed,
Lay Thy hands about my head;
Let me feel Thee very near,
Jesus Christ, our Saviour dear.

Be beside me in the light,
Close by me through all the night;
Make me gentle, kind, and true,
Do what mother bids me do;
Help and cheer me when I fret,
And forgive when I forget.

Once wert Thou in cradle laid,
Baby bright in manger-shade,
With the oxen and the cows,
And the lambs outside the house:
Now Thou art above the sky;
Canst Thou hear a baby cry?

Thou art nearer when we pray,
Since Thou art so far away;
Thou my little hymn wilt hear,
Jesus Christ, our Saviour dear,
Thou that once, on mother's knee,
Wert a little one like me.

FRANCIS TURNER PALGRAVE.

MORNING HYMN

Now the sun is in the skies,
From my bed again I rise;
Christ, Thou never-setting Sun,
Shine on me, Thy little one.

Watch me through the coming day,
Guard me in my work and play;
Christ my Master, Christ the Child,
Make me like Thee, Jesu mild.

Christ, Almighty King above,
Thee I pray for all I love;
Christ, who lovest more than I,
Help them from Thy throne on high.

Christ, of Mary born for me,
To Thy name I bow the knee;
Saviour, bring us, by Thy grace,
To Thy happy dwelling-place.

R. F. LITTLEDALE.

THE GOOD SHEPHERD

Kind Shepherd, see, Thy little lamb
  Comes very tired to Thee;
O fold me in Thy loving arms,
  And smile on me.

I've wander'd from Thy fold to-day,
  And could not hear Thee call;
And O! I was not happy then,
  Nor glad at all.

I want, dear Saviour, to be good,
   And follow close to Thee,
Through flowery meads and pastures green
   And happy be.

Thou kind, good Shepherd, in Thy fold
   I evermore would keep,
In morning's light or evening's shade,
   And while I sleep.

But now, dear Jesus, let me lay
   My head upon Thy breast;
I am too tired to tell Thee more,
   Thou know'st the rest.

H. P. HAWKINS.

EVENING HYMN

Now the day is over,
   Night is drawing nigh,
Shadows of the evening
   Steal across the sky.

Now the darkness gathers,
   Stars begin to peep,
Birds, and beasts, and flowers
   Soon will be asleep.

Jesu, give the weary
   Calm and sweet repose;
With Thy tenderest blessing
   May our eyelids close.

Grant to little children
   Visions bright of Thee;
Guard the sailors tossing
   On the deep blue sea.

Comfort every sufferer
  Watching late in pain;
Those who plan some evil,
  From their sin restrain.

Through the long night-watches
  May Thine angels spread
Their white wings above me,
  Watching round my bed.

When the morning wakens,
  Then may I arise
Pure, and fresh, and sinless
  In Thy holy eyes.
                    S. BARING-GOULD.

THE TENDER SHEPHERD

Jesus, tender Shepherd, hear me:
  Bless Thy little lamb to-night;
Through the darkness be Thou near me,
  Keep me safe till morning light.

Through this day Thy hand hath led me,
  And I thank Thee for Thy care;
Thou hast warmed me, clothed, and fed me,
  Listen to my evening prayer.

Let my sins be all forgiven,
  Bless the friends I love so well;
Take me, when I die, to heaven,
  Happy, there, with Thee to dwell.
                    MARY L. DUNCAN.

A CHILD'S PRAYER

God, make my life a little light
   Within the world to glow;
A little flame that burneth bright,
   Wherever I may go.

God, make my life a little flower
   That giveth joy to all,
Content to bloom in native bower,
   Although the place be small.

God, make my life a little song
   That comforteth the sad;
That helpeth others to be strong,
   And makes the singer glad.

God, make my life a little staff
   Whereon the weak may rest,
That so what health and strength I have
   May serve my neighbours best.

God, make my life a little hymn
   Of tenderness and praise;
Of faith—that never waxeth dim,
   In all His wondrous ways.

                    MATILDA B. EDWARDS.

JESUS BIDS US SHINE

Jesus bids us shine
   With a pure clear light,
Like a little candle
   Burning in the night;
In the world is darkness,
   So we must shine—
You in your small corner,
   And I in mine.

Jesus bids us shine
  First of all for Him:
Well He sees and knows it,
  If our light grows dim;
He looks down from heaven
  To see us shine—
You in your small corner,
  And I in mine.

Jesus bids us shine,
  Then, for all around:
Many kinds of darkness
  In the world are found;
Sin and want and sorrow;
  So we must shine—
You in your small corner,
  And I in mine.

EMILY H. MILLER.

ALL THINGS BRIGHT AND BEAUTIFUL

All things bright and beautiful,
  All creatures great and small,
All things wise and wonderful,
  The Lord God made them all.

Each little flower that opens,
  Each little bird that sings,
He made their glowing colours,
  He made their tiny wings.

The rich man in his castle,
  The poor man at his gate,
God made them, high or lowly,
  And order'd their estate.

THE GOLDEN STAIRCASE

The purple-headed mountain,
  The river running by,
The sunset and the morning,
  That brightens up the sky.

The cold wind in the winter,
  The pleasant summer sun,
The ripe fruits in the garden,
  He made them every one.

The tall trees in the greenwood,
  The meadows where we play,
The rushes by the water,
  We gather every day;—

He gave us eyes to see them,
  And lips that we might tell
How great is God Almighty,
  Who has made all things well.

C. FRANCES ALEXANDER.

GOD, WHO HATH MADE THE DAISIES

GOD, who hath made the daisies
  And ev'ry lovely thing,
He will accept our praises,
  And hearken while we sing.
He says though we are simple,
  Though ignorant we be,
'Suffer the little children,
  And let them come to Me.'

Though we are young and simple,
  In praise we may be bold;
The children in the temple
  He heard in days of old.

And if our hearts are humble,
  He says to you and me,
'Suffer the little children,
  And let them come to Me.'

He sees the bird that wingeth
  Its way o'er earth and sky;
He hears the lark that singeth
  Up in the heaven so high;
But sees the heart's low breathings,
  And says (well pleased to see),
'Suffer the little children,
  And let them come to Me.'

Therefore we will come near Him,
  And solemnly we'll sing;
No cause to shrink or fear Him,
  We'll make our voices ring;
For in our temple speaking,
  He says to you and me,
'Suffer the little children,
  And let them come to Me.'

E. P. HOOD.

PSALM XXIII

The God of love my Shepherd is,
  And He that doth me feed,
While He is mine, and I am His,
  What can I want or need?

He leads me to the tender grass,
  Where I both feed and rest;
Then to the streams that gently pass:
  In both I have the best.

Or if I stray, He doth convert,
  And bring my mind in frame:
And all this not for my desert,
  But for His holy name.

Yea, in Death's shady black abode
  Well may I walk, not fear;
For Thou art with me, and Thy rod
  To guide, Thy staff to bear.

Nay, Thou dost make me sit and dine
  Ev'n in my enemies' sight;
My head with oil, my cup with wine
  Runs over day and night.

Surely Thy sweet and wondrous love
  Shall measure all my days;
And as it never shall remove,
  So neither shall my praise.

GEORGE HERBERT.

EARLY PIETY

By cool Siloam's shady rill
  How sweet the lily grows!
How sweet the breath beneath the hill
  Of Sharon's dewy rose!

Lo! such the child whose early feet
  The paths of peace have trod;
Whose secret heart, with influence sweet,
  Is upward drawn to God!

By cool Siloam's shady rill
  The lily must decay;
The rose that blooms beneath the hill
  Must shortly fade away.

And soon, too soon, the wintry hour
    Of man's maturer age
Will shake the soul with sorrow's power,
    And stormy passion's rage!

O Thou, whose infant feet were found
    Within Thy Father's shrine!
Whose years, with changeless virtue crown'd,
    Were all alike Divine;

Dependent on Thy bounteous breath,
    We seek Thy grace alone,
In childhood, manhood, age and death,
    To keep us still Thine own!

BISHOP HEBER.

EX ORE INFANTIUM

Little Jesus, wast Thou shy
Once, and just so small as I?
And what did it feel like to be
Out of Heaven and just like me?
Didst Thou sometimes think of there,
And ask where all the angels were?
I should think that I would cry
For my house all made of sky;
I would look about the air,
And wonder where my angels were;
And at waking 'twould distress me—
Not an angel there to dress me!
Hadst Thou ever any toys,
Like us little girls and boys?
And didst Thou play in Heaven with all
The angels that were not too tall,
With stars for marbles? Did the things
Play 'can you see me?' through their wings?

And did Thy mother let Thee spoil
Thy robes, with playing on our soil?
How nice to have them always new
In Heaven, because 'twas quite clean blue!

Didst Thou kneel at night to pray,
And didst Thou join Thy hands this way?
And did they tire sometimes, being young,
And make the prayers seem very long?
And dost Thou like it best that we
Should join our hands to pray to Thee?
I used to think before I knew,
The prayer not said unless we do.
And did Thy mother at the night
Kiss Thee and fold the clothes in right?
And didst Thou feel quite good in bed,
Kissed, and sweet, and Thy prayers said?

Thou canst not have forgotten all
That it feels like to be small:
And Thou knowest I cannot pray
To Thee in my father's way—
When Thou wast so little, say
Couldst Thou talk Thy Father's way?
So, a little child, come down
And hear a child's tongue like Thy own;
Take me by the hand and walk,
And listen to my baby talk
To Thy Father show my prayer
(He will look, Thou art so fair)
And say: O Father, I, Thy Son,
Bring the prayer of a little one;
And He will smile, that children's tongue
Has not changed since Thou wast young!
FRANCIS THOMPSON.

SONG

(From The Husband of Poverty)

There was a Knight of Bethlehem,
　Whose wealth was tears and sorrows;
His men-at-arms were little lambs,
　His trumpeters were sparrows;
His castle was a wooden cross,
　Whereon He hung so high;
His helmet was a crown of thorns
　Whose crest did touch the sky.

　　　　　　HENRY NEVILLE MAUGHAN.

CHRIST AND THE LITTLE ONES

'The Master has come over Jordan,'
　Said Hannah the mother one day;
'He is healing the people who throng Him,
　With a touch of His finger, they say.

'And now I shall carry the children,
　Little Rachel and Samuel and John,
I shall carry the baby Esther,
　For the Lord to look upon.'

The father looked at her kindly,
　But he shook his head and smiled:
'Now who but a doting mother
　Would think of a thing so wild?

'If the children were tortured by demons,
　Or dying of fever, 'twere well;
Or had they the taint of the leper,
　Like many in Israel.'

THE GOLDEN STAIRCASE

'Nay, do not hinder me, Nathan,
   I feel such a burden of care,
If I carry it to the Master,
   Perhaps I shall leave it there.

'If He lay His hand on the children,
   My heart will be lighter, I know,
For a blessing for ever and ever
   Will follow them as they go.'

So over the hills of Judah,
   Along by the vine-rows green,
With Esther asleep on her bosom,
   And Rachel her brothers between;

'Mid the people who hung on His teaching,
   Or waited His touch or His word,—
Through the row of proud Pharisees listening,
   She pressed to the feet of the Lord.

'Now why shouldst thou hinder the Master,'
   Said Peter, 'with children like these?
See'st not how from morning to evening
   He teacheth and healeth disease?'

Then Christ said, 'Forbid not the children,
   Permit them to come unto Me!'
And He took in His arms little Esther,
   And Rachel He set on His knee;

And the heavy heart of the mother
   Was lifted all earth-care above.
As He laid His hand on the brothers,
   And blest them with tenderest love;

As He said of the babes in His bosom,
   'Of such are the kingdom of heaven'—
And strength for all duty and trial,
   That hour to her spirit was given.

                          JULIA GILL.

EVENTIDE

At cool of day, with God I walk
    My garden's grateful shade;
I hear His voice among the trees,
    And I am not afraid.

I see His presence in the night,—
    And, though my heart is awed,
I do not quail beneath the sight
    Or nearness of my God.

He speaks to me in every wind,
    He smiles from every star;
He is not deaf to me, nor blind,
    Nor absent, nor afar.

His hand, that shuts the flowers to sleep,
    Each in its dewy fold,
Is strong my feeble life to keep,
    And competent to hold.

I cannot walk in darkness long,—
    My light is by my side;
I cannot stumble or go wrong,
    While following such a guide.

He is my stay and my defence;—
    How shall I fail or fall?
My helper is Omnipotence!
    My ruler ruleth all.

The powers below and powers above
    Are subject to His care:—
I cannot wander from His love
    Who loves me everywhere.

Thus dowered, and guarded thus, with Him
  I walk this peaceful shade;
I hear His voice among the trees,
  And I am not afraid!

CAROLINE MASON.

THE GOD OF MY CHILDHOOD

O GOD! who wert my childhood's love,
  My boyhood's pure delight,
A presence felt the livelong day,
  A welcome fear at night!

Oh let me speak to Thee, dear God!
  Of those old mercies past,
O'er which new mercies day by day
  Such lengthening shadows cast.

They bade me call Thee Father, Lord!
  Sweet was the freedom deemed,
And yet more like a mother's way
  Thy quiet mercies seemed.

At school Thou wert a kindly face
  Which I could almost see;
But home and holyday appeared
  Somehow more full of Thee.

I could not sleep unless Thy hand
  Were underneath my head,
That I might kiss it if I lay
  Wakeful upon my bed.

And quite alone I never felt,—
  I knew that Thou wert near,
A silence tingling in the room,
  A strangely pleasant fear.

Holy, Holy, Holy,
I heard the mocking scorn:
But Holy, Holy, Holy,
I sang against a thorn.

Holy, Holy, Holy,
Ah, His brow was bloody:
Holy, Holy, Holy,
I sang against a thorn!

Holy, Holy, Holy,
Ah, His brow was bloody:
Holy, Holy, Holy,
All my breast was ruddy.

Holy, Holy, Holy,
Christ's Bird shalt thou be:
Thus said Mary Virgin
There on Calvary.

Holy, Holy, Holy,
A wee brown bird am I:
But my breast is ruddy,
For I saw Christ die.

Holy, Holy, Holy,
By this ruddy feather,
Colum, call thy monks, and
All the birds together.

FIONA MACLEOD.

A CHILD'S EASTER

HAD I been there when Christ, our Lord, lay sleeping
Within that tomb in Joseph's garden fair,
I would have watched all night beside my Saviour—
Had I been there.

THE GOLDEN STAIRCASE

Close to the hard, cold stone my soft cheek pressing,
I should have thought my head lay on His breast;
And dreaming that His dear arms were about me,
      Have sunk to rest.

All through the long, dark night when others slumbered,
Close, close beside Him still I would have stayed,
And, knowing how He loved the little children,
      Ne'er felt afraid.

'To-morrow,' to my heart I would have whispered,
'I will rise early in the morning hours,
And wand'ring o'er the hillside I will gather
      The fairest flowers;

'Tall, slender lilies (for my Saviour loved them,
And tender words about their beauty spake),
And golden buttercups, and glad-eyed daisies,
      But just awake:

'"Grass of the field" in waving, feath'ry beauty,
He clothed it with that grace, so fair but brief,
Mosses all soft and green, and crimson berry,
      With glossy leaf.

'While yet the dew is sparkling on the blossoms,
I'll gather them and lay them at His feet,
And make the blessèd place where He is sleeping
      All fair and sweet.

'The birds will come, I know, and sing above Him,
The sparrows whom He cared for when awake,
And they will fill the air with joyous music
      For His dear sake.'

And, thinking thus, the night would soon be passing,
Fast drawing near that first glad Easter light.
Ah, Lord, if I could but have seen Thee leaving
      The grave's dark night!

I would have kept so still, so still, and clasping
My hands together as I do in prayer,
I would have knelt, reverent, but oh, so happy!—
    Had I been there.

Perhaps He would have bent one look upon me;
Perhaps in pity for that weary night,
He would have laid on my uplifted forehead
    A touch so light;

And all the rest of life I should have felt it,
A sacred sign upon my brow imprest,
And ne'er forgot that precious, lonely vigil,
    So richly blest.

Dear Lord, through death and night I was not near
    Thee;
But in Thy risen glory can rejoice,
So, loud and glad in song this Easter morning,
    Thou 'lt hear my voice.

ANNIE SLOSSON.

INDEX OF FIRST LINES

	PAGE
A baby is a harmless thing	330
Abou Ben Adhem (may his tribe increase !)	259
A chieftain, to the Highlands bound	174
Across the narrow beach we flit	230
A fair little girl sat under a tree	8
A little fairy comes at night	82
A little lonely child am I	278
All in the pleasant afternoon	2
All things bright and beautiful	342
A mouse found a beautiful piece of plum-cake	13
An ancient story I'll tell you anon	210
'And where have you been, my Mary	135
A pair of steady Rooks	18
Are you a Giant, great big man, or is your real name Smith?	29
As Joseph was a-walking	316
At cool of day, with God I walk	350
Augustus was a chubby lad	23
Auld Daddy Darkness creeps frae his hole	118
Away in a manger, no crib for a bed	315
A wet sheet and a flowing sea	105
Baby, baby, hush-a-bye	301
Bartholomew	300
Behold a silly tender Babe	331
Beside a green meadow a stream used to flow	51
Beside the ungathered rice he lay	166
Be useful where thou livest, that they may	275
Bird of the wilderness	254
Breathes there the man, with soul so dead	275
But the Consul's brow was sad	161
By cool Siloam's shady rill	345
By the shores of Gitchee Gumee	213
Come, dear children, let us away	279
Come live with me, and be my love	265
Creep awa, my bairnie,—creep afore ye gang	117
'Dear me! what signifies a pin!	24
Dear mother, if you just could be	68
'Dear mother,' said a little fish	5
Did you hear of the curate who mounted his mare	225
Down by a shining water well	47
Effingham, Grenville, Raleigh, Drake	187
Eilidh, Eilidh	310
Eleven men of England	194
Eliza and Anne were extremely distress'd	13
Fair daffodils, we weep to see	264
Five little pussy-cats, invited out to tea	12
For a cap and bells our lives we pay	274
For many a year I've watched the ships a-sailing to and fro	232

	PAGE
From out Cologne there came three kings	327
Gay Robin is seen no more	110
Get up, little sister, the morning is bright	25
Gloomy night embraced the place	332
God, make my life a little light	341
God rest you merry, gentlemen	319
God who created me	227
God, who hath made the daisies	343
Good-bye, good-bye to Summer!	90
Good King Wenceslas looked out	323
'Good-night, Sir Rook!' said a little Lark	61
Go, prettie child, and beare this Flower	334
Great, wide, beautiful, wonderful World	108
Had I been there when Christ, our Lord, lay sleeping	354
Half a league, half a league	185
Hamelin Town's in Brunswick	216
Hear what Highland Nora said	199
Heaven's fairest star	334
He comes in the night! he comes in the night!	43
Here a little child I stand	64
He that is down, needs fear no fall	228
He was a rat, and she was a rat	39
Hie away, hie away	104
Holy, Holy, Holy	353
Home for the Holidays, here we go	72
How doth the little busy bee	21
How sleep the brave, who sink to rest	275
Hush-a-bye, baby, on the tree top	297
Hush! my dear, lie still and slumber	309
I am coming, little maiden	35
If no one ever marries me	41
I have a little shadow that goes in and out with me	15

	PAGE
I have got a new-born sister	37
'I have no name	305
I hear a pretty bird, but hark!	36
I know a funny little man	21
I know the ships that pass by day	106
'I'm a merry, merry squirrel	11
In all the land, range up, range down	270
In summer, when the grass is thick, if mother has the time	38
In the bleak mid-winter	326
In winter I get up at night	1
I once had a sweet little doll, dears	44
I sprang to the stirrup, and Joris, and he	189
It almost makes me cry to tell	33
It is not growing like a tree	258
It was an old, old, old, old lady	97
It was a summer evening	141
It was Earl Haldan's daughter	207
It was the schooner Hesperus	171
It was the time when lilies blow	202
I've found my bonny babe a nest	303
I've never travelled for more 'n a day	234
I've plucked the berry from the bush, the brown nut from the tree	116
I was four yesterday: when I'm quite old	41
I wish I lived in a caravan	32
I would like you for a comrade, for I love you, that I do	22
Jesus bids us shine	341
Jesus, tender Shepherd, hear me	340
Jog on, jog on, the footpath way	201
John Gilpin was a citizen	235
John Grumlie swore by the licht o' the moon	259
Joy to Philip! he this day	112
Kind Shepherd, see, Thy little lamb	338

INDEX OF FIRST LINES 359

	PAGE
King Bruce of Scotland flung himself down	66
King Francis was a hearty king, and loved a royal sport	168
Lady Moon, Lady Moon, where are you roving?	64
Let dogs delight to bark and bite	43
Let others looke for Pearle and Gold	337
Lips, lips, open!	308
Listen, lordlings, unto me, a tale I will you tell	335
Little baby, lay your head	297
'Little bird! little bird! come to me!	9
Little children, never give	16
Little Jesus, wast Thou shy	346
Little ladies, white and green	40
Little Lamb, who made thee	62
Little one, come to my knee!	71
Look! Look! the spring is come	109
March, march, Ettrick and Teviotdale	184
Mary, the mother, sits on the hill	317
May Margaret stood in her bower-door	288
Merrily swinging on briar and weed	74
My beautiful! my beautiful! thou standest meekly by	145
My fairest child, I have no song to give you	227
My heart's in the Highlands, my heart is not here	93
My mind to me a kingdom is	251
My tea is nearly ready and the sun has left the sky	3
Nay, only look what I have found!	77
News of battle!—news of battle!	176
No stir in the air, no stir in the sea	143

	PAGE
Not a drum was heard, not a funeral note	245
Now ponder well, you parents dear	98
Now the day is over	339
Now the sun is in the skies	338
O Captain! my Captain! our fearful trip is done	244
Och, Modereen Rue, you little red rover	231
Of all the birds from East to West	119
Of Nelson and the North	197
Oft I had heard of Lucy Gray	169
O God! who wert my childhood's love	351
Oh hush thee, little Dear-my-soul	302
O, hush thee, my babie, thy sire was a knight	303
Oh, in my garden every day	2
Oh! I wish I were a tiny browny bird from out the south	111
Oh, the mother she loves her only son	63
Oh, the white Sea-gull, the wild Sea-gull	91
O little town of Bethlehem	329
'O Mary, go and call the cattle home	254
Once a little round-eyed lad	84
Once in royal David's city	328
One cannot turn a minute	70
One day Mamma said: 'Conrad, dear	15
One ugly trick has often spoiled	27
Orpheus with his lute made trees	201
'O well is me, my gay goshawk	283
O, young Lochinvar is come out of the west	155
Pibroch of Donuil Dhu	183
Remember us poor Mayers all	252

Right on our flank the sun was dropping down . . .	192
Ring, sing! ring, sing! pleasant Sabbath bells	204
Said an ancient hermit, bending	249
Shiv, who poured the harvest and made the winds to blow .	267
Sleep, my little Jesus . .	315
So here hath been dawning .	226
Soldier, rest! thy warfare o'er .	182
Sure, he's five months old, an' he's two foot long . . .	299
Sweet and low, sweet and low .	305
Tell us, thou cleere and heavenly Tongue	335
Tell you a story, children? Well, gather round my knee . .	127
Thank you, pretty cow, that made	10
The blackbird has a mouth of gold, though sombre be his feathers	111
The breaking waves dashed high	158
The camel's hump is an ugly lump	83
The captain stood on the carronade:—'First lieutenant,' says he	243
The days are cold, the nights are long	306
The dew was falling fast, the stars began to blink, . .	52
The door was shut, as doors should be	73
The first Nowell the angel did say	321
The flowers in the garden . .	17
The friendly cow all red and white	10
The Giant sat on a rock up high	55
The God of love my Shepherd is	344
The King sits in Dunfermline toun	260
The King was sick. His cheek was red	133
The little toy dog is covered with dust	253
'The Master has come over Jordan'	348
There dwelt a miller hale and bold	60
There's a breathless hush in the Close to-night . . .	186
There's no dew left on the daisies and clover . . .	65
There was a Knight of Bethlehem	348
There was a little girl, and she wore a little curl . . .	39
There was a sound of revelry by night	246
There was one little Jim . .	17
There were dolls in grand confections	131
There were three sailors of Bristol city . . .	107
The rhyme of the Monk Molios .	268
The Rock-a-By Lady from Hushaby Street . . .	304
The rooks' nests do rock on the tree-top	307
The Sea! the Sea! the open Sea!	104
The Son of God is born for all .	322
The spearman heard the bugle sound	138
The splendour falls on castle walls	266
The sun is weary, for he ran .	114
The warrior bow'd his crested head, and tamed his heart of fire	148
The Wind one morning sprang up from sleep . . .	88
The wind whistled loud at the window-pane . . .	306
The world's a very happy place .	95
The year's at the spring . .	228
They went to sea in a Sieve, they did	45
Thou must be true thyself . .	258

INDEX OF FIRST LINES

	PAGE		PAGE
Thou that once, on mother's knee	337	When icicles hang by the wall	257
Tiger, tiger, burning bright	228	When in my youth I travellèd	78
'Tis the voice of the sluggard; I heard him complain	87	When I was sick and lay a-bed	4
To Heaven's Meadows, bright with flowers and sunshine	122	When the sun has left the hilltop	311
'Tu-whit! tu-whit! tu-whee!	6	When the table-cloth is laid	26
Twinkle, twinkle, little star	4	When the voices of children are heard on the green	229
		Where are you going, my little children	317
Under a spreading chestnut tree	80	Where did you come from, baby dear?	298
Under the greenwood tree	256	Where the bee sucks, there suck I	201
Up from the meadows rich with corn	208	Where the pools are bright and deep	103
Up the airy mountain	86	Who is Silvia? What is she	255
		Who would true valour see	264
Waken, lords and ladies gay!	115	'Why weep ye by the tide, ladie?	273
Wee Davie Daylicht	119	'Will you walk into my parlour?' said the Spider to the Fly	48
Wee Willie Winkie rins through the toon	116	With some good ten of his chosen men, Bernardo hath appeared	151
What does little birdie say	299	With sweetest milk and sugar, first	121
What have I done for you	276	Wynken, Blynken, and Nod one night	31
'What means this glory round our feet,'	325		
What shall he have that kill'd the deer?	200		
What tents gleam on the green hillside, like snow in the sunny beam	153	Ye Mariners of England!	157
		You can take a tub with a rub and a scrub in a two-foot tank of tin	26
Whene'er I take my walks abroad	109	You know, we French stormed Ratisbon	160
When Father goes to town with me to buy my Sunday hat	94	You spotted snakes with double tongue	256
When father takes his spade to dig	1		

Printed by T. and A. CONSTABLE, Printers to His Majesty
at the Edinburgh University Press